THE PSYCHOANALYST, THE THEATRE OF DREAMS AND THE CLINIC OF ENACTMENT

THE PSYCHOANALYST, THE THEATRE OF DREAMS AND THE CLINIC OF ENACTMENT

R. M. S. Cassorla

LONDON AND NEW YORK

First published 2018
by Routledge
2 Park Square, Milton Park, Abingdon, Oxon OX14 4RN

and by Routledge
711 Third Avenue, New York, NY 10017

Routledge is an imprint of the Taylor & Francis Group, an informa business

© 2018 R. M. S. Cassorla

The right of R. M. S. Cassorla to be identified as author of this work has been asserted by her in accordance with sections 77 and 78 of the Copyright, Designs and Patents Act 1988.

All rights reserved. No part of this book may be reprinted or reproduced or utilised in any form or by any electronic, mechanical, or other means, now known or hereafter invented, including photocopying and recording, or in any information storage or retrieval system, without permission in writing from the publishers.

Trademark notice: Product or corporate names may be trademarks or registered trademarks, and are used only for identification and explanation without intent to infringe.

British Library Cataloguing-in-Publication Data
A catalogue record for this book is available from the British Library

Library of Congress Cataloging-in-Publication Data
A catalog record has been requested for this book

ISBN: 978-1-78220-507-4 (pbk)

Typeset in Palatino
by V Publishing Solutions Pvt Ltd., Chennai, India

CONTENTS

ACKNOWLEDGEMENTS	vii
ABOUT THE AUTHOR	ix
PREFACE TO THE ENGLISH EDITION	xi
PREFACE TO THE BRAZILIAN EDITION	xvii
INTRODUCTION	xxiii
CHAPTER ONE The analytic field and dreams-for-two	1
CHAPTER TWO Dreaming non-dreamed dreams	11
CHAPTER THREE The theatre of dreaming	27

CHAPTER FOUR
Non-dream and enactment 43

CHAPTER FIVE
Symbolising traumas: acute enactment 51

CHAPTER SIX
From bastion to enactment: intersubjective models 63

CHAPTER SEVEN
Enactment and implicit alpha-function in the analysis
   of borderline configurations 79

CHAPTER EIGHT
Dreaming bizarre objects and early traumas: the continuum
   dream <-> non-dream 99

CHAPTER NINE
What happens before and after acute enactment: the
   validation of clinical facts 119

CHAPTER TEN
When the analyst becomes stupid: between Narcissus
   and Oedipus 147

CHAPTER ELEVEN
Oedipus, Tiresias, and the Sphinx: from non-dream
   to transformations into dreams 165

REFERENCES 179

INDEX 197

ACKNOWLEDGEMENTS

I thank the *International Journal of Psychoanalysis* for permission to reprint parts of the following papers:

Cassorla, R. M. S. (2001). Acute enactment as resource in disclosing a collusion between the analytical dyad. *International Journal of Psychoanalysis, 82*: 1155–1170.
Cassorla, R. M. S. (2005). From bastion to enactment: the "non-dream" in the theatre of analysis. *International Journal of Psychoanalysis, 86*: 699–719.
Cassorla, R. M. S. (2008). The analyst's implicit alpha-function, trauma and enactment in the analysis of borderline patients. *International Journal of Psychoanalysis, 89*: 161–180.
Cassorla, R. M. S. (2012). What happens before and after acute *enactment*? An exercise in clinical validation and broadening of hypothesis. *International Journal of Psychoanalysis, 93*: 53–89.

I thank the *Psychoanalytic Quarterly* for permission to reprint parts of:
Cassorla, R. M. S. (2013). When the analyst becomes stupid: an attempt to understand enactment using Bion's theory of thinking. *Psychoanalytic Quarterly, 82*: 323–360.

ABOUT THE AUTHOR

Roosevelt M. S. Cassorla, MD, PhD, is a titular member and training analyst of the Brazilian Psychoanalytic Society of São Paulo and the Campinas Study Group. He is Full Professor of Psychological Medicine and Psychiatry at the Medical School of the State University of Campinas, and is a member of the editorial board of the *International Journal of Psychoanalysis* and collaborator on the International Psychoanalytic Association's *Encyclopaedic Dictionary of Psychoanalysis*. He has edited five books and is author of a number of book chapters and papers on psychoanalysis and medical psychology. He is the 2017th recipient of the Mary S. Sigourney Award for Outstanding Achievement in Psychoanalysis.

PREFACE TO THE ENGLISH EDITION

The Psychoanalyst, the Theatre of Dreams and the Clinic of Enactment is the culmination of Roosevelt Cassorla's creative and penetrating exploration of the nature of psychoanalytic process, a project he has been pursuing for more than twenty years. Although his ideas are strikingly original and resist easy characterisation, one way to describe what he has done is to say that he first combines the field theory that is native to the Rio de la Plata region with Bionian thinking in a way that at least until recently has been more familiar to Latin Americans and Continental Europeans than it has been to Anglophone psychoanalysts. With the publication of this book, English speakers will have the opportunity to immerse themselves more fully in the work of one of the world's truly innovative psychoanalytic thinkers.

When analysis is going well, Cassorla believes, analysts listen to their patients' associations and use those associations as a kind of day residue that inspires dreams. Dreams—which, following Bion, occur when we are fully awake—give new meaning to the patient's thoughts, meaning that is conveyed to the patient through interpretation. In turn, the patient uses the analyst's interpretation as the day residue around which a new dream can be formed, and communicates this to the analyst. The process goes on indefinitely, creating what Cassorla calls "dreams-for-two" which give rise to the "Theatre of Dreams" that is part of the book's title. As each participant redreams the dreams of the other, new meanings emerge and deepen. It is a process that is both highly rigorous and ineluctably personal.

But this description covers only one aspect of what happens in the consulting room. Cassorla, again following Bion, knows that there are times when we cannot dream; inevitably there are proto-experiences (Bion's beta-elements) that resist symbolisation. When this happens, the analyst tries to dream what the patient cannot; this is sometimes but not always possible. When attempts to dream fail, the analysis devolves into what Cassorla calls "non-dreams-for-two", creating the "Clinic of Enactment" that is the last part of the title.

Cassorla knows that although dreams-for-two and non-dreams-for-two seem to describe dichotomously alternative processes, both may go on simultaneously. That is, there are always likely to be elements of the analytic relationship that cannot be dreamed by either participant. These undreamed elements are expressed in what he terms "chronic enactments", which are unspoken, collusive agreements between analyst and analysand about how the relationship will be configured.

The use of the term "enactment" is unusual for a non-Anglophone analyst; it reflects Cassorla's attempt to build bridges to concepts of enactment that are native to North American thinking. This is a project that is not easily (and certainly not frequently) undertaken and that is even less easily fulfilled; Cassorla is successful not only because of his innovative use of theory but even more so because of the warmth, openness, and honesty that he brings to both his clinical work and his writing.

The concept of enactment has a long history in North American psychoanalysis. But even as analysts representing many different theoretical persuasions have become aware of the centrality and even ubiquity of enactment, and even as we learned that enactments of one kind or another could be useful sources of information about the analysand's personal history and internal world, there was still a lingering sense that it might be best if they were avoided. For many years, when enactments were discussed, either in oral presentations or in written reports, the analyst's tone was either vaguely embarrassed about having broken the rules or vaguely boastful about having courageously thrown away the book. It is one of the great strengths of this book that Cassorla is neither.

Instead, his work offers us a thoughtful and matter-of-fact approach to the problem of enactment. He begins by making a crucial and seminal distinction between what he calls "chronic" and "acute" enactments. Chronic enactments may go on quietly for years, he teaches; they are unlikely to be noticed, at least for a very long time, and they occupy a narrow space between collusive disavowal and the building of a working alliance. Acute enactments, the explosions that demand attention and lead to guilt and shame, may (if we allow ourselves to think about them matter-of-factly) be steps forward in the analytic process. They can be the beginning of the end of chronic enactments, introducing triangular reality into what had been a sequestered dyad. Of course, to use what happens in this way the analyst has to get past both the shame and the pride about his or her part in the explosion.

This is where Cassorla's extraordinary openness, honesty, and humility allow him to explore the problem of enactment with unique depth and nuance. His willingness to acknowledge his own participation in the "acute enactments" that many find embarrassing and to explore their implications is one example of this. And of course, there is his willingness to entitle one of his chapters "When the analyst becomes stupid …". When this chapter first appeared in 2013 as an article in *The Psychoanalytic Quarterly*, I found it enormously helpful. As a result, I frequently recommended it to students and supervisees who, knowing only the paper's title, were not surprisingly taken aback by the suggestion. After reading it, they had a very different reaction, because it presents a point of view of the analyst's participation in enactments that is as compassionate as it is incisive. I cannot think of a better combination for facilitating both learning and personal growth.

A couple more examples of Cassorla's thinking will drive the point home. In Chapter Six, he writes about a moment when he realises that in the course of his work with a patient, "I had made myself into a suffering victim, a martyr, who bore the pain masochistically, with no awareness that I was counteridentified with those same aspects of [my patient]". This insight (the result of self-reflection or a kind of Barangerian "second look") is interesting and important; it is the kind of thing that analysts need to find in themselves in every analysis if that analysis is to move forward. But that said, it is also a kind of self-awareness that is frequently described in contemporary clinical reports.

What is remarkable, perhaps even unique, is what Cassorla says next; he finds that his submission to his patient "was unconsciously pleasurable, letting myself take satisfaction in being a patient analyst". I can't recall another author who has acknowledged the pleasure that he or she takes from enactments, but grappling not only with our participation but also with the various pleasures that derive from and shape that participation is certainly essential if we are going to deepen our understanding of what has happened.

Cassorla is particularly forthright in addressing a problem that haunts our clinical practice but that has not been widely theorised. In Chapter Five, he develops his idea that there is a close relationship between chronic enactment and working alliance. This formulation will ring true to every practising psychoanalyst, especially to those who do not adhere rigidly to a prescribed set of rules for doing treatment. In this chapter, he discusses a patient who accuses him of having "deceived" her. Eventually, he comes to the conclusion (again, a remarkable example of his honesty) that "I had let myself deceive her by not picking up on her symbiotic, omnipotent, linking fantasies". This reminds me of a patient of mine who I came to believe I had deceived by not picking up on—or not addressing, I can't quite be sure which—her fantasy that she was married to me. In both cases, there seems to be a thin line between enactment, on the one hand, and tact and timing, on the other. Paradoxically, Cassorla's ideas about chronic enactment simultaneously abrogate and deepen the distinction; on his view, it matters less what we call it and more that we understand ourselves in relation to the analysand, including the personal anxieties and pleasures that unconsciously shape our participation.

These thoughts lead me to reflect on the impact that this book is likely to have on readers of all theoretical persuasions and all levels of experience. Although Cassorla's focus throughout the book is clinical practice and the way it can be theorised, in another sense his target is dogma of all kinds. This includes the dogmas contained in formal theories, which can lead to what he calls "hallucinatory understanding that obstructs contact with the unknown", but even more importantly the personal dogma that can lead any of us to lose contact with who we are and with what we are experiencing. In Cassorla's terms, this is what happens when the analyst—for whatever reason—becomes unable to dream and the analytic situation devolves into "non-dreams-for-two". When this happens, the analyst temporarily loses his or her commitment to pursuing truths that are personal to both participants. Under these circumstances, interpretations become what Cassorla—certainly influenced by his political and social background and sensibilities—evocatively characterises as "propaganda".

On virtually every page of the book, Cassorla reminds us that that analyst's interventions can be understood only within the personal and intersubjective context in which they are formed and expressed. Thus, in his creative and illuminating reading of *Oedipus Rex* he wisely and movingly shows us that truth, the end product of insight and the key to therapeutic progress, can also be destructive. Seamlessly weaving Sophocles and Bion, he notes that when Tiresias confronts Oedipus with the truth about his birth he does so hatefully, and Oedipus becomes enraged. The problem, Cassorla concludes, is that "The truth charged with hate only supports Oedipus' hatred of the truth …". Analysts need to be mindful of this, of course, and to consider not only that they are trying to communicate to the patient (whether they reflect a personal truth or propaganda), but also the emotional soil within which the ideas have grown. The ever-present danger is that "truth, contaminated by hate, [will be] useless for stimulating thinking". And, of course, stimulating thinking is always Cassorla's treatment goal.

Few authors are able to convey a sense of both the intellectual discipline and the personal involvement that are essential if psychoanalytic treatment is to succeed. Cassorla is one of those few, and his book both challenges and guides the thinking of anyone who seeks to work in depth with those who seek help.

Jay Greenberg

Training and supervising analyst of the William Alanson White Institute; editor of *The Psychoanalytic Quarterly*; recipient, in 2015, of the Mary S. Sigourney Award

PREFACE TO THE BRAZILIAN EDITION

When Roosevelt Cassorla invited me to write the preface to this book, I felt honoured by the distinction. I have considered the various ways in which to introduce him and his work. I could describe the loyal friend with whom I have been exchanging ideas for twenty-eight years. I could comment on his work, his academic career, or on the stories he has told me about his life. Since I cannot decide which to choose, I intend to speak a little about each of these aspects.

For nearly fifteen years, I attended a study group where we would meet once a month to discuss topics in psychoanalysis. This was a group of people who were highly engaged, competent, and sensitive; the meetings were unforgettable and a great source of pleasure for me. The person who proposed these monthly meetings was Roosevelt Cassorla. I had only recently returned from thirteen years abroad in Europe, having spent ten years in England where my wife Elizabeth and I underwent our psychoanalytic training. This invitation was, to my mind, one of the kindest ways to welcome us (my wife and I, that is), and an expression of confidence in my ability to contribute to Brazilian psychoanalytic thought. This was many years ago, during a period when certain psychoanalytic circles still regarded those who had recently arrived from places considered to be centres of colonialism, as was the case for England, with a certain hostility. Given this context, Cassorla's invitation was more than just a welcome; it was an act of courage. This courage is a defining feature of Cassorla's work, particularly in relation to his research in recent years dedicated to the thorny subject of enactment, which he seeks to illuminate and to develop through understanding and exposition.

Enactment is a broader term than acting or acting-out, although it does bear some kinship. While I was in London, I used to attend a seminar run by Professor Joseph Sandler on "Enactment and/or Acting Out" where he jokingly defined these concepts as comprising everything the patient did that the analyst didn't like, and which also applied to the analyst when he did things that the IPA didn't approve of (Joseph Sandler was the president of the IPA at the time). It was a joke, of course, but the joke contained a warning that we were entering a minefield and working with a border concept that could be considered an ethical breach of boundaries. Hence the degree of courage required to study the subject in greater depth, which Cassorla does masterfully and with great sensitivity. These qualities are written in his face and in the very titles of his articles, titles that are often inspiring and provocative and thus invite close reading and reflection. Let's remind ourselves of some of these works: "Reflections on non-dreams-for-two, enactment and the analyst's implicit alpha-function"; "When the analyst becomes stupid: an attempt to understand enactment using Bion's theory of thinking"; "From bastion to enactment: the 'non-dream' in the theatre of analysis"; "What happens before and after acute enactments?", are good examples.

Perhaps what best characterises contemporary psychoanalysis, contrary to what it initially set out to do, is its focus on intersubjective processes and, as a result of this approximation, on finding a means of interpretation to incorporate analytic listening and the subsequent process that takes place in our minds as a result of this particular type of approach. In this characterisation of psychoanalysis, it is clear that we cannot ignore the impact the patient has on the analyst and the analyst on the patient, as a direct result of its method. Cassorla investigates these processes and the ways in which they are manifested, coining concepts in the course of his research that have come to be effective tools for clarification in understanding how the mental processes operate within the analyst–patient pairing. We can cite such concepts as "chronic enactment", "acute enactment", and "non-dreams-for-two". Today, Cassorla is the author of concepts that form part of the baggage of the international culture of psychoanalysis.

In this book, we will find a collection of reflections, illustrated by an abundance of clinical material, concerning the complex interaction and mutual impact that occurs in an analytic relationship, which demands profound reflection given its extensive implications. The way in which the patient engages with us through their presence followed by their speech has an effect upon us—whether it takes the form of feelings experienced, thoughts evoked, bodily sensations, desires that are delineated, states of mind that surface, sometimes pleasant, other times deeply unpleasant—and suggests the existence of a peculiar phenomenon at work. Since psychoanalysis is a unique kind of relationship, it cannot avoid inquiring into what to do with these experiences. Do we ignore them? See them as neurotic manifestations, and thus discard them? Seek to understand them as a means of communication operated by an intense traffic of projective identifications telling us something about the patient and part of the lived relational context? How do we process them? Should we become attentive observers of what takes place in our inner world and attempt to put feelings awakened in us by the patient's presence into words?

Pierre Fédida (1991), reflecting on the French appropriation of the concept of countertransference and concerned about the possibility of psychoanalysis becoming a psychology of communication and/or of interpersonal relations, warns of the need for us to construct a metapsychology of countertransference. Countertransference would have as a model the metapsychology of dreams and, above all, the logic articulated by oneiric work. The target of his criticism in this reflection was the description of countertransferential phenomena in terms that are limited to the communication processes at work, associated in the majority of cases with hidden latent thoughts, whilst relegating to the background the issue of unconscious scenarios being acted in the relationship with the analyst. As a result of an ever broader approach to countertransferential processes, we have come to seek to uncover the intersubjective phenomena present in the analytic session.

René Roussillon has been stressing that modern psychoanalysis is angled more towards an understanding of complex psychic processes, and using these to develop metapsychological concepts enables us to better understand the current clinic.

Roosevelt Cassorla, in his study of enactment, places this concept within the framework of the aforementioned preoccupations. Enactment cannot be summed up by one action or response, but instead refers to a complex and often lengthy process that manifests itself in the clinic, but is equally a metapsychological concept.

Cassorla's ideas were discussed in depth by the IPA's Committee of Clinical Investigation, in a Report presented at the IPA Congress in 2011. Its author, Donald Moss (2011), writes:

> Cassorla offers us his vision. The vision is deep and elaborate, a thick mix of developmental, structural, and clinical dimensions. The vision is, in my view, quite beautiful, reminiscent, I think, of the kind of beauty available in some Renaissance paintings—iconography and technical mastery combining to produce a picture of extraordinary narrative force and conviction. [...] Cassorla brilliantly generates a clinical/conceptual molecule by which he can simultaneously ask and answer a set of questions posed by way of a moment of clinical surprise.

Cassorla has approximately two hundred publications to his name: papers in scientific journals, five books, and various book chapters. He has been awarded many prizes for his research. These include the Parthenope Bion Talamo Prize (Boston, 2009) and the IPA Best Research Prize on Symbolization (Prague, 2013).

Professor Cassorla has not limited his contributions to psychoanalytic societies (he is training analyst of the Society of São Paulo and the Campinas Study Group, Brazil) and has developed a prolific academic career. He became a professor at the State University of Campinas, where he established community studies and the post-graduate course *sensu stricto* in mental health. He was also a professor at the Pontifical Catholic University of Campinas, and has collaborated as a visiting professor at several universities.

His interest in teaching and research led him to create the working party "Microscopy of the Analytic Session", recognised by the Brazilian Federation of Psychoanalysis (FEBRAPSI) and by the Latin-American Federation of Psychoanalysis (FEPAL).

I will conclude by saying that reading this book will not only teach us a great deal, but it will also give us great pleasure, thanks to the enjoyable, profound approach of Professor Roosevelt Cassorla.

Happy reading.

Elias Mallet da Rocha Barros

Training and supervising analyst of the Brazilian
Psychoanalytic Society of São Paulo; recipient, in 1999,
of the Mary S. Sigourney Award

INTRODUCTION

Psychoanalysis is a "thing for two". Although this statement, coined by Grinberg (1996), may seem obvious, it contradicts certain ideas that assume that the analyst "analyses the patient". Analysis requires the participation of both members of the analytic dyad, a fact that has been discussed by contemporary psychoanalysis in great depth. Patient and analyst both become emotionally involved in the meetings and misunderstandings that take place during the sessions. The analyst, using his analytically trained intuition, maintains a distance from what he is experiencing at the same time as he participates in the emotional exchanges, observing what occurs between the pair and imagining what might be done with these observations to enable development. The patient, for their part, learns emotionally through their experiences. Gradually, the personal contributions from the patient and analyst combine and the dyad finds itself with products of the analytic field, the fruits of the intersubjective relationship.

The impression that psychoanalysis is focused on understanding the patient's unconscious leads towards the study of the phenomena that present themselves in the analytic field, deformed facts both conscious and unconscious as transference/countertransference phenomena. One more step and the analyst realises that he must value what is going on within himself—the analyst. The analyst has always known that he can only be an analyst if he is able to know himself. This self-knowledge, of the real or unique person that he is, protects him from the realisation of countertransferential fantasies but is also related to understanding his own mind, the tool with which he works.

The analyst might imagine that he is in touch with what is happening in the analytic field, only to soon realise that he merely has access to his own mind, that is, to the way in which perceptions, feelings, and intuitions relating to the analytic field are represented within himself. In observing himself, he will be seeing the reflections of what he has captured from the relationship with his patient. As his capacity for observation develops, he will gain greater contact with the intersubjective facts, the "thing for two". This is one of the reasons that have led psychoanalysis to focus increasingly on the analyst as a person, in particular on the qualities that make the analyst similar to, and at the same time different from, all other analysts. Each analytic dyad, each analysis, will be totally different from the rest, although common features do exist. These common features allow our art to approximate hegemonic scientific understanding, but individual peculiarities lead us to other more necessary and interesting forms of understanding, that make up part of the science-art that is psychoanalysis.

In this book, I intend to share with the reader the emotional experiences that occur in the analytic field. This expression—emotional experience—already reveals certain presuppositions on the part of the author. It assumes that human beings are made up of and develop through experiences, and that these experiences are of an emotional order.

Scientific writing is insufficient to represent these experiences. They simply *are*. Artistic communication, on the other hand, is limited by the means of expression and by the author's deficiencies. The reader before a book, just like the analyst, can only be aware of what he is experiencing by observing himself, during the reading process and afterwards when the product of this reading is decanted. One hopes that, if he is a psychoanalyst, the text will reverberate within him—he will feel as though what he is reading is not strange to him, even though he may not know it. Just like the analytic process, reading is a product of emotions. This suggestion follows on from a bigger idea: that thinking is an emotional process. Contemporary authors have been developing this idea, influenced, each in their own way, by Bion.

The range of emotions can be understood along three basic dimensions: love, hate, and knowledge. Human links draw on these emotions, positive and negative alike. Negativity results in transformations whereby these emotions' capacity for linking is attacked. The desire to know is replaced by the desire to not know, or to bring about misunderstandings. Idealisation as the negative of love, and hypocrisy as the negative of hate, together amount to misunderstanding and can predominate over positive linking. In this scenario, the thinking that accompanies the creative processes become impossible.

On the other hand, emotional experiences can only be felt, or given meaning, if it is possible to represent them. For this, the mind activates its capacity for symbolisation. In writing, I seek to transfer emotional experiences relating to psychoanalytic events and knowledge into verbal symbols that are transformed in turn into written symbols. If I am successful, I can transfer my ideas to colleagues. The term "transfer" implies the psychoanalytic concept as well as the common communication between human beings (Cassorla, 2012b).

Therefore, the reader is faced with transformations of emotional experiences realised by the author, transformations whose meaning will be created by him—the reader—according to his personal experiences and understanding. The practising psychoanalyst reader will have greater facility for this, though other readers may be able to overcome the difficulties.

I am drawing a distinction between analytic experiences and the various theories that simultaneously facilitate and impede contact with the emotional experience. Aversion to totalising theories is one characteristic of contemporary psychoanalysis, for they can become rigid, making it difficult for the analyst and patient to become "themselves". Theoretical analysis can become adaptive to the conscious or unconscious expectations of the analyst's theory. We must not forget that theories are hypothetical constructions that seek to organise clinical facts and shed light on their understanding, and must be modified or discarded whenever necessary. Otherwise they establish a suppositional, hallucinatory understanding that obstructs contact with the unknown. Explicit theories (branded with the names of certain authors) can serve to create the illusion of a group identity. These theories can transform themselves into dogmatic facts. The analysts who question the dogmas are considered enemies. "Religious" wars are waged within psychoanalysis, in much the same way as they are in the other areas of the sciences and humanities.

These features tend to diminish thanks to the development of the psychoanalytic thinking and the questioning of authoritarian stances. The transition has been slow in some psychoanalytic cultures. The tendency, however, is that each psychoanalyst sees himself in his own identity, as the fruit of his experience and reflections. It will be this identity that allows him to engage in creative dialogue with his colleagues, each of whom has their own identity. They all share something in common: psychoanalysis, a body of knowledge, practices, and methods of investigation, with invariant factors that unite the different theoretical and practical vertices. This dialogue can be difficult at times, due to diverse conceptual foci, but when dealing with the practice, the clinic, the field common to all theories, it always remains possible.

Beyond explicit theories, the analyst draws upon the implicit theories that are being unconsciously created from the dyad's emotional experiences. Implicit theories go far beyond the supposed explicit theory that the analyst believes he is using, which occasionally goes in the opposite direction, but the analyst fails to realise this. The identification and comprehension of implicit theories forms part of the analytic process. Typically, the analyst uses dialogue with his colleagues in order to identify them. It is impossible to be a psychoanalyst without the exchange of experiences with other colleagues, because the unknown is only revealed through intersubjectivity.

Communication between analysts, including through scientific publications, arises from this necessity. In this book, I seek to describe the clinical experience using the minimum of theoretical constructions. This minimum is indispensable for both scientific and artistic communication and may cause a feeling of strangeness to readers used to theoretical digressions. The author posits that the risks of simplification are lesser than those of saturating the reader. Evidently the reader will notice the theoretical preferences of the author. The author in turn is certain that his preferences would be different if he lived in other cultures and times, and if he had had the opportunity to interact with other experts. Theoretical constructions arise not only from the personal characteristics of each analyst but also from random factors, sociocultural and historical.

The author hopes and wishes for readers to construct their own theoretical hypotheses according to their personal experience. This is a reason for the emphasis on clinical material. Some psychoanalysts scorn clinical accounts, seeing them as contrivances used simply to justify the ideas the author desires. These considerations must be taken into account.

On the other hand, we know that the patient wants to take the analyst wherever she imagines will alleviate her suffering, even if it hinders her development. Every psychoanalyst or psychoanalyst reader knows this. The analyst, confronted with the clinical material, compares the facts he is experiencing, consciously and unconsciously, against his own experience, and the result—in the analysis as in the act of reading—will be the creation of new facts, new experiences that will be validated or invalidated in sequence. Analyses or texts that are idealised by the patient—or by the reader—refer to inductive discourses that, while appearing to develop thinking, generally obstruct it. The risk of this occurring with clinical accounts is minimal when the reader is a practising analyst.

One perennial problem for the psychoanalyst author lies in how to relate clinical material while maintaining ethical discretion. For this, he can use the authorisation of the patient, which must be given a good while after the analysis has been concluded. This occurs easily when the patient also commits herself to psychoanalysis. Every psychoanalyst knows that this solicitation is not without consequences. It is more common for the author to distort the material, in such a way that it becomes vignettes, scenes, and passages from a hypothetical story. Not dissimilar to the work of a novelist. We know that fictional literature often relates the facts of life more successfully than historically accurate stories when the author manages to transmit the emotions involved in an authentic way. The psychoanalyst author is attempting something similar, even if he lacks the literary dimension. In this way, the reader must view the clinical material as facts of life that have been constructed in such a way as to maintain consistency with clinical facts. They are the product of clinical experiences, supervisions, clinical seminars, and the analyst's own facts of life. Some of the transformations put into effect follow Gabbard's (2000) suggestions.

The author imagines that the previous paragraphs have made sense to the reader. This "imagining" is a fantasy on the part of the author. Studying this fantasy suggests some possibilities:

> The author (A) could suppose that the reader (R) perceives and experiences the reality that he communicates in the same way that he, the author, does. In this case, the author "imagines" that R's mind is similar to A's in this area. This relationship can be represented by $1 + 1 = 1$. It deals with an undifferentiated dual relationship, dual in the sense that there is no separation between self and object.

In psychoanalytic jargon, they say that A projects and identifies parts or aspects of his own mind (represented by the text's ideas) in R. The terms "transference" and "projective identification" form part of the jargon. Let us suppose, however, that the author's mental health is not disturbed and that he knows that his "imagining" that R will experience the facts communicated in a similar way to himself is only a hypothesis, supposition, or preconception. The author (A) knows that the reader (R) would never be able to experience the facts in the same way as A, because he is a different person. A's hope is simply for R to understand what A desires to communicate, in a way that will be possible for R.

The certainty that R, being another person, will have different experiences, opens up the possibility that the author might have to endure the frustrations of not having his text understood in the way that he imagines or would wish it to be. He will have to deal with his own narcissistic aspects, even more so if he is criticised. If this is a possibility, the author would benefit from the fact of R being another person. It is difference that promotes fertilisation and new ideas.

If the author (A) treats his text as if it were a dream being dreamed while awake, he will be able to treat the criticism like a dream of the reader (R) who is re-dreaming his dream (the author's). The author will then be able to re-dream the critic's dream and so on, establishing creative dreams-for-two that will broaden the scope of the text's ideas. In this situation, the author maintains his capacity for dreaming and thinking, being able to live in the triangular reality where self and object are distinct and have their own minds. We can represent this situation as $1 + 1 = 3$. Number 3 represents himself and all subsequent numbers. The minds of A and R alter, each in their own way, and we have at least two texts that fertilise to result in new texts, and so it continues.

The opposite will occur if the psychotic part of the author's mind predominates. Confusing his text with himself, he will experience criticism as a threat of annihilation. In this situation, the author can be dominated by a kind of delirium, a non-dream in which he will treat the critic reader as a personal enemy. The dual relationship, once idealised (when A imagined that R would experience the facts in the same way as him), becomes persecutory. The triangularity is destroyed.

In the event of the author feeling insecure and fragile, he will be able to project his need for protection onto the reader, who will become idealised. The reader's potential criticism will then be accepted without thinking. The need to please, to make R=A, would make the author attack his own capacity to think. Not being able to endure 1 + 1 = 3 means maintaining the configuration 1 + 1 = 1.

The situations described here are similar to those that can occur between the members of the analytic dyad. In areas of possible symbolisation, patient and analyst "dream", each in their own way but also together, what occurs in the analytic field. Differentiation exists between self and object, so there is the possibility of oedipal triangulation. The transformation of (1 + 1 = 1) into (1 + 1 = 3) is possible. It is important for these configurations to oscillate, that is, that (1 + 1 = 1 <-> 1 + 1 = 3). The provisional dual identification is necessary and anticipates triangular differentiation. And the triangular differentiation should enable new identifications, that is, provisional dual relations. Therefore, in an area of dream and thought, that is, a non-psychotic area, the primordial function of projective identification is to communicate emotional states in symbolic form, since there is self–object differentiation.

When the patient cannot endure the triangularity, the configuration 1 + 1 = 1 is maintained, or reverted to in desperation. There is an important difference between the author–reader and patient–analyst situations. In the latter, thanks to the devices of the analytic framework, projective identification is stimulated. The patient imagines—unconsciously—that the analyst is a part of himself, even though he knows consciously that it is another person.

The model above, however, is more complex. This is because the analyst also unconsciously places internal objects and parts of his own mind within the patient. These aspects are commonly activated or stimulated by the projective identifications of the patient. The personal analysis, the supervisions, and the contact with other analysts all serve to make the analyst's own aspects better understood, so that they do not interfere with the analytic work. However, this interference is inevitable and the best the analyst can do is to take advantage of it, even if it occurs afterwards, as a "second look", a "listening to listening", or while recuperating from a psychological catastrophe that has threatened to destroy the analytic field.

I imagine that the reader, still patiently poring over this Introduction, is waiting to find out "In the end, what is enactment?". This is the title of a text dedicated to curious analysts in training (Cassorla, 2013c). The previous paragraphs, on dual and triangular relations, introduce the theme.

Psychoanalysis has been devoting itself to the in-depth study of complex situations, where imperceptible resistance organisations attack the capacity for thinking and dreaming. The analyst enters into contact with these areas when confronted with dual relationships, lack of self–object differentiation, of which he is unaware. These constitute what will be called "chronic" enactments. When this relationship is suddenly undone, the analytic field is traumatised due to the difficulty of living in the triangular reality. These events are called "acute" enactments. The chapters of this book will discuss the origins, factors, dynamics, consequences, and theories of these phenomena. Their study leads us to obligatorily address aspects of psychoanalytic theory and technique when we deal with patients who are difficult to access. Beyond the clinic, we will rely on the help of artistic and mythical models.

Some of the main ideas in this book have already been published in scientific journals. These texts were modified for the present publication. The main core of the book, which progressively discusses the clinical events and their theorisation, constitutes Chapters Five, Six, and Seven. These are based on the following works cited in the References at the end of the book as Cassorla (2001, 2005a, 2008a, and 2009a). The international clinical validation of the hypotheses raised in these chapters is found in Chapter Nine, based on Cassorla (2012a). Chapter Ten, which introduces the term "stupidity", has been modified from Cassorla (2013b, 2013d, 2014c). Chapter Three, which discusses artistic models for the events that take place in the analytic field, is based on Cassorla (2003) and (2005b). Chapter Eleven turns to mythical stories as literary models to describe emotional experiences, and is based on Cassorla (2008b, 2010a, 2010b).

If the reader were to read the chapters of this book in sequence, they would come across some repetitions of ideas discussed in earlier chapters. The author hopes that the reader considers these to be tolerable. It is possible, as the clinic attests, that repetitions—in forming part of new contexts—can broaden the understanding of themselves.

CHAPTER ONE

The analytic field and dreams-for-two

Psychoanalysis takes place between two people. The patient seeks to reveal themselves in their subjectivity to the analyst, albeit with potential difficulty. The analyst, for his part, participates in the analytic process, receiving and interpreting what the patient reveals and/or hides. It is debatable as to whether the analyst is committed to objectively understanding his patient's mental functioning or whether he experiences emotional states that emerge during the encounter on a subjective level. In other words, we may ask to what extent the analyst will be objective or subjective. Here, we encounter two extreme hypotheticals: in the first, we have the ideal of the *objective* analyst, one who does not become involved with the patient and simply observes the material from the outside, like a cold scientist in the lab; at the other extreme, we have the analyst who eschews all objectivity and focuses on what he *feels*, believing this *feeling* to be the only reliable tool for this activity.

For psychoanalysis, the objective <-> subjective paradigm is limiting. Analyst and patient become emotionally involved with one another and this turbulence is a constitutive part of human relationships. It is important for the analyst to be able to allow himself to be led by what is happening in the analytic field, at the same time as meticulously observing the events in which he is a participant. Thus the analyst seeks to objectivise, for himself, whatever he may subjectively experience.

We consider *analytic field* (Baranger & Baranger, 1961–1962) to refer to the space/time in which the analytic process occurs. Both members of the analytic dyad are mutually influenced, and nothing occurs for one of them without repercussions for the other. These factors are linked to the idea of transference as a total situation. Klein writes that "in unravelling the details of the transference it is essential to think in terms of *total situations* transferred from the past into the present, as well as of emotions, defences, and object-relations" (1952, p. 54). Betty Joseph reminds us that *total situation* refers to everything that the patient brings to the relationship. She tells us that this can be calibrated by focusing our attention on what is happening within the relationship, understanding "… how patients act on us to feel things for many varied reasons; how they try to draw us into their defensive systems; how they unconsciously act out with us in the transference, trying to get us to act out with them; how they convey aspects of their inner world built up from infancy—elaborated in childhood and adulthood, experiences often beyond the use of words, which we can often only capture through the feelings aroused in us, through our counter-transference, used in the broad sense of the word" (1985, p. 157).

This author focuses our attention, in great detail, on what patients do unconsciously with the analyst. It is clear that the analyst will be able to *capture experiences*, or *learn through feelings aroused in him*, only if these aspects can be thought by the analyst. I am using the term "think" here to signify the transformation of these experiences by the professional into something symbolic, in other words to endow them with a psychic quality. And the first step towards thinking will be to *dream* these experiences.

At this point, we encounter what Bion (1962b, 1992) calls *dreamwork-alpha* or simply *alpha-function*, a hypothetical mental function that transforms raw elements (those that have not acquired a psychic quality), called *beta-elements*, into *alpha-elements*. The beta-elements cannot connect or link with each other, and thus cannot be deployed for dreaming, thinking, or memory. The opposite occurs with alpha-elements, which already have a psychic quality and constitute the raw materials required for dreams. The linking together of alpha-elements forms a contact barrier, a barrier that separates and at the same time allows for communication between the conscious and unconscious.

Dreaming takes places as much when we sleep as in unconscious waking life. In its broadest sense, dreaming includes daydreams and night dreams (category C in Bion's 1977 grid). In the case of dreams that occur during sleep, we can have some access to their latent content from the understanding of the manifested content that continues with associations, images that are attracted or sequential to the account of the night dream. This means that the dream continues to be dreamed when we are awake. In relation to the dream or unconscious waking thoughts, its latent content tries to manifest itself through daydreams. These are visual pictures that pass through the mind of the waking dreamer, generally if they keep themselves in a state of suspension of desire and memory. The concept of projective identification aids the understanding of what takes place in the analytic field. The patient, in their fantasy, places parts of the self, objects, and their relations, within the analyst who is seen in a deformed manner, as though containing aspects of the patient. However, if these projective identifications are pathological, massive, then they can act beyond the fantasy, invading the receiver with the ability to control them from within. The analyst is recruited to become a part of the patient and coerced into acting out the projected aspects.

In Bion's container–contained model (Bion, 1962b), the understanding of these facts is amplified. If the alpha-function is damaged and the container is unable to transform external and internal perceptions into something which passes for thought, we find ourselves faced with dysfunctional configurations where the analytic dyad cannot dream and think adequately. This results in situations of sterility or rigidity of thought that can be referred to as "non-dreams", the raw material for what will be described later on as "enactment". These non-dreams are comprised of configurations that behave like beta-elements, seeking release. The qualifying *non* indicates that we are dealing with a potential dream that has not yet taken place, but which could be dreamed if it were to find a containing, dreaming, thinking mind. The difficulty in dreaming and thinking occurs in what Bion (1957, 1962a) calls the psychotic part of the mind. This extends into archaic, traumatised areas and areas with no representation (Cassorla, 2009a, 2014a) that can be somehow superposed over the unrepressed unconscious described in Freud's second topography (Bollas, 1989; Freud, 1923b; Sapisochin, 2007).

The alpha-elements constitute the first level of meaning; sketches of thought in images that link together to constitute the initial thinking.

The imagetic symbols then seek verbal symbols. When dreaming occurs, it is because this symbolisation is already taking place.

Let us remember that symbols are elements that allow us to manage reality in their absence. They are characterised by the capacity for linking, for articulating in networks, in symbolic webs, whose connections broaden the capacity for thought. For example, a word heard in a strange language, since it has no meaning, cannot enter into any symbolic network. Thinking does not take place. The opposite will occur if we know its translation in our own language, its word-symbol that will attract other symbols, thus entering into the symbolic web. Another example: in the present text, the word *alpha* would be no more than a Greek letter, devoid of meaning, unless it connects to the symbolic web in Bion's theory of thinking. We must also remember that these symbolic networks do not represent the thinking, they *are* the thinking, and their capacity for connection enables the creation of new thoughts and possibilities.

Alpha-function deficiency will mean that the symbols lose their functions. The symbolic networks are inadequately formed, they come undone, or a stagnation takes place in which the supposed ideas become hardened. This last transformation would occur, for example, if the term *alpha-function* were to be used not as a hypothesis to broaden the capacity for thinking but as an irrefutable, unshakeable belief: an ultimate certainty. In this case, it would act in the service of *non-thinking*, emerging in the mind to form part of a *non-dream*. The patient externalises these non-symbolised aspects in the analytic field, through affects, sounds, non-thought acts, beliefs, symptoms, and voids. Such discharges can invade the analyst through massive projective identifications. They stimulate his feelings more than his capacity to hear. They are non-dreams that can be potentially transformed into dreams by an analyst with available alpha-function.

The situation described above, in which the term *alpha-function* becomes a belief, transformation in hallucinosis (Bion, 1965), and refrains from being a usable symbol, a thought, demonstrates what is called the *reversal of alpha-function* (Bion, 1963), the destruction of the symbolic formation. What previously served as thought becomes something devoid of this capacity that functions in a similar way to beta-elements.

In this way, elements that never acquired thinkability form part of the non-dream, just like those that are a product of the reversal of the alpha-function, which are manifested as somatisations, symptoms, actings, beliefs, delirium and hallucinations, and any other form of non-thinking. Caper (1996) distinguishes a synthetic alpha-function that deals with non-mental states (raw sensations and perceptions) and an analytic alpha-function that deals with unbearable mental states, that is, delirium, hallucinations, bizarre objects, moralist hate, and so on, products of the reversal of the alpha-function, or of a hypothetical anti-alpha-function (Sandler, 1997).

The oneiric process requires work towards developing emotional experiences that seek expression through images, that is to say figurability. The migration towards figurability (Freud, 1900a) occurs in an affective atmosphere that unconsciously determines the dream, producing images that capture and express the initial constitutional forms of these experiences' meanings, in a kind of metabolisation of emotional life (Barros, 2000). Barros refers to what he calls "affective pictograms" to denote the first form of mental representation of emotional experiences, which constitutes the beginning of oneiric thinking. We could say that the alpha-function turns the experiences without meaning into pictographic form. The affective pictogram, in the process of its constitution and in the figuration itself, potentially contains hidden and absent meanings, which pressure the mind to broaden its range of tools for representation.

The analyst is called upon to respond to this pressure, with his mind acting in tandem with the imagetic elements brought to the scene. Running the risk of being engulfed by this pressure, the analyst's function is to try and uncover it, demonstrating and creating meanings and direction for new forms of representation, primarily through words—the ultimate symbols. In the first instance, or even later on, it is possible that he is also unable to find them, and the scene will continue in its search for meaning, until verbal symbols emerge. These attract new symbols, mainly verbal but also sensory and imagetic, broadening the meanings. With this, the mental universe expands, opening up the experience to new symbolic connections, new meanings, greater emotional development, and greater richness in the dyad's work. Scenes and plots that take place in the analysis theatre broaden out and refine themselves in a process that is never complete; a continuous amplification of the inner world (Cassorla, 2015, 2016a).

In this model, we are confronted with an exertion, an effort on the part of a mind, a personality required in giving meaning to the world. When we refer to the transformation into pictographic images manifested in the analytic field, we consider that it has already taken place with a certain degree of symbolisation. At the very least with enough to enable the constitution of these images and plots. The patient can dream and the function of the analyst will be to dream, from different angles, the dream that the patient dreams. That is, the analyst re-dreams the dream and in capturing new meanings amplifies the symbolic web. At this point, we are in a non-psychotic area, where symbolisation is possible.

When dealing with psychotic and traumatic areas, it is not possible to dream, and the patient brings us non-dreams to be dreamed by the analyst. To summarise, in the non-psychotic area we re-dream the patient's dream, and in the psychotic area we attempt to dream the patient's non-dream.

A non-dream can occasionally simulate a dream—however, it may be identified as false because it repeats itself, stereotyped, and seems to recruit the analyst who is non-dreaming it. It will be static, without movement in the plot, or with only a paralysing pseudo-movement. Traumatic dreams have this characteristic while they are being non-dreamed (Cassorla, 2005b).

For example, Helen Keller experienced trauma in the form of a brain lesion at nineteen months old, resulting in blindness and deafness. The description that follows is not very different to those related by patients who have experienced psychotic and traumatic areas of non-dreaming, once they have recuperated.

> I lived in a world that was a no-world. […] I did not know that I knew aught, or that I lived or acted or desired. I had neither will nor intellect. I was carried along to objects and acts by a certain blind natural impetus. I had a mind which caused me to feel anger, satisfaction, desire. These two facts led those about me to suppose that I willed and thought. […] I never contracted my forehead in the act of thinking. I never viewed anything beforehand or chose it. […] I also recall tactually the fact that never in a start of the body or a heart-beat did I feel that I loved or cared for anything. My inner life, then, was a blank without past, present, or future, without hope or anticipation, without wonder or joy or faith.
>
> It was not night—it was not day……
> But vacancy absorbing space,
> And fixedness, without a place;

There were no stars—no earth—no time—No check—no change—no good—no crime.

My dormant being had no idea of God or immortality, no fear of death.

(Keller, 1908, pp. 113–121)

The dream-for-two

From the considerations put into effect, it emerges that the analytic situation is made up of *dreams-for-two* (or, if the analytic process does not develop, a complex of non-dreams). The analyst allows himself to be taken by the patient's dream and re-dreams it. This new dream is then recounted to the patient through interventions. Once these are connected to the patient's symbolic network, the patient re-dreams the analyst's dream, and so on and so forth. In this way, it constitutes a web of *dreams-for-two*. In this model, Ogden's (1994a, 1994c) ideas may be applied—the dreams-for-two maintain a dialectic relationship with the dreams of each member of the dyad—and those of Ferro (1992)—the dreams-for-two are formed like affective holograms of the field. These ideas derive largely from Bion's thinking.[1]

To quote Meltzer:

> What seems to happen is that the analyst listens to the patient and watches the image that appears in his imagination. It might cogently be asserted that he allows the patient to evoke a dream in himself. Of course that is his dream and will be formed by the vicissitudes of his own personality. [...] From this point of view one might imagine that every attempt to formulate an interpretation of a patient's dream could imply the tacit preamble, "While listening to your dream I had a dream which in my emotional life would mean the following, which I impart to you in the hope that it will throw some light on the meaning that your dream has for you".
>
> (1983, p. 90)

In perceiving that the dream dreamed by the analyst, despite attempting to dream that of the patient, is a dream that belongs to the analyst, it becomes clear that factors belonging to the analyst as a *real* person enter into play. The lesser the patient's capacity for symbolisation, the more these factors shall be required.

Grotstein (2000, 2007) affirms that the analyst is called upon, provoked, or urged to respond to the emotions and associations of the analysand with personal emotions of his own. The analyst, in contact with those derived from his oneiric thinking, observes the visual images that pass through his mind. His alpha-function means that his own emotions and experiences that resonate with the patient's emotional truth are localised and unconsciously grouped together, indicating the clinical truth of the moment as *sense or common sense* (Bion, 1963; Sandler, 2005). The patient in turn, while re-dreaming the dream recounted by the analyst, shows him, as the analyst's "best colleague" (Bion, 1963; Ferro, 1996) the effect of his work, and so on and so forth. Therefore, both members of the dyad dream and are dreamed simultaneously.

The analyst's daydreaming, or *reverie*, refers to the *spontaneous* emergence of images in his mind. This spontaneity refers to the necessity to curb memory and desire. For this to occur, an active exercise can be necessary on the part of the analyst, to go against the mental tendency to seek images, ideas, or past affects that make up part of the memory, or desired ideas and affects. In other words, to withstand the *not knowing*, the chaos, until something naturally takes shape. With practice, this active exercise tends to become automatic.

I think that this apparently simply rule, one that demands intense discipline and self-knowledge for its execution, is part of psychoanalysis's greatest technical discovery, the rule of *fluctuating attention*, counterpart of the fundamental rule of *free association*, that is solicited of the patient.

However, even in believing himself to be alert to fluctuating attention, the analyst often fails to recognise that the attention has hardened, and in some areas has stagnated. This hardening is manifested in various ways and involves non-dreams. One of these is the employment of theories (the analyst's or those of another author) that are described to the patient, almost always with an explanatory purpose, where the patient's material is embedded, rigidly packaged, a fact that the patient who resists thinking can accept with pleasure.

Another factor that hardens the fluctuating attention is when the analyst directs his attention towards past events or expectations of the future, without the necessary patience to wait for the dyad's dream to emerge. In these situations, the analyst seeks to explain what is happening through the reductionisms relative to what has already taken place before, or tries to foresee the patient's life, sometimes transforming the patient in doing so, according to expectations and desires for the future. If in the first case (reductionism to the past) the analytic process is limited to the area in question, in the second (the analyst's expectations) the process also ceases to be analytic and becomes propaganda, in the sense that the analyst is employing suggestion or directing the patient's life.

It is possible that the utilisation of explanatory theories and their communication to the patient have their origins in Freud's efforts to test his ideas out on his patients, as we can observe in some of his texts. However, his brilliance makes him alter theories and sometimes radically modify them. Other authors have done the same, but the analyst runs the risk of identifying adaptively with his masters, other analysts, and theories, devoting to them a reverential awe. In these situations, the analyst, even when potentially capable of capturing emotional phenomena, has compromised his capacity to dream and think.

Some authors, chiefly those of recent decades, have drawn attention to the possibility of stagnation in technical procedures. The emphasis Bion (1967) has placed on the necessity for the analyst to work in a state of *no memory, no desire, no intention to understand*, was an important contribution. A consequence of this technical rule was the re-assessment of the emphasis upon conscious fantasies, in the analyst's daydreams, in the revalorisation of images, of the scenes organised visually, as privileged aspects in the identification of the repressed and its return (Freud, 1915e; Isaacs, 1948). However, we must draw a distinction between the *memory-dream* and the *desire-dream* (Bion, 1970), fruits of the analytic dyad's dreaming that emerge spontaneously and naturally in the prepared mind of the analyst, and the utilisation of memory and of desire, fruit of the anxiety to fill in the not-knowing.

To summarise, during the analytic process of the model in question, there are two possibilities:

a. When the patient communicates their dreams to the analyst, that is to say, when the patient communicates something that has already acquired a psychic quality (resulting from the alpha-function), we say that projective identification has taken place as a form of communication, normal or realistic. The analyst will dream the dreams dreamed by the patient from other angles, seeking to broaden their meaning;

b. When the patient presents non-dreams, they can enter the analyst through normal or massive projective identifications, and it will become part of the analyst's function to untangle them, and attempt to dream the non-dreams that have been non-dreamed by the patient, so that they can acquire a psychic quality. If they are not untangled, they will also be *non-dreamed*.

In this way, the analytic process is a result of an intersubjective relationship in which everything that occurs in the analytic space/time is important to us, both dreams and non-dreams alike, when observed and worked on by a prepared mind. The analyst makes use of his *psychoanalytically trained intuition* (Sapienza, 2001) to do this. As a result, he can become involved with the patient and allow himself to be influenced by their dreams and non-dreams, at the same time as observing what takes place within himself, his own dreams and non-dreams.

A dream-for-two takes place, an outsourced product of the dreams and non-dreams being dreamed, involving both members of the dyad and going beyond their simple sum. For each individual patient, the analyst seeks to uncover how each aspect is dreamed or non-dreamed and will look for ways to dream them, dreaming from other angles those which have already emerged as dreams, and transforming the non-dreams into dreams.

When the patient's non-dream is projected within the analyst in such a way that their capacity to dream deteriorates, we say that *non-dreams-for-two* are taking place. Since the analyst does not realise what is happening, the non-dreams-for-two result in collusions which are imperceptible to both members of the analytic dyad. They constitute the raw material of what will be studied, during the ensuing chapters, as chronic enactment.

Note

1. Bion's thinking has been further developed by various contemporary authors. For example, Meltzer (1978, 1983, 1986, 2005); Ferro (1992, 1996, 1999, 2002a, 2002b, 2006, 2009); Ogden (1989b, 1994c, 2005, 2013); Rezende (1995); Tabak de Bianchedi (1999); Symington and Symington (1996); Grotstein (2000, 2007, 2009); López-Corvo (2006); Brown (2011); Chuster (2003); Junqueira Filho (2003); Sandler (2005, 2009, 2011, 2013); Pistiner de Cortiñas (2011); Civitarese (2013b); Levine and Brown (2013).

CHAPTER TWO

Dreaming non-dreamed dreams

As we have seen, the alpha-function transforms emotional experiences into alpha-elements, which constitute the raw material for oneiric thinking. On the other hand, we know from Freud (1900a) that unconscious oneiric thinking is transformed into manifest dreams through the work of figurability, which involves condensations, displacements, and secondary revisions.

The manifest dream communicates to the dreamer (and to the analyst) the unconscious dream, thoughts that have been disguised in order to escape notice by the censor which would block the dream thought from consciousness. The dream is connected with verbal symbols and in this way the dreamer transforms imagetic symbols, initially unconscious, into conscious verbal thinking. This transformation allows new conscious and unconscious connections with other experiences and thoughts, broadening the thinking capacity.

This broadening can be exemplified by the discovery of the benzene formula: the chemist Kekulé transformed his emotional experiences derived from his researches into unconscious thought. The work of dreaming transformed this unconscious thinking into an image in which some snakes were biting each other's tails, forming a hexagon shape. Only when Kekulé woke up did he associate the dreamed image with what he was researching, that is, the chemical formula for benzene.

It is known that a nightmare can wake up the dreamer. These dreams or non-dreams are interrupted (Ogden, 2005) because the symbolising process is inadequate to contain the powerful affects; thus the sleeper is awakened. In contrast, at other times, the dreamer wakes up in order to make contact with the solution to a problem realised during his unconscious dream which has been expressed in some way by the manifest dream. The creative awakening of Kekulé is different from the awakening from a nightmare/traumatic non-dream.

The idea that the dream can be thought of as a "theatre generator of meaning" (Meltzer, 1983) refers, therefore, to the constitutional and transformational processes of the symbolic unconscious network. The generated meanings, that is, dreamed unconsciously, also search for unconscious comprehension by the dreamer (Grotstein, 2000). When we state that the subject dreams both during the day and during the night, we are referring to the unconscious dream thought, which like breathing and digestion, occurs twenty-four hours a day. The manifest dream, whether a waking or asleep dream, reveals the conflict between the truth and the mechanisms that try to hide it. During the analytical session, the patient dreams unconsciously what is happening here and now, and these thoughts are expressed in a deformed way through the verbalisation of conscious fantasies, feelings, and ideas that cross the patient's mind. The analyst is included as a transferential object into these dreams and the understanding of the transference/countertransference, as total situations, reveals the meanings of these dreams. The statement "the analyst dreams the session" (Bion, 1992) can be broadened into "patient and analyst dream the analytical session".[1]

The capacity to symbolise is dependent upon to the capacity to live through the complexities of the oedipal triangulation. This triangulation develops during the depressive position (Klein, 1940), and the depressive situation is a result of the same triangulation. Self and object are experienced separately, having their own lives. The capacity to symbolise depends not only on the capacity of the container (mother, analyst, etc.) to transform beta-elements into alpha-elements, but also on the proper oscillation between disperse facts of the schizo-paranoid position (PS) and the organisation (including oedipal) of the depressive position (PS<–>D) (Bion, 1962a,b).

The capacity to symbolise is connected to the patient's ability to observe himself and to realise his separateness from others. The occasional confusion between internal and external reality is acknowledged, on a second glance (when the patient takes a distance) or when it is shown by the analyst. Here, we are describing a non-psychotic, or neurotic, area of the personality (Bion, 1962a) in which dreaming is possible—whether sleeping or awake. The patient is able to realise that he dreamt during the night or that he had been daydreaming during the day.

In this area of the personality (non-psychotic), the patient externalises aspects of his internal world that contain representations of drives and defence, that is, objects and internal object relations that are unconsciously symbolised. As we have seen, the analytical field is composed of dreams that are dreamt by the patient—here and now—and which include transferential fantasies regarding the analyst's dreams and the analyst himself. The dreams have an impact on the analyst who, through the use of his analytical capacity, re-dreams the patient's dreams (conscious and unconsciously), broadening their meaning. At the same time, the analyst is able to take a distance and observe what is happening between the two members of the analytical dyad. The analyst's dreams (which includes the patient's) can be transformed into interventions, which, in turn, broaden the patient's and the analytical dyad's dreaming capacity. As the analytical process develops, the dreams of both members of the analytical dyad constitute a complex, dreams-for-two, in which it is not always possible to differentiate the contribution of each one.

In the psychotic part of the personality, the oedipal triangle has been disturbed and the patient cannot discriminate himself properly from the object. The capacity of symbolisation is impaired and a confusion between the internal and external world occurs. The analytic field is dominated by formations that can be called non-dreams. The non-dreams manifest themselves through discharges in acts and in the body, through compulsions, repetitive scenes and plots, fanaticism, omniscience, other delusions, and transformations in hallucinosis. The non-dreams penetrate the analyst's mind, and he must transform them into dreams. On occasion, the analyst may be so penetrated by the patient's non-dreams that his symbolic capacity is attacked; thus giving rise to non-dreams-for-two. The non-psychotic area coexists, in all human beings, with the psychotic one. The latter should be expanded to include the traumatic and primordial areas that are part of the non-repressed unconscious.[2]

We can identify a spectrum for the non-dream, involving a continuum from beta-elements towards alpha, thus moving in the direction of the dream. As examples, at one of the extremes we would have a catatonic patient who is absolutely incapable of speaking or moving and nothing is happening with the analyst; near the other extreme of the non-dream (closer to the dream) the patient issues forth meaningless noise, but in conjunction communicates visual images that seek to sketch out a narrative, but there is obstruction in the symbolic verbalisation and the scenes remain stagnant.

It is known that psychoanalysis faced serious problems when the first analysts became more involved emotionally with their patients. The analytical process became stagnant and ended in repetitive dual collusions. The access to the symbolic network was impaired and the analyst's capacity to dream was also impaired. The technical recommendations of Freud (1912e, 1913c) indicated how to deal with such situations, aiming to transform discharge into thoughts. Due to the development of his theory, Freud gave priority to what we have been calling "dream areas". But he also pointed to non-dream situations, when he referred to *Agieren* (Freud, 1914g) (acting-out) and to hypothetical constructions or reconstructions in relation to traumas that do not have the potential of being recalled (Freud, 1937d).

In the last decades, psychoanalysis has been searching for ways in which to work with borderline, perverse, psychotic, and autistic configurations in which difficulties, blocks, and attacks that impede the adequate development of the symbolic network of thinking are found. The analyst, facing these configurations, works in hazardous conditions and is subject to having his own mental functions attacked.

Significant technical advances were developed from object relations theory. The idea of projective identification as something that described a phenomenon beyond unconscious fantasy (Bion, 1959; Grinberg, 1957; Rosenfeld, 1987), that is, which evoked powerful emotions in the analyst, reinforced the importance of the use of countertransference as an instrument of the analysis (Heimann, 1950; Money-Kyrle, 1956; Racker, 1948, 1953). Even though controversies persist, countertransference is seen as an important instrument and as a common ground by which to compare contemporary psychoanalytic approaches (Gabbard, 1995). When countertransference is effectively used, it becomes a powerful resource that allows for the analyst's capacity to get in touch with areas of impaired symbolisation. The emphasis on the intersubjective nature of the analytic dyad, a characteristic of contemporary psychoanalysis, has developed from these clinical ideas (Brown, 2011).

There is a tendency to broaden the concept of countertransference with that of reverie, which would now encompass (Barros, 2013; Barros & Barros, 2016; Civitarese, 2013a; Ogden, 1999) previously unappreciated aspects of the analyst's imagination, visual images, fantasies, perceptions, feelings, daydreams and dream, somatic sensations. Bion (1962b) tells us that reverie is that open state of mind that is receptive to any emotional state of the loved object, that is, of the projective identifications felt as both good and bad. As it occurs with the mother of the baby, the analyst also uses his reverie capacity during the session. It is necessary that the analyst gets lost in his thoughts and feelings until the reveries start to make some sense. The non-trained analyst tends to ignore his reveries or considers them as products of his own perturbations and thus does not bother to investigate them (Ogden, 1999).

The reverie capacity involves an active mental state that searches for contact with this kind of "natural reserve" (Freud, 1911b) where the primary process predominates: an area of fantasy or daydreaming. The analyst allows himself be lost in the reveries but, at the same time, he observes them and tries to comprehend them. The state of reverie allows raw emotional experiences to be captured and transformed into unconscious waking thought, and here we can see alpha-function at work. These experiences are connected to other emotional experiences, either conscious or unconscious, which had already been signified and/or are being signified. These reverie images that come to the mind of the analyst constitute fantasies or manifest daydreams which reveal the dream thoughts that are being generated and worked unconsciously by the analyst and by the analytical dyad (dream-for-two). Besides the figurability, the reveries are also formed by the other mechanisms found in dream work: condensation, displacement, and secondary revision. These mechanisms also rely on what happens in the analytical field, and manifest themselves in the transference/countertransference experience and are dreamed in the here and now. It is likely that the secondary revisions produced during this process are more sophisticated since the patient, being awake, has access to the secondary processes. It is for this reason that the way the patient presents his ideas may seem logical and organised, using facts and memories that conceal the truth/reality (Cassorla, 2016b).

Non-dreams that manifest themselves through discharges, somatisations, transformations in hallucinosis, and voids are "imagined" by the analyst, who interprets the conscious and unconscious meaning of these experiences. In primal areas of the mind, the analyst can be solicited to use constructions (*via di levare*) (Freud, 1937d). The constructions that appear in the analyst's mind can be also reveries.

The functions of the mental apparatus described by Freud (1911b) (consciousness, attention, memory, judgement, thought, and actions) must be altered in order to allow for the reverie capacity to emerge. The analyst's attention, which is used to "periodically search the external world" (Freud, 1911b, p. 219), must keep fluctuating without giving major or minor importance to what is observed (evenly hovering or fluctuating attention) (Freud, 1912e). Memories, desires, expectations are also actively blocked. This results in an altered state of conciousness between sleep and wakefulness. This state of mind can be achieved by following Bion's recommendations (1967, 1992): the analyst must work without memory, without desire, without intention to comprehend. This process becomes circular: the reverie state is a product of these recommendations, and these recommendations are possible when this state is reached. The analyst knows that he has lost his capacity for reverie when he realises he is dominated by desires and memories.

The factors that favour the reverie capacity and its clinical use are not clear. I think that an important factor is the active search for atemporality. When past and present (memory and desire) are ignored, everything that happens in the analytical field seems to happen at a present time, although the term "present time" is opposed to the past and future time. As these categories of past and present cease to exist, we are in the atemporal terrain where present, past, and future, the time of the conscious, do not exist. The addendum "without intention to comprehend" will not be pertinent since intention is a fact that refers to the future. I think that the insistence on this recommendation shows that Bion perceived how it would be difficult to experience the "not-knowing". Thanks to this attitude of "not-knowing", the analyst can experience another type of knowledge which manifests itself in other ways—encompassing the dream thought—behind and beyond the secondary process.

Throughout his work, Bion uses other models to explicate his technical suggestions. They are related to the analyst's containing capacity to bear frustration and attacks and to keep himself alive and thinking.

Bion (1970) proposes that the analyst develop his "negative capability", an expression that was found in a letter of Keats: "when man is capable of being in uncertainties, mysteries, doubts, without any irritable reaching after fact and reason". Bearing the capacity of not-knowing is also reinforced by the idea of Maurice Blanchot (that he took from André Green): "*La réponse est le malheur de la question*".

Bion (1970) also uses the term *intuition* as an instrument capable of capturing emotional phenomenon. It must prevail over the observation of the sensorial organs. In other places, Bion (1967) reminds us of the letter from Freud to Andreas-Salomé in which he suggests that the analyst should artificially blind himself in order to better see the light.

Derived from the theory of thinking, Bion proposes that the analyst bear the chaos until the selected fact arises. This fact will make the chaos meaningful. The chaos is related to the facts of the paranoid-schizoid position (PS) and the organisation to the facts of the depressive position (D). The analyst must oscillate between these two positions—he must bear the chaos and, at the same time, he must not attach himself rigidly to D (a premature sense of order). The capacity to tolerate fluctuations (Ps↔D) between states of relative fragmentation (Ps) and integration (D) depends upon the strength of one's analytical capacity (and also his capacity of thinking). Bion recommends patience during the PS phase in order to allow the unconscious work of dreaming to take place. As a result of the analyst's ability to tolerate states of PS, a sense of security arises as the chaos slowly organises itself (PS→D). This sense of security offers only a brief respite until it is undone in order to allow for new experiences to emerge. Bion proposes that the analyst have faith in the capacity of his unconscious to dream and attribute meaning to non-dreams.

In the same direction, Meltzer (2005) proposes that the analyst should maintain a state of repose which is at the same time highly alert, waiting patiently for incipient meanings to emerge as the fruit of his receptive imagination, open to what might be possible without taking probability into account. The analyst is a "poetry generator" who abandons thought (science) in favour of intuition (art, poetry).

Let us return to studying the capacity for reverie when the analyst is faced with areas in which symbolisation is found to have been damaged. The analyst hears the patient but mainly *suffers* the action of the projective identifications within himself. The analyst experiences the product of these identifications as discomfort, mental anguish, symptoms, difficulties or blockages in thinking, accompanied (or not) by sketches of scenes. These sketches are poor, they lack emotional resonance, and they point to contact with failed sketches of symbols, at times symbolic equations, that exert pressure on the mind of the analyst to find meaning.

The analyst feels pressure to liberate himself from the non-dreams that the patient introduces to him. Concomitantly, thanks to his analytic function, he feels stimulated to find ways in which to symbolise them. Initially, as we have seen, through the images that pressure for new forms of representation, principally through words. In the first instance, or even later on, it is possible for the analyst not to find them. The situation will continue in a search for meaning, while the analyst maintains his negative capacity until the selected fact emerges. The images attract new symbols, sensory, imagetic, and principally verbal, and broaden meanings. The experience is opened up to new symbolic connections, new meanings, greater emotional development, and greater richness in the dyad's work. This process is never complete, as meanings keep being generated in a continual expansion of the mind. We are faced with what Imbasciati (2006) calls *simbolopoese* which occurs within the so-called *constantly expanding oneiric holographic field* (Ferro, 2009).

The analyst may not tolerate the not-knowing that forms part of the non-dream, while trying to dream it. This occurs due to flaws in his capacity to maintain the state of reverie or because the non-dream has mobilised areas of the analyst himself, which have not been sufficiently dreamt in his own life, or that—although dreamt—do not tolerate being re-dreamed at that time. The analyst's "indigestion" when faced with the raw elements of the patient involves factors from both members of the dyad. In these situations, the not-knowing will be experienced as an internal persecutory object. For this, the analyst can call upon the *already-known*, memories, wishes, theories, beliefs, used not because they are true, but as ways of appeasing the persecutory object. This substitution of the *non-knowing* for the *already-known* is stimulated by the non-neutralised presence of the destructive superego from the psychotic part of the personality (Bion, 1959), moralistic and omniscient, that attacks any *not-knowing*, transforming it into the supposed *already-known*.

When the analyst also finds himself prevented from dreaming the patient's non-dream, both members of the dyad can become involved in *non-dreams-for-two*. The analyst's mind is possessed by the patient's non-dream that *falls upon the analyst's ego* (Cassorla, 2007; Freud, 1917e), as is the case in melancholia, blocking his capacity for dreaming and thinking. Its substitution for *already-known*, that is, for defences that involve omniscience, is presented as repeated stagnant scenes with manic and obsessive characteristics, that conceal melancholy and persecutory narratives.

However, the analyst does not realise these things. His mind finds itself numbed, as though stupid (Bion, 1958, 1961; Cassorla, 2013b, 2013d).[3] The "without memory and without desire" will be replaced by the saturation of memories, wishes, theories, and apparent knowledge. Interpretations, according to this information, result in adaptive suggestion and not in psychoanalysis. Rational or theoretical interpretations serve to label the patient and impede her development.

The analyst can intuit certain signs that reveal his obscurement. He must remain alert to exaggerated feelings of pride in relation to the potency of his own analytic capacity (when the analytic process seems to be going very well) or in relation to his patience and capacity to contain (when the analyst supposes that he is dealing well with frustration and violence). These exaggerations are usually arrogant and demonstrate stupidity. Chronic irritation and constant admiration in relation to the patient are other indicators. The analyst must leave a certain laziness aside when he feels impelled to write down the clinical material, even if he lacks clarity in relation to motives. This indicates the need for a "second look" (Baranger, Baranger, & Mom, 1983), for a "listening to listening" (Faimberg, 1996). Countertransferential night dreams and intuitions of daydreams can provide us with other clues.

I think that the analyst works simultaneously in all mental areas. Interpretations in the symbolic area indicate a present analyst who, at the same time, helps to symbolise and to create mental structures. His work, therefore, also benefits the psychotic and traumatic areas of the patient's mind. Moreover, when the analyst works in an area of the mind where the capacity to symbolise is impaired, he is also stimulating the symbolic network that exists in a non-psychotic area of the mind.

This perspective helps us to move away from a moralistic view about what is "right or wrong" in the analytical work. The moralistic superego should be quieted by the validation of the analyst's work (Cassorla, 2012a), that is, observe how this work creates, develops, blocks, or reverses the dreaming capacity and the symbolic network of thinking.

The analytical work, particularly with more challenging patients, stimulates self-knowledge in the analyst as he inevitably makes contact with his own traumatised areas. An analytical process promotes development in both members of the dyad. Although we expect the patient to undergo personal development more than the analyst, if the analyst does not develop personally then this is an indication that obliges us to consider that something has gone wrong.

Some of the ideas described here will be illustrated by clinical material that will also serve as an introduction to the clinical feature of enactment. Let us bear in mind that writing is a poor method of illustrating emotional experiences.

The clinic

It is dawn. I have difficulty in getting out of bed. I suppose it is because I went to bed late last night. I have a quick breakfast and leave home in a hurry. I arrive at my office five minutes late, at 7:05 a.m. I am upset with myself because of my delay but remain calm. I know my patient John usually arrives between 7:08 and 7:10 a.m. But, this time, I meet John in the hall waiting for me to open my office. It is the first time John arrives earlier than me. I feel bothered.

When the session starts, I remember that John missed his last session, without giving me previous notice. I wondered if he had travelled on business, a common issue in his life as a businessman.

The analyst's discomfort for arriving later than John is, for a while, a non-dream in search of meaning. He knows that there is a relation between his delay and John's constant delays. The analyst's "manifest dream" does not go beyond that. The fact that "I went to bed late last night" is real, but it is a rationalisation for the delay, a false dream (Cassorla, 2008a) covering his not knowing. The analyst must bear the uncertainty of this false dream until something takes form in his imagination. Recalling that John had missed the last session is a dream-like memory (Bion, 1970), something that came spontaneously to the analyst's mind, therefore it is not an obstructive memory. However, the subsequent memories about the patient's trips must be abandoned in order for the analyst to remain receptive to new thoughts. The analyst is aware that he knows nothing about the reasons of the patient's current absence. His memory was only associated to an hypothesis, a preconception (Bion, 1962b), which will have to be either confirmed or not. If the analyst felt completely certain that John had missed the session because of his trip, his mind would be dominated by psychotic functioning and omniscience.

> John starts the session by telling me details about problems in his job. I observe the same moaning tone with which I am familiar. He complains and complains as if he were a victim of the world. His complaints are unreal, not justified, but I feel that if I show him that, he is going to say that I despise his suffering and that I do not understand him. I keep on listening, downhearted, trying to keep my mind in a reverie state, "without desire, without memory".
>
> I find my thoughts wandering. I remember that on the previous night, I was trying to write a psychoanalytical text and I felt blocked in my ideas. I went to bed frustrated. In another part of my mind an idea came up—if I were not a psychoanalyst, I could tell John how unpleasant he is. Later, I would realise that I was attempting to transform into a dream the impotence and anger I was going through with John, which came from the previous night as well as my present frustration with him.

The analyst knows that John's complaints are discharges and that he communicates his incapacity to dream and think through them. His reveries reveal attempts at connecting facts that are happening in the analytical field with personal experiences, like the ones from the previous night. The fact of realising his annoyance and dismay alerts the analyst to the risk of being recruited by John's non-dreams, and the analyst perceives the risk of giving back the discharges to John.

> In a sequence, I remember arriving late to the session. I can identify and name part of my discomfort: shame. This feeling connects to another memory: the one from last night in which I wondered if I could sleep some extra minutes more because John was my first patient and was always late. Having admitted my feelings of shame removes any obstructions to the expansion of my symbolic network that permits me to realise that John's delays were convenient to me—they gave me more time to read my morning newspaper ... I had come to count on John arriving late and so felt "permission" to do the same. I feel sad and, at the same time, satisfied for being able to make contact with painful facts about myself.
>
> On the other hand, I know that I have not fully dealt with the issue of either my patient's lateness nor with my failure to bring this to his attention

in the analysis. Therefore, I am obliged to ask myself whether or not I have dealt with this issue with the necessary potency.

The analyst is aware that he was involved in a collusion with John and that its origins and consequences are not sufficiently clear. These mutual and repetitive delays correspond to what I have called chronic enactments. The patient and analyst have behaved like actors in a miming theatre in which they act, without words, the mutual latenesses. These are a type of symbolisation in actions that are in search of verbal symbolisation. It was about this issue that the analyst was trying to write the previous night, when his symbolic network was blocked.

The memories of the late arrivals and the difficulty writing the previous night show how unconscious dream thoughts of the analyst are revealed to him, and are in a search for signification and broadening of meanings. Initially, the analyst was unable to realise the chronic enactment, but this idea was already part of his thinking. When this realisation comes to his mind, he feels creative and knows he will register the fact through writing after the end of the session.

Subsequently, reviewing the session, the analyst will perceive that John's moaning could be in response to the analyst's delay. If he had he realised this earlier, then the analytical process during this session would have taken other paths.

> Now I hear John talking about a business meeting he had in city X, from where he had just come back. I see, inside my mind, the city X: images of my visit to this tourist destination when I was young. I wonder about the building where John could have been, in the H square. In fact, John doesn't say a thing about any buildings or places. This scenery is a creation of my mind. John talks about a former military officer who was in the meeting and who put obstacles to the negotiations. In my mind, I "see" an officer with medals on his uniform.
>
> While John tells me about the negotiation, I feel bothered. This feeling of nuisance is transformed into an impression that John is hiding something from me. I think about bribery, corruption. I don't know whether it is a dream of mine or it is related to what John is telling me.

When writing the session, the analyst will further dream the session by adding more details of his own images, the city X, the H square, and the officer. The analyst recalls a situation when he was a teenager and he took his first trip with other teenagers. He was euphoric with his sense of freedom while he was in the H square. He was playing mindlessly with his wallet when a thief, running past, robbed his wallet. His friends ridiculed him for being distracted, "with his mind elsewhere". This made him recall his childhood, when he was accused by adults of being "asleep" when he got lost in his own thoughts. The H square, dreamed, was also a dirty place, closer to a red light district. The worst consequence of having his wallet stolen was losing his ID card.

Still during the process of writing about the session, the analyst realised that his daydream indicated the consequences of being "with his mind elsewhere", "sleeping", also as an analyst who is late for his patient because of his sleepiness. He could lose his analytical identity for not realising "thefts" (delays and absences) which were corrupting the analytical process. The H square (where there were prostitutes as well as historical museums with masterpieces) represented not only the dirty aspects of the analytic field, but also the resources and treasures that existed, and had the potential of being rediscovered. The image of the officer reminded the analyst of deceptive and destructive situations that he had experienced during his adolescence.

> Returning to the session, John says "I dreamed of you". "I came to the session and you were mad at me, because I had missed the previous session. You said: 'just wait there, I do not know when I will see you'. It was a punishment. In the waiting room, there was an athletic type of guy, a sailor, who was on holiday. He was dribbling, crazy. You put a straitjacket on him, he reacted by becoming violent, and then you bound him. Afterwards, another crazy guy suggested we robbed G (anti-psychotic medicine) from a cabinet. We were being careful so you could not see us. Then I woke up. The dream seemed like a loony bin, madness."
>
> I feel invaded by a profusion of vague ideas. Although I did not have John's associations, I began an attempt at formulating an interpretation. I say that maybe John is afraid of not counting on me. I talk about his absences and our late-starting sessions, which may not contain the madness permeating our work. We would have to resort to straitjackets and anti-psychotics. I realise that my formulation is not one of my best, and I am aware that I did not wait for his associations. But, as I speak, each word attracts another word and I feel creative. But, soon I realise the risk of talking too much, which might cause an "indigestion", in other words, giving him too much to mentally process; thus I interrupt my intervention and wait.

John is thoughtful. I wonder if my complicated intervention made sense to him. Then, he recounts a "hard to tell" episode. He had not come to the previous session because while in the city X, he took drugs and got involved in sexual and social situations dangerous to his own life. It is not the first time that he has engaged in such risky behaviour. Hearing about his dangerous activities makes me feel dismayed and worried.

The "hard to tell" episode is a manifestation of discharges, non-dreams, happening outside of the sessions, which keep a certain invariance in relation to what is happening in the analytical field. All the stories and scenes, dreamed and non-dreamed by the analytical dyad, are expressions of madness, destruction, corruption, dirt, imprudence, sedation, involving relations of John with himself, with other people, and with his analyst.

After John told the "hard to tell" episode, it became more clear to the analyst why John arrived punctually to his session. He needed my help to dream the horrific non-dream related to the dangers he lived in and outside of his mind. John intuited that this non-dream was another version of his internal deadly sabotage and corrupted relationships. The analyst also made contact with his own personal aspects that were similar to those of John.

In other words, it is as if John (like all patients) said to the analyst: "I will make you participate in my dreams and non-dreams again, in another way—please, see if you are able to signify them or give them new meanings". And, in case the analyst is unable to do so, then the mind of the patient will continue to try again and again … .

After this session, the following hours and the analysis continue without any further delays either from the patient or from the analyst.

The study of this material shows that when the analyst is also delayed, the dual collusion (chronic enactment) is undone and the dyad enters into contact with the triangular reality. The sudden discrimination of self and object is acute enactment and involves a mixture of discharges, non-dreams being dreamed, and dreams reverting to non-dreams. We shall return to this theme in the following chapters.

Notes

1. Bollas (2007) reminds us that ancient peoples needed to interpret their dreams. Even powerful religious beliefs could prove insufficient to counter anxiety. It was essential to have the assistence of someone else in order to survive mental life.

2. Non-dream areas of the non-repressed unconscious (Freud, 1923) have been studied by contemporary authors, such as Green (1986, 2002a); Marucco (2007); Ferro (2009); Barros (2002, 2011); Levy (2012); Levine (2012); Levine, Reed, and Scarfone (2013); Botella and Botella (2013).
3. This obscuring, that renders the analyst stupid, will be discussed in Chapter Ten.

CHAPTER THREE

The theatre of dreaming

As an analysand tells us a nighttime dream or describes a dream scene or passes from one scene to another, he might make a verbal slip. He might say that he saw a certain scene in a "movie", instead of calling it a "dream". Observing these situations, it is not hard to note that the analysand "watches" a "movie" as a subject at the same time that he might see himself in a "dream-movie" in a clear or deformed way. The presence of a subject who is distinct from the characters in a dream indicates to us that we are observing a part of the mind where the self and the object are seen as separate. This kind of dream takes place when oedipal triangulation is possible. Being able to discriminate between outside reality and psychic reality occurs at the same time that the capacity to symbolise is developed. Another description leads us to say that the dream occurs in an experiential, depressive mode. This expression refers to the depressive position from Kleinian theory as studied by Ogden (1994c) or in a non-psychotic part of the personality (Bion, 1957). These occur not only when the patient relates the dream-movie, but also while he is dreaming it.

Nighttime dreams that emerge in the analytic field are told to the analyst by means of other dreams or daydreams that the analysand is having, due to stimulation by emotional experiences that are being dreamed in the here and now. The analyst also dreams the emotional experiences that are occurring as he lets himself become involved by the analysand's dream.

Therefore, when patient and analyst work in areas of the mind where symbolisation is possible, scenes, plots, and narratives emerge in the field with a strong visual component. Both members of the analytic dyad can imagine in their minds what is being related, or narrated.

The emotional experiences that are dreamed by the patient are communicated to the analyst through symbols, especially verbal symbols, as well as through normal projective identification. The analyst, using his capacity for reverie, takes in the patient's dream and experiences it, and is thus able to perceive defences that mask meaning and deform oedipal conflicts. By calling attention to defences, the analyst's dream transforms the patient's dream into another dream that now takes on a broader meaning. In other words, the analyst re-dreams his patient's dream.

The analyst's dream, told to the patient through unsaturated and modulated interpretations (Ferro, 2002a), connects to the patient's symbolic network and is re-dreamed by the patient. This new dream of the patient is told to the analyst, and so forth. *Dreams-for-two* are developed, thus expanding the thinking capacity and the work of the analytic dyad. They can be overlaid by what Ogden (1994a) calls the "analytic third". This element is a product of the two members of the analytic pair, and maintains a dialectic relationship with dreams.

It is important to note that, even though the analyst's dream is part of the *dream-for-two*, it is a dream of his own. Therefore, the *real person* of the analyst is important beyond his analytic capacity (Levine & Friedman, 2000).

The symbolic area that allows for dreams-for-two to appear in the analytic field corresponds to what Bion (1957) called the non-psychotic part of the personality. It co-exists, in all human beings, with a non-symbolic area called the psychotic part of the personality.

We can imagine that the feeling of watching "movies", by either analysand or analyst, is due to the density of the visual images. In contrast, the audience in a movie theatre requires darkness in order to watch the movie projected on the screen. Other visual stimuli are thus blocked out by the absence of light.

The darkness can be considered as equivalent to everything that is covered over, hidden, or suppressed by the dream (or the dream-movie), that is, to everything that does not appear on the screen. The screen itself is, at one and the same time, real and virtual, being a barrier that separates light from darkness. Likewise, it is similar to the barrier that separates consciousness from the unconscious. In fact, even at a movie theatre, the concrete screen is not necessary. The image is produced simply by photograms that blink on and off in rapid sequence on any surface that will receive them (such as a wall or a ceiling), and this is what happens in dreams.

This description is similar to Bion's (1962b) concept of the *contact barrier*, made up of alpha-elements, which, in effect, are pictograms the sequence of which is seen in the photograms or frames that make up a dream-movie. The illuminated screen is in contrast to the darkness in the movie theatre, and it is irrelevant whether the darkness is "in front of", "behind", or "beside" the screen permeated with light. This shows us that the unconscious is not to be found in any specific "place", but in the contrast with the illuminated screen.

When movies are "bright", their light partially illuminates some of the darkness in the theatre, and shapes in the surroundings can be made out. The sharper and clearer are the images on the screen and the better the projection equipment is, the easier it will be to perceive shadowy areas that are partially illuminated by the light coming from the screen. In like manner, when there is separation between consciousness and the unconscious, they insinuate one another, and between light and darkness there is an intermediate space of more or less illuminated shadows. The study of these spaces can give us indications about areas that remain in the dark in the same way that compromise formations help us come into contact with the unconscious.

In "dark" movies, for lack of light in the scene or problems with the projection equipment, a movie theatre can fall into complete darkness. Sometimes not even what is happening on the screen is very clear. In this type of dream-movie we might imagine, analogously, that there is no clear separation between consciousness and the unconscious, and that analysand and analyst must constantly deal with darkness and mysterious chimeras that can create frightening atmospheres.

Strange things can happen when the projectionist has to deal with mechanical problems, and photograms are projected into the faces in the audience. With light in their faces, people in the audience are unable to see anything, not even the images. Some may think that this visual confusion is funny, but the fun turns to anxiety if the situation continues on for too long. In the world of dreams, it would be as if the dreaming apparatus had broken down and resulted in indistinction between self and object, between persecutory and confused states, and even in manic defence reactions. These states come up as nightmares, dream-like states, and sleep disturbances. When the disturbance is serious, the person is unable to either sleep or stay awake, much less to dream, even if an analysand might refer to her hallucinatory discharges as "dreams".

When an analysand narrates this kind of "dream", she does not make any slip of the tongue by calling it a "movie". Analysands may tell us they "dreamed" about "Noise, thunder, and that's all ...", or "Something was going to fall in", or "People were hurt and there was blood all over".

In these "dreams", there is no plot and the analysand does not use subjective expressions such as "I saw" or "I was afraid". Sometimes dreamers may refer directly to themselves, as in: "There were people who wanted to kill ... I ran away desperately", "A very high place ... I was going to fall and I woke up in sweat and trembling with fear". But any suggestion of subjectivity is quickly avoided. The atmosphere of the dream is terrifying and scary, and the analysand feels passive in the face of uncontrollable forces. She is the object of the dream that attacked her, rather than a participating subject. These types of dreams can be called *non-dreams*.

In non-dreams, there is neither screen nor any perceptible separation between the observer and what happens in the scene, since the observer is absent. Isolated scenes can be noted but there is no connection between them, or else it is incipient. There is no plot or story to be told even though a certain theme might be proposed. Commonly, the analysand lives out the dream as being concrete and expresses terror when telling it to the analyst. The dream continues as a hallucination in the "here and now" of the field. Confused states indicate indiscrimination between internal and external realities, between being asleep and being awake.

A non-dream may include the outline of a plot, but it is closed in on itself and leaves no room for metaphors or analogies. The analysand might say that she "Saw a stranger ... who scared me out of my wits ...". Then she may remember another scene where things were very dangerous and she woke up in terror and had to look under the bed for fear of a murderer in hiding. The associations are poor, and it will fall to the analyst to help transform this plot-discharge into something comprehensible, using his capacity for reverie. In these situations, together with the elements to be discharged, the patient uses some material which is suited to the dream, but insufficient.

In these types of dreams, the differentiation between light/darkness, like conscious/unconscious, will make less sense. The so-called beta-elements will correspond to that which cannot be "visible", "thinkable", because neither symbols nor sequential linking between the possible outlines exist. Grinberg (1967) appropriately named these discharges of beta-elements, which appear as dream, as evacuative dreams and mixed dreams (when they mix together with thoughts). Segal (1981) calls them "psychotic dreams".

If a movie projector breaks down, it might tear sections of the film, screws can come loose, only residues of images might remain, all at the same time (Ferro, 1996). The analogy that comes to mind is a situation where bizarre objects resulting from an explosion in the mind appear and there is a violent projection of the container and the contained, leading to strange configurations (Bion, 1957).

The movie model can be used for dreamlike flashes (Ferro, 1992; Meltzer, 1986) but it does not apply to bizarre objects that come up in visual hallucinations, especially if the visual aspect is unimportant, as in cases of discharge into acts, somatisation, and other transformations into hallucinosis, such as beliefs, fanaticism, and delusions.

In this way, it is viable that whenever the "movie" model does not apply to the "dream" then we are dealing with functioning from the psychotic part of the personality, or the schizo-paranoid and autistic-contiguous mode of generating experience (Ogden, 1989a), like non-dreams.

The theatre model

Now let us go back to nighttime dreams that take place when there is sufficient symbolising capacity and that the analysand equates with movies. When the analysand tells these dreams, he uses neither the theatre model nor the literature model, even though he may be a playwright or a writer. Like a writer's imagination, the scenery and the stage in a theatre might be equivalent to the screen in a movie theatre. The preference for the metaphor of the movie might be due to the contrast that exists between light and darkness.

Before going on, let us look at some differences between the three narrative arts: literature, theatre, and cinema. The art involved in all these modes of representation consists in creatively reconciling the happenings, reflections, and feelings that are part of the story that is being written, staged, or filmed. I am looking for parallels between the art of dreaming and the art of its manifestation in the analytic field.

Strictly speaking, literature, as a written art, shows us nothing beyond graphic characters, or symbols, which, when deciphered, can lead us to imagine, think, and feel. The author transforms his dreams into verbal symbols that, in turn, are transformed by the readers into imagination and dreams of their own.

On the other hand, storytellers stir up emotional movements in their listeners through the expressiveness of their voice and their body. At times, they may even assume roles in order to make the characters more real or give emphasis to certain aspects of the narrative. In this case, storytelling is similar to theatrical performances.

In the cinema, we come into visual contact with scenes that were filmed in the past. The objective of the director (who is the narrator) is to show the audience how he dreamed the story, in an attempt to touch us so that we can dream his dreams and the dreams of the characters played out by the actors.

In movie productions, there has been time to build the scenery beforehand, edit the film afterward, and work it through (as it occurs in dreams). And even when a director hides certain parts of the scenery, as they often do in suspense movies, clues are planted to be deciphered later. The audience becomes curious about the director's "intentions" and, as they watch the scenes, they accumulate information and test possible conclusions. But these "intentions" are resolved at "The End".

When books are the form of communication, the text has already been edited and the reader knows that the story will finish at the end. Readers might even risk scanning pages ahead in order to find out what is going to happen. Unexpected events can come up in the story but not in the form of narration. Novels also finish at "The End", even if this is not made explicit.

Both movie audiences and book readers have full control over how the story will be absorbed, since a movie can be interrupted and a book can be closed. Both text and images continue to be available, unchanged. Everything is already "given".

But just the opposite happens in the theatre, where the story is presented "live". Although there may be a script where the text of the play is in written form (but there is definitely no such thing as a script in the "theatre of dreams"), the important thing is that the action takes place "here and now". No theatrical presentation is the same as any other, even if the actors and the script are the same, because human beings can never be identical.

Anything can happen in a "live" theatre. An actor can forget his lines, invent new lines, collapse, or even die on stage. A dialogue on stage might reflect a personal dispute between actors, sabotage against the author or director, or a challenge to a critic. In fact, an actor, or the whole cast, can walk off the stage. The lights might go out, the sound system could crash, the theatre can catch fire, a fight might break out in the audience, somebody might decide to go up on the stage, or other such happenings. The police might invade the theatre to arrest actors or persons in the audience. Films or books can also catch fire, or they can be censored or confiscated by the police, but there are usually copies.

In contrast, dream-scenes in the theatre of the mind and the theatre of analysis will never be replayed. Nor is there a script before things begin. The analyst observes and participates in a total improvisation, implying an unpredictable story with unpredictable actors. During the analysis, a multiplicity of plots and stories can come up according to certain standards, but if the analyst sticks too closely to standards and patterns, he will never notice the new things that are going on all the time, in each scene.

In a theatre, there is a separation between audience and actors but it can easily be breached. In some modes of theatrical presentations, the audience can be induced to participate in the scene (even though they might feel uncomfortable about this) or a scene can take place in the midst of the audience, virtually eliminating the separation between stage and audience. This often happens in plays for children and in circuses, where individuals in the audience are called up and they run the risk of identity confusion since the reality principle is maintained stably by the presence of adults.

This is impossible in cinema. Only Woody Allen—in *The Purple Rose of Cairo*—managed to show a spectator walk on screen and interact with the characters in the movie. As the audience to this movie observe the main character who herself is watching a movie and unexpectedly walks into the screen, they continue feeling like subjects who are independent of both films. The director's art manages to convey the character's emptiness, which leads her to fuse with her desired object. It is this art that allows us to identify with this character without running the risk of confusing ourselves with her, except momentarily and under control, until the theatre lights go on. If the involvement is intense, we may need a few minutes after leaving the theatre to pull ourselves together again. The same thing happens in analytic work, and we sometimes need a few minutes to re-establish contact with ourselves before opening the door for the next analysand.

There is another characteristic of the theatre that is of interest to psychoanalysts. In both literature and cinema, the writer can easily take the narrative to other times and places. In the theatre, however, events and feelings take place in the "here and now" even if a given actor, in a different scene, represents the same character at some other time or place. But this is usually bad theatre. A good author or narrator will make things happen in the "here and now" to transport us to other times and places without changing the scenery.

The analyst is not interested in reading a text written by an analysand nor watching a movie or videotape she brought to the session. But he will certainly pay close attention to the reading of a text or the screening of a video when presented by the analysand "here and now" and associated with everything else that is happening in the analytic field.

Another characteristic of the theatre is its need for economy. In contrast to a novelist, a playwright cannot make comments or clarifications about behaviour except through inclusions in the action. In classical theatre, the narrator and the chorus would often describe internal states of the characters. Hamlet's famous monologue in modern theatre is more interesting when spectators want to hear it because they want to observe how such and such an actor will interpret it on that day, and it will always be different from other actors or other days. In his office, an analyst may have to listen to more or less sterile monologues but must still be on the alert for the emotions and behaviour beneath the analysand's discourse.

Theatre is basically action. Thus, in *Hedda Gabbler* Ibsen cannot tell us, like a novelist might do, about Hedda's disdain for her husband and his family. Ibsen has Hedda hold the hat she knows belongs to her husband's aunt and say that it is unforgivable for the maid to have forgotten her ridiculous hat in the living room. This is how the narrator precisely conveys to us this aspect of Hedda without any need for descriptions or narrations (Mendonça, 2000). The psychoanalyst will find analogies with this situation, in the oneiric work as much as in its externalisation during the session, but here the author-patient seeks not only to reveal, but also to hide. These two things often occur at the same time, using condensation and displacement to do so, in the characters and plots that will be presented in the form of images (in the dream) and of behaviour accompanied or not by words (in the analysis). This artifice will occur with greater intensity when the patient does not have the words at her disposal to refer to her affects.

The above observations lead us to an important conclusion. Although analysts see themselves talking to their analysands through coherent verbal symbols, they must also be constantly observing and participating in the scene, seeking to catch those aspects that are struggling to be symbolised or that are resisting symbolisation. These aspects emerge between the lines in the analysand's outwardly adequate verbal discourse as well as during their periods of silence. Also important are the analysands' tones of voice, the musicality or volume of their discourse, their gestures, whether obvious or subtle, contractions in facial and throat muscles, the body in general, hairs standing on end, sweating, smells, changes in skin colour, ways of moving their eyes, and everything else that is taken in by the senses. The indescribable aspects that take place when affects, emotions, and feelings become manifest as part of the emotional environment also come into play, especially if this manifestation is so subtle that only an analyst's intuition can capture it.

The analyst will also note how all these aspects appear in himself, since he realises that he is observing products of the field to which he belongs. It should also remain clear that such observation will not be "objective", but the result of his spontaneous capacity to dream and think about what is happening.

In this sense, we must remember that the affect is the flesh of the signifier and the signifier of the flesh (Green, 1973). That is, the affect has a semantic function, like a link in the chain of signifiers (Green, 1983); its overflowing potential, that would break the chains of thought, will find containment in the analytic situation.

McDougall (1982, 1999) uses the model of the theatre as a metaphor of psychic reality, based essentially on the intuition of Anna O, who described her daydreams as her "private theatre". The analyst is invited to take part in the drama and to interpret his own interior theatre before interpreting that of the analysand. Breuer, in contrast, had not been able to bear the role attributed to him by Anna O.

Dora repeats with Freud (1905e), as if on a stage, Mr. K's having abandoned her, and Freud notes that:

> Another advantage of transference, too, is that in it the patient produces before us with plastic clarity an important part of his life-story, of which he would otherwise have probably given us only an insufficient account. He acts it before us, as if it were, instead of reporting it to us.
>
> (Freud, 1940a, p. 174)

Klein (1932) noticed that her little analysands personified their toys and transformed them into real or fantasised human beings that interrelated among themselves. Strachey (1934) shows that, in the analytic process, we are living in a current and immediate situation where analysand and analyst play the leading "roles". Loewald (1975) used the metaphor of the theatre to study transference, including the analyst as a participant in the scenes.

Joseph (1989) shows that analysands use verbal and nonverbal means to recruit the analyst into representing certain mental states, just as a director prepares an actor for a role, but without the actor knowing that he or she is being prepared (Caper, 1999). Lothane (2009) proposes models that approach both what he calls dramatisations in thoughts (images and scenes lived out in dreams and fantasies), and dramatisations in acts, "dialogues, and other interactions between *dramatis personae* involved in plots of love and hate, faithfulness and adultery, ambition and failure, triumph and defeat, fear and death, despair and hope" (p. 140). The scenes represent the truth of the emotions (Marcus & Marcus, 2010). Civitarese (2013b) proposed a comprehensive and detailed model that involves the interaction between characters, actors, casting, and ways of focusing the scenes.

"Total situation" is everything the analysand brings into the relationship (Klein, 1952), and the analyst should observe everything that is happening, including what is happening to himself (Joseph, 1989).

The ideas expressed here on the analytic field make use of and broaden the proposals of the authors cited above. Besides observing "everything", the analyst finds himself participating in the field without failing to take into account the real person of the analyst and whatever happens outside his office, in other spaces and at other times, when these facts are part of the analysis.

Functions of the analyst

I suggest using here the theatre model to study some of the functions of the analyst as an observer-participant in the analytic field, where she is both the object of fantasies and a real person.[1] When facing scenes placed in the analytic theatre, an analyst, with her analytic function intact, will carry out the following functions *simultaneously*:

1. *Character*, by interacting with the other characters who come into the field.
2. *Spectator*, by observing and trying to understand what is happening (The power to participate and observe at the same time allows her to exercise the functions described below).
3. *Co-author*, to the extent that, when interacting with the characters in the field, the analyst does not necessarily do so simply according to the pressure she feels. Much of her analytic activity will consist of pointing out this pressure in order to make it understandable for the analysand (for whom it is not conscious).
4. *Director*, by analytically acting together with the characters in the field as she seeks the best way for the original plot to be understood and changed.
5. *Theatre critic*, by standing back from the scene and using her knowledge to critically evaluate how the drama was carried out, how the characters behaved, or whether the scene could have occurred in some other way (here, she will emphasise the analyst's critical function). She may also evaluate what explicit and implicit psychoanalytic theories were used for both observing and understanding the phenomena and how they could be understood on the basis of other theories, or even if new concepts or models are required. The role of critic becomes more powerful after the dramatisation has occurred. In short, *the analyst's critical capacity* is an important factor for defining her vertices of observation.
6. *Light and sound technician*, by aiding the director in seeing and hearing what is happening. Theatrical presentations are impossible without sound or lighting and, for this reason, technicians should seek to

light up dark aspects or aspects that are trying to disappear into the wings. A good lighting technician throws light on the characters with appropriate nuances of brightness and colour.

The darkness/light dialectic expresses the conscious/unconscious model, and we use the word "insight" when we gain consciousness of something, or when something comes to light.

The analyst's lighting function depends on her capacity to enter into the context of the scenes and live them "at-one-ment" (Bion, 1970). Adequate lighting is equivalent to psychoanalytically trained intuition (Sapienza, 2001). Since the analyst is simultaneously co-author, character, and/or director, these functions will complement her capacity for psychoanalytic observation. Focusing on direction and lighting by the director-analyst (who is also co-author and actor) is the spontaneous product of dreams that are being dreamed. The capacity to make the adequate splits becomes an important factor for these functions to be carried out as well.

Although at the beginning of the analytic scene it is possible to identify who (generally the patient) is placing their internal "characters" on stage, it soon becomes clear that these "characters" end up mixing together, and presently we no longer know to whom they belong. Moreover, we know that they are the result of the interaction between the minds of the patient and analyst, and it can be postulated that even the beginning of a scene already includes this mixture.[2] In this way, new "characters" are created, products of the fertilisation of aspects of the analyst and patient. Remembering that these "characters" are not necessarily people, they can be, for example, a symptom, a letter, a journey, an ideal, a relationship, an institution, and so on, that can be "outsourced" creations of the patient <–> analyst dyad.

Another highly important characteristic of the analytic theatre, already highlighted, is the lack of knowledge of or absence of the previous text: then, there are no indications as to which ones are the characters or how they should behave—they emerge in the here and now, they call others, acting together, and the plot is created, without being able to predict what will take place. The model is closer to that of a theatrical improvisation, although we know that this "improvisation" is to an extent being partially determined by the structures that are initially placed on stage.

In an analytic relationship, the possible scenes are innumerable, and it will be the focus of the direction and lighting of the director-analyst (who is also co-author and interpreter) to determine what appears on stage and can be identified.

> The patient describes in detail a six-month trip he took thanks to the scholarship he worked so hard to earn. He is happy and enthusiastic about this. Then he surprises me by aggressively complaining about the cost of a course he is taking, even though we know that this does not cause him any financial problem. The trip, the course, and the money enter here as "characters" of the analytic field. The emotions related to money are strong for me, as a selected fact (Bion, 1962b) of the field. I feel concerned with the impending interruption of the analysis. What if he has a crisis during the trip? At the end of the session, when he pays me, he appears irritated and indignant for having to pay for a session he missed. He complains that when I go out of town, I don't pay him for sessions that were missed. In other words, there is a double standard here. The missed session and the emotions involved enter into the analytic field. I had not perceived that my own trips had also entered the field. That night, I dream that my son had an accident, and when I wake up the patient comes to mind. I have the feeling that the dream has something to do with my fear that there might be an "accident" during his trip because he is not under my care. The next day, he once again complains angrily about my being insensitive and about the injustice he is being subjected to. It's absurd to pay for the session he missed, because his son had had an accident. At this moment, my dream comes into the field and I can broaden its meaning for myself.
>
> The analytic work allowed the patient and myself to perceive that the trip and the course were metaphors for our analytic "trip", and the emotions involving money indicated the unjust emotional "costs" of the interruption of analysis, costs for both members of the dyad. The "lack of sensitivity" indicated the need to depreciate the analyst in order for the patient to be able to leave analysis. At the same time, it showed the momentary difficulty of the dyad in facing the emotions involving their separation. The "accidents", one involving the analysand's son and the other occurring in the analyst's nighttime dream, represent the accidents that are happening in the field. With the expansion of dreams-for-two, we come into contact with the sabotage by envy that had made it difficult for the patient to "travel" better through life, this difficulty being a traumatic repetition of experiences that had not been adequately signified. The analyst, in turn, comes into contact with the guilt he feels for having charged for the session, and wonders whether he has not been travelling too much. And he thinks he should be giving more time to his children, and to himself.

In this account, pictograms are placed in sequence, providing narratives laden with visual aspects—course, trip, missed session—that include sadness and anger (in the scene, between patient and analyst), as much those that are told as, principally, those that are felt in the dyad's emotional contact. It will be live in this "theatre" that tears, traces of hate, tones of scorn, affection, beseeching, hope will be perceived, as well as everything else that the plot requires in order to exist.

The facts described could lead to the continuation of the plot with infinite possibilities besides those that have already occurred: reschedule the missed session, don't charge for it, ignore the facts, apologise, promise to pay the patient when the analyst misses a session, and so on. But here we would no longer be in an analytic process.

The theatre model must be complemented by addressing the analyst's participation in greater detail. I think, like Barros (2000), that the analyst's interpretations allow unconscious mental representations of emotional situations to be transformed into images and acquire meaning. Remember that there is a privileged link between affect and image, due to the linking of affect to the representation of the unconscious thing. In order to develop the affect it must be linked to words (Canelas Neto, 2003). As we have seen, Barros (2000) proposes the term "affective pictogram" for a first form of mental representation of emotional experiences, resulting from the operation of the alpha-function. Powerful expressive and evocative elements form part of the process. Their manifestation becomes clearer when we use the theatre model. The images in action broaden the possibility of perception of the affective envelope of the verbal symbols.

There is a tendency to reserve the name "interpretation" for the classic interpretations that deal with the common meaning of transference. Many, however, do not refer to the transformation of beta-elements into alpha as "interpretation", to alpha-betisation as giving emotion "thinkability". I propose that the model of the arts can encourage us to recuperate this meaning.

In the model of giving "thinkability" to emotion, we can say that a musician "interprets" a composer who transforms his emotions into music. This was registered ("alphabetised") by the composer, in the piece, through graphic symbols. This piece makes the music "interpretable" by an artist, who will transform the sequence of graphic elements into evocative sound. Similarly, actors will "interpret" the theatre script; an art critic will "interpret" the work of an artist, who, for their part, "interpreted" their own feelings in creating it. And all the art *aficionados* will "interpret" the work through their own emotions and knowledge.

The analyst, for her part, when intuiting and naming beta-element emotional states, or even when re-signifying sequences of alpha-elements, also "interprets" them, in the same way as the artist. Remember that modulating affects accompany verbal symbols. The analyst and the patient, as well as the artist, not only interpret (in the sense of painting, staging, performing music, alpha-betising elements of the patient) but make this new interpretation usable within the symbolic networks that make up part of the mental world, modifying them, opening the way for other derivations, and even creating symbols and new networks. In this way, the mental universe and its perception is amplified.

Once the model where the scenes will take place has been defined, it could be asked *what* will be staged. In fact, this is a false problem: what will be staged is the product of the externalisation of the contents and mental containers of the patient, signs of how his mind functions, and also the same in relation to the analyst performing her work, and even structures that are products of the interaction between aspects of the patient and analyst. These products will depend, therefore, on the functioning of the minds in question. The forms that could be used (story accounts, facts, myths, memories, dreams; acts, discharges, silences; corporal manifestations, affective states, symptoms, hallucinations, etc.) will be varied and will indicate forms of functioning and characteristics belonging to each patient.

What these aspects placed on the scene represent will basically depend on the model of observation ("listening" for some), or better yet, the *analyst's critical capacity*, where she situates herself as a theatre critic observing the stage—or the analytic field—using certain suppositions. In other words, the scenes will be taking shape under the influence of the vertex of observation of the theatre analyst-critic. One hopes that this vertex arises from the cohesion of her analytic identity, in which she feels she is herself. Ideally, a continuous oscillation of numerous vertices occurs, the analyst functioning as a satellite dish that captures everything that occurs in space, at a certain wavelength, this wavelength having been prepared and worked on by the analyst. And each prepared analyst mind will be transmitted through similar waves but also differently. The predominant "sub-frequency" of the wave must be tuned to where the most significant events can be illuminated—and the analyst must resonate with them. On the other hand, we know that it is these events and characters that best conceal themselves in the dark hidden corners of the stage and in the wings.

It doesn't hurt to reinforce the fact that the model of the satellite dishes and the wave frequencies does not bear relation with saturated theories seeking to "box in" the observed structure: on the contrary, hopefully the analyst's theory includes the capacity to allow herself to be penetrated by the scene and to live it, in a controlled manner; and this "living" will be brought about using certain patterns, corresponding to the way in which the analyst lives the analysis, as a process and understanding.

Notes

1. I have always dreamed a good deal, and when I was a child I had a feeling that my dreams would enrich my life and make things clearer, although I didn't know how. I think this was one of my first steps toward my future choices.
2. This previous emotional turbulence occurs in every human relationship. The terms "anticipatory transference" and "anticipatory countertransference" are ways of naming this potentiality.

CHAPTER FOUR

Non-dream and enactment

When the theatre was suggested in the previous chapter as a model for occurrences in the analytic field, the expression "placing on stage" was used fairly imprecisely, in reference to the externalisation of aspects of the mental functioning of both patient and analyst.

This expression has been in use in English-language psychoanalytic literature for a while, through the word *enactment*. In its colloquial sense, enactment refers to theatrical representation, staging, and placing on stage, similar to the English words *to act, to represent, to play*. The same use is found in psychoanalytic texts both old and recent where the verb *to enact* refers to the externalisation of the patient's internal dramas, during the session or outside it. The term *re-enactment* is also used, meaning that the scenes initially take place in the internal world and are then re-staged within the analytic relationship. However, in recent years, the term *enactment* has come to be employed as a concept. Jacobs' study (1986) would have been the first to include the term in the title, but the definition has been the object of divergences (Ellman & Moskovitz, 1998; McLaughlin, 1991; McLaughlin & Johan, 1992; Panel, 1999). For some, it came to replace the term *acting-out*, which had become pejorative and conceptually confused.

A new connotation from the legal world has contributed towards greater conceptual precision. In legal terms, *enactment* signifies something with the force of the law, a statute, something that must be obeyed. With this, the psychoanalytic term comes to encompass both meanings, that is to say, it refers to a placing on stage that occurs necessarily. To these characteristics we can add another important factor: *enactment* occurs between patient and analyst, meaning that both participate in what is taking place. This is different from *acting-out*, in which the actions are the patient's alone and the analyst simply observes them.

An initial approximation leads us to consider enactment as a compromise-formation in which actions and behaviours involving both members of the analytic dyad simultaneously conceal and reveal unconscious aspects.

Before expanding upon this idea, we will return to the differences between enactment and acting-out. There is a phrase from a classic study by Greenacre (1950) that is significant: "Acting out… is a special form of remembering, in which the old memory is re-enacted in a more or less organised and often only slightly disguised form" (p. 456). This quote demonstrates that *to act out* and *to re-enact* had virtually the same meaning at the time. Let us remember that *acting-out* is the English translation of the term *Agieren*, used by Freud (1914g) to describe situations where the patient stages, through his behaviour, things that he is unable to remember. The notion of *Agieren* became confused with the idea of transference.

However, in common usage, analysts tend to use the term *acting-out* in reference to more or less one-off impulsive discharges, and it is scarcely used to refer to staged representations that elapse over a longer period of time. The adverb *out* suggests something that is placed outside (of the internal world) quickly. Acting-out used to be seen as an obstacle to analysis, something unwelcome. It was common for analysts to accuse the patient of having *acted-out* instead of associating freely, as though the patient were "refusing" to remember.

The term *acting-out* was also used to label impulsive and sociopathic personalities. The concept broadened in scope, with a moralistic bent, to enter the language of mental health professionals. The term came to be commonly used to refer to patients and people who were supposedly transgressive. Curiously, it was not taken into account that many perverse acts may have been the fruit of sophisticated reasoning.

This moralistic connotation is disturbing because it is obvious that if a patient is *acting* he does so because he lacks the sufficient conditions to do anything else, and not necessarily because he wishes to contravene the supposed rules of the analysis.

The conceptual confusion surrounding the term *acting-out* can be clarified if we consider the following possibilities: when the patient dramatises—through his behaviours—situations that cannot be remembered, we are confronted with *Agieren* as described by Freud. From another angle, the term *acting-out* has come to be used predominantly to refer to impulsive discharged acts. Studying *enactment* will provide us with clues to be able to differentiate, at least in certain situations, between the two meanings.

These considerations lead us to consider forms of repetition that constitute features of transference. They include such transferential phenomena as "actualisations", re-experiences, repetitions, and so on, if we refer to the strict Freudian framework, and the externalisation of unconscious fantasies in the object relations framework. However, in certain psychoanalytic cultures, there exists a tendency to differentiate between the phenomena that occur in "desirable" transference and those that are usually not considered to be "welcome". Therefore, some psychoanalysts reserve the term *enactment* (and also *acting-out*) for non-verbal behaviours and verbal behaviours in which the words serve less to symbolise than to discharge, and so would not be "desirable". But other authors (Chused, 1991; Roughton, 1993) value the communicative aspect of enactments and the great usefulness to be had in their understanding. We are gradually discovering that the most useful feature of enactment lies in its potential for revealing failures and successes in initial development that can be neither remembered nor forgotten, because these capacities have not yet been developed.

Bateman (1998) describes the controversies around the term *enactment*, dividing them into two main areas. First, actions that involve the patient and the analyst, to lesser or greater degrees of severity. At the mildest extreme, we have "actualisations" (Sandler, 1976), which satisfy transferential desires in relation to the analyst. In the most severe cases, the analyst's capacity is compromised, causing her to cross the boundaries of analytical treatment (Gabbard, 2006). The difference between this and *acting-out* lies in the fact that, in the latter, the analyst is not included, participating only as an observer of the patient's actions. However, in an enactment, the analyst contributes, subject to her own transferences and blind spots, to being led by the relationship instead of accompanying it. Second, enactment implies a positive strength in treatment. Once the analyst has understood it, she separates her own conflictive contribution from that of the patient, thus making the event useful to the progress of the treatment. Nevertheless, Bateman himself (1998) criticises this last meaning because, given that the analyst plays this role constantly throughout the analytical process, this would mean the whole process becoming an enactment, thus making the term redundant. Renik (Panel, 1999) says something along the same lines, and believes that we can sometimes separate and identify a number of enactments that are small parts of the wider enactment that occurs throughout the analytical process.

The concept of normal enactment (Cassorla, 2001) refers to realistic projective identification that occurs normally between the members of the analytic dyad. It forms part of non-psychotic transference. Normal enactments are undone through the analyst's interpretations. We will return to this subject in the following chapters.

Despite the fact that, in the literature, the concept of enactment generally refers to acute situations, the performance of the dyad in the analytic field can last for longer and hence becomes a prolonged collusion, which is not sufficiently perceived by the analyst. This is chronic enactment. The patient and analyst perform certain behaviours, as though in a kind of theatrical mime, or silent cinema. We can consider chronic enactment to be similar to *Agieren*, with the difference that the analyst is also involved.

Acute enactment, on the other hand, corresponds to sudden behaviours that at first simply seem to be discharges. This suggests that it is acting-out, but since it involves both members of the dyad, it would be acting-out for two. However, this comparison is incorrect. As we will see later, acute enactment involves not only discharges but also non-dreams being dreamed, and dreams reverting to non-dreams.

A deeper exploration of this idea leads us to see enactment as behaviours involving the patient and analyst that make archaic situations or fantasies present, a reflection of transferential and countertransferential hopes and fears, with real or fantasised traumatic situations from the past being placed on stage and occurring unconsciously. The behaviours replace verbal communication, which is limited. For this reason, they occur within analytic processes that deal with psychotic and borderline configurations, in which verbal communication is limited or impossible. Since in enactment both members of the dyad are involved, the concept goes beyond acting-out and *Agieren*, both of which are described as belonging to the patient.

Another way of looking at enactment leads us to consider it as an intersubjective phenomenon in which the analytic field, as a result of mutual emotional induction, is taken over by conducts and behaviours that involve both members of the analytic dyad without them sufficiently realising what is happening, and refers to situations in which verbal symbolisation is impaired. When words do exist, they serve as tools for discharges or ways in which to express affects that emotionally involve the interlocutor. The word functions as an act, in that "to say is to do" (Austin, 1962). It is a way of remembering through feelings, what Klein (1957) refers to as *memory in feelings*. Or, to expand upon her idea, memory in behaviours.

Close examination of enactments ascertains that the performance is initiated by one member of the analytic dyad, generally the patient. The initiator's involving behaviour puts pressure on the other member to respond in a complementary way, recruited by projective identifications. The phenomenon occurs in a dual direction, with analyst and patient mutually influencing one another. We can observe that some aspect of the analyst is involved in the enactment, making her more susceptible to the patient's induction. The patient suffers induction from the analyst, and the instigator of the enactment is often unknown. Some authors place greater emphasis on the role of the analyst and employ the term *countertransferential enactment*.

Chronic enactment results in crossed projective identifications in which analyst and patient perform roles together. Other, more primitive forms of identification may also be in play (Franco Filho, 2000; Sandler, 1993). In the analysis of children, adolescents, and severe cases, the involvement of parents and other people around them creates a tangle of crossed projective identifications (Cassorla, 1995, 1997, 1998e, 2009b, 2013d) which can make it difficult to perceive the facts involved.

Related phenomena already intrigued me long before I was faced with these situations; for example, health team mistreatment of certain patients, such as somatisers and suicide attempts (Cassorla, 1985, 1998c; Cassorla & Smeke, 1995). The professionals, not knowing how to deal with their own limitations, allowed themselves to be recruited by aggressive aspects projected by the patient, thus developing them without being able to think them. I also noted that a therapist's "failures", when getting the appointment time wrong, using the wrong name, adopting an impatient, ironic, or seductive tone of voice, and so on, in response to the patient's recruitments, could become productive once they had been recognised by the therapist and discussed with the patient.

There was a memorable situation that took place before I became an analyst. At the end of his session, a patient informed me that he had forgotten the cheque and would pay me at the next session. I told him to leave the cheque at reception that same day, because I had a payment that would be required the following day. I felt forced, in the explanation as in the payment. In the next session, the patient told me that he never imagined that I needed money. Using this information, we could work on his fantasy that I was some sort of inexhaustible breast who was always there simply to satisfy him, without a life of my own. It was not hard to see that we were both involved in a collusion of gratification and submission, within certain areas of the relationship. It was what would years later be called chronic enactment. This was undone when the charge was paid and the traumatic contact with the self/object discrimination, the acute enactment, ended up being productive. I gained awareness of the previous collusion only after this had occurred.

Thus, chronic enactments point to collusions between the members of the analytic dyad that have not been thought, and can anticipate a possible rupture in the analytic field. This rupture occurs as a result of abrupt behaviours that impose upon the analyst's observation due to their intensity: acute enactments. Only then does the analyst realise what had occurred during the previous chronic enactment. This retroactive re-signifying corresponds to the Freudian idea of *Nachträglichkeit*, usually translated as "deferred action" or *après-coup* (Freud, 1918b).

The idea of chronic enactment (not the term) can be broadened to include social situations in which charismatic leaders emotionally recruit people, groups, and populations who allow themselves to be drawn in, attacking their own thinking capacity. Perverse collusions are established in which people are emotionally manipulated. These situations demonstrate how fragile human beings are when it comes to emotional induction. The tragic consequences are familiar, manifested through intolerance, prejudice, fanaticism, and other forms of attacks on thinking.

Many analysts have described situations similar to those we are calling enactments without clearly naming them. Freud presents them, for example, in the case of Dora (Freud, 1905e) and in the dream of Irma's injection (Freud, 1900a). Breuer and Anna O together possibly constitute the first collusion described in psychoanalysis. Currently, the term tends to be incorporated by analysts of various origins (for example, Bohleber et al., 2013; Britton, 1999; Feldman, 1997; Hinshelwood, 1999; Mann & Cunningham, 2009; Steiner, 2000).[1] Brown (2011) reviews pioneering authors who pointed towards similar facts. In Chapter Ten, we shall study situations prefigured by Bion when the analyst becomes stupid, similar to those that take place during enactments.

Within the proposed model, enactments, principally the chronic kind, must be understood as a product of non-dreams-for-two. They are manifested through stagnant scenes and plots that do not involve visual clarity, or when this does exist it is fragile and motionless. The material does not have a meaning, there is no space for linking, emotional resonance for new connections does not exist, and the analyst is engulfed by the situation, not perceiving what is happening. For this reason, the scenes and plots could be better described as non-scenes and non-plots in which both members of the dyad feel afflicted.

The study of chronic enactment has led me to see it not only as a result of the incapacity for symbolisation on the part of patient and analyst, but also as a consequence of the need for initial linking mechanisms to be revived. In this revival, the patient receives the analyst's alpha-function, even if this happens unconsciously. It is gradually introjected, which also happens unconsciously. When it becomes sufficient, the symbiotic chronic enactment is suddenly undone as acute enactment. The non-dreams are transformed into dreams, with retroactive re-signification.

Chronic enactments include, potentially, clues that would show us the genesis of non-dreams, the obstacles to thinking capacity, reversals of the alpha-function, and the primitive functioning of the mind. In these situations, the analytic process allows us to see, *in statu nascendi*, how the intersubjective relationship develops symbol formation. These aspects will be addressed in greater depth in the following chapters.

Doubt remains as to whether a new term would be necessary for what underlies crossed identifications, which necessarily occur between analyst and patient with simultaneously obstructive and communicative purposes. Nevertheless, it seems to me that the term *enactment* is useful, at least for four reasons:

1. it draws attention to something that had not been clearly named, although it had already been described;
2. it does not share the pejorative sense attributed to the term *acting-out*, and goes further than this concept;
3. by insisting upon the role of both members of the analytic dyad, mutually influencing one another, it emphasises the intersubjective aspect;
4. by defining a concept, it has allowed the study of it to become more extensive, as we will see in the following chapters.

Nowadays, the term has come to form part of the common ground of psychoanalysis, used by psychoanalysts of various theoretical orientations. Like any new term, it was initially viewed with aversion and distrust. Then it came to be accepted, with criticism and reticence. The use has broadened, but it remains necessary to make its meaning explicit, as is the case for the majority of psychoanalytic terms.

Note

1. See also endnote 4 in Chapter Nine, which names other authors.

CHAPTER FIVE

Symbolising traumas: acute enactment

This chapter will discuss situations in which the analytic process appears to be productive while at the same time a chronic enactment is taking place, imperceptible to both members of the dyad. A sudden event undoes the chronic collusion. This event, acute enactment, leads to contact with once sealed-off primitive traumas, the consciousness of which will be experienced as intolerable. The facts described will become clearer when illustrated in a clinical situation.

Tania came to me during a psychotic break, terrified and imagining she could kill herself. The beginning of her analysis included fairly detailed and intense accounts of traumatic childhood situations, in which she showed herself to be a victim of disturbed parental figures. The facts of her past struck me as so traumatic that I doubted their veracity. With time, I managed to convince myself that they could correspond to real facts. These were revealed somewhat in her unusual relationships with relatives and work colleagues. Suddenly someone would be offended by something trivial and they wouldn't talk to each other for months; on other occasions, there would be verbal and physical aggressions; then moments of passion, which would explode into violent hatred. The same would occur during the analysis, with abrupt oscillations between her need for and dependence on the analyst, when she seemed hypersensitive to the smallest details, and periods or phases in which violent and disdainful attacks would predominate, when she was feeling superior and invulnerable.

I soon realised that Tania was mobilising me to enter into solidarity with someone who had suffered so many injustices and difficulties. She seemed to me to be a "borderline" patient, corresponding in general to the "thin-skinned narcissist" type described by Rosenfeld (1987), hypersensitive to real or imaginary frustrations and terrified of not feeling accepted, even though she tried to defend herself from this by presenting herself—in a caricatured way—as "superior" and inaccessible. In this way, she enveloped her "thin skin" with a shell of "thick skin" and these mechanisms alternated, although generally they appeared combined.

Gradually, these oscillations came to be perceived and transformed into dream by the analytic dyad. After some years of analysis, Tania was acquiring better tools to be able to experience her mental suffering, tolerate it, and give it meaning. The analytic process seemed productive, despite the existence of a certain oscillation between phases during which her mental world expanded and phases during which the analytic process was attacked.

Given the length and progress of the analysis, I considered our work to be productive and developing satisfactorily. Sometimes I would surprise myself, awaiting Tania's arrival with, perhaps too much, pleasure. This led me to consider what was happening: whether the process was not going "too well", perhaps captivated by one thing and blind to something else. I even thought of discussing a session with colleagues, but this was postponed.

The acute enactment

At the beginning of the third year of analysis, I moved my consulting room. I left my home for a business complex, in a building exclusive to doctors. Tania was informed several weeks in advance that the address was changing to an office block, without further details. There occasionally emerged a number of fantasies in relation to the move, which had the possibility of being deepened and worked through. The analysis went through an atmosphere of turbulence that was felt to be sufficiently creative.

I will now describe our first session in the new consulting rooms. On entering, I saw that she was disturbed, and her expression reminded me of our first interview, as if she were psychotic. Her look frightened me, and I felt shocked to see her like this. She neither sat nor lay down. Standing, aggressively, she told me she was not going to continue with the analysis, after what I had done to her. She obsessively repeated the accusation, extremely ill at ease, not going into details. Her speech was forceful, omniscient, totally closed to any questioning. Her hatred was obvious, and I was afraid she might jump on me and attack me physically.

I felt quite embarrassed, sceptical, surprised, and without the least idea of what was going on. I had never seen or heard her like this before. Automatically, I sat down in a chair I use for initial interviews and not in the one I use as an analyst, behind the couch. She remained standing, close to the door, which she had not shut, complaining, defiant, and threatening to leave.

I told her I did not understand what was going on and that I wanted her to explain what she was saying. I had to raise my voice, trying to get her to listen to me.

At that moment she sat down, in front of me, also on a chair used for interviews. At the top of her voice, she machine-gunned me with accusations, in a confused and delirious torrent. I wondered if she could be heard throughout the whole building. But, although ill at ease, I found myself quite curious to work out what was going on. I was still afraid she might suddenly get up and leave the room without giving me the time to find out.

Her rabid speech was uncoordinated and rather confused, her words seemed like explosions, but I managed to understand that she was telling me something about how I had deceived her by not telling her that the new address was a building for medical surgeries. She said she felt offended by the building, it was horrid and dirty. And that she had seen a sick child in the lift and that was horrible too. And more: the doorman was unpleasant and had a backward look about him. And she complained that I had not told her "any of this" prior to the move.

I tried to tell her that I had informed her that it was in an office block, but she interrupted me. She said, yes, I had told her it was in a building but I had not told her it was specifically for doctors' surgeries. So it was a "commercial" building because everyone was there to make money. And to make matters worse, my nameplate in the entrance hall was dreadful. She insisted that she would not continue analysis with me. I felt I now had some clues: she was going to leave me because I was a different analyst, not the one in which she had placed her trust. I continued hearing similar phrases; I was no longer afraid that she might leave suddenly, but nothing came to mind, and so I stayed quiet, observing Tania and also my own sensations and feelings.

Gradually, I became convinced that her greatest anxiety came from having felt deceived. After one or two attempts, I managed to interrupt her, and I told her that I was very surprised by her reaction, and that I did not concur with the accusation that I had deceived her. I noted that she was listening to me. I continued: she was right that I had not told her the building was specifically for doctors' surgeries, but I had not told her because I had not considered it important. And, furthermore, I was intrigued and curious to know why the presence of doctors so disturbed her. I added, "Perhaps you are afraid of appearing ill?"

Less aggressively, she replied, "Maybe, but it's not that. After all, I don't know any doctors in this building and, even if I did, I could say I was coming to study here with you or to undergo supervision." But she immediately continued by saying that I had changed, that she had been let down, and that she was going. The end of the session arrived, and I told her that things still needed clarifying and that I would expect her the next day. She left annoyed, but I was sure she would return.

Clues triggered by the acute enactment

I shall now summarise what happened in the two following sessions. Tania arrived in a calmer frame of mind, we picked up the issue once more, and she listened to what I had to say and my interpretative hypotheses. They revolved around her anxieties and reactions linked to unconscious fantasies about exclusion. This exclusion was expressed in fantasies of humiliation, jealousy, and envy, through feeling obliged to follow me where I went, because she depended on my resources as an analyst and, on top of this, she had to pay me for this.

This was also made worse by her raging feelings of guilt that prevented her from becoming established as a self-employed professional, charging for her services. Associations and facts of this kind are followed by the memory of a dream that she had had the night after the session described above. This dream continues in the analytic field and, as a dream-for-two, we were able to perceive that Tania was reliving something incomprehensible to her: the intimate relationship between her parents, which was equated with the sexual and mental relations of the analyst. The analyst has links with his own internal objects and also with external objects. Tania has neither these links nor these objects, which makes her feel terribly excluded. In the dream, the mysteries surrounding inclusion and exclusion appear as situations of fertility and decadence, which confusedly merge with life and death. Tania does not understand the deceits and betrayals she has experienced, with great suffering. Faced with this confusion, she tries to "not see" what is happening, including her oedipal attraction and jealousy, but this is not entirely possible. In the dream, there is also the death of the analysis and of all the links that exist within the analyst and with him. At the same time, she recognises the analytic dyad's resources. However, she has to attack them, jealously disdaining them because she needs them so much. But without them, she would not survive. And all of this makes her feel sad and frightened.

During these sessions, Tania appears keen to collaborate, her speech is coherent, and the relationship is creative. Among her rich dream associations, Tania tells me about the various changes in residence she has experienced throughout her life. Her mother was never satisfied with her earnings and would suddenly warn that they were going to move. She claims that her mother never thought about the children, who would leave their friends, their surroundings, and most importantly their teachers, with whom they maintained strong links. She felt this to be like the death of herself and of everyone else. The work and the money were the most important things, and her mother did not accept complaints. It was clear that the change of consulting rooms caused Tania to relive these situations. She had to leave my residence, the welcoming environment, because I had changed address due to money, because I was "commercial". At the same time, I maintained the links that she had lost with my family, with my wife, and with myself. Feeling excluded and deceived, she tried to take revenge by abandoning me. But this left her alone, increasing her despair and hatred, at the same time as it seemed that she would not survive, just as she had felt during childhood in the face of every separation or exclusion.

Discussion

The situation that took place during the first session in the new consulting rooms constitutes an acute enactment. It undoes a configuration that had been established over a prolonged timeframe between analyst and analysand. In that session, Tania invaded me with massive projective identifications, triggering the acute enactment, and I followed her, unconsciously accepting to participate in the scene by sitting in the interviewing chair rather than the analyst's chair.

One possibility is that I may have counteracted due to the counter-transferential commitment. Otherwise, I would have sat in my usual chair, not giving in to Tania's fantasies and thus showing her that I continued to be the same analyst. If this was done consciously, it could be an interpretative action (Ogden, 1994b).

The way in which events developed, however, led me to another hypothesis. On sitting in the interviewing chair, I confirmed the patient's perception: yes, I was another analyst. Only then did I come into contact with the unconscious "perception" (which later became more conscious) that we had been experiencing an idealised symbiotic relationship at my family home. Tania experienced the analytical relationship as if she were a part of my family, as if she were the daughter, wife, sister of her analyst and of my wife and children. And I, her analyst, not only did not see this but contributed to it. Now, I had elements with which to understand the reason for my pleasure when waiting for her, my moments of suspicion that the process was going "too well" (but, delaying the investigation through this perception), and the little importance I gave to possible transferential interpretations that might objectively include my family. Thus, although the analysis was productive in many ways, the described symbiosis was a prior and subtle enactment that had been occurring for some time, without the analyst realising it. The analyst, in part, took on the role of idealised object or parental couple and protector that defended her from the terrible parents, internalised as destructive and disintegrating objects of her mind. My role in the chronic enactment avoided contact with these latter aspects.

Thus the accusation that I had deceived her was not totally mistaken. She had been deceived and I had let myself deceive her, by not having picked up on her symbiotic, omnipotent linking fantasies. When these collapsed, through the consultancy move, a new dyad emerged: a new analyst and a new patient, the symbiotic fantasy, the prolonged enactment unveiled.

I suggest that, when we talked in the interview chairs, it was as if we were reviewing the contract, acting out another unconscious need on the part of both of us. I also think that, intuitively, I deduced that, if I sat in my analyst's chair, she would leave, feeling misunderstood.

The hypothesis proposed above, evidently, only became clearer in the subsequent sessions, and the writing and discussion of materials organised my ideas. There is one thing more: when Tania sat down, I automatically got up to close the door. This act could, at first glance, be considered as a precaution to prevent her from leaving. I do now believe that this is what actually happened, but I think its role was also to maintain a private space, a signal that I accepted her as she was, that I would not leave her or throw her out, even though we had both deceived each other. Closing the door and coming to sit back down in front of her were both parts of the "performance", like a "story" made up of several scenes forming part of the enactment: a) commencement, with her arrival, disturbed, shouting, standing, and the open door; b) the analyst feels invaded, frightened, and he automatically sits in the interview chair, without knowing why; c) the patient remains standing, accusing the analyst; d) the analyst is frightened that the patient may assault him or may leave, before he has understood what is going on; e) the analyst speaks, increasing the normal volume of his voice; f) the patient sits down in front of the analyst; g) the analyst feels less threatened and quite curious, but there is suspicion that the patient may leave; h) the analyst gets up to close the door—the patient continues shouting and appears unaware of the analyst's movement; i) the analyst sits down again; j) the communication begins to become more comprehensible and the analyst waits, observing the patient, himself, and the atmosphere of the meeting; k) the symbolic communication is clearer; l) the analyst interrupts the patient and makes himself heard, and so on. Between these stages, and also accompanying them, in addition to the words, there were lesser acts, difficult to describe, which included facial expressions, movements, voice tones, as occur in any performance between two actors, with the important difference being that all this took place, largely, unconsciously.

Continuation of the analysis confirmed the previous hypotheses, enabling deeper consideration of aspects that resisted clarification. It was possible to access a certain defensive eroticisation of the transferential relationship, which she had also defended herself against in my residence by displacing it onto imaginary lovers and fantasising that we were living together as a happy, integrated family, with her included. She also confessed to me that she had had the idea that my change of consulting rooms was due to me separating from my wife, but she did not tell me this at the time. This fantasy was terrifying for her; feeling as she did simultaneously abandoned by the parental couple and guilty about her oedipal desires to have me alone all to herself.

Conclusions

This description of acute enactment also has the purpose of demonstrating its communicative value for the analytical process, encouraging its understanding. As Bateman (1998) indicated, in the case of narcissistic patients, this phenomenon frequently occurs at the moment of alternation between "thick-skinned" and "thin-skinned" defences, as happened with my patient, because on changing direction (thick <-> thin), both narcissistic positions, rigid and static, exposed her highly dangerous instability during which both violence and self-destruction, previously controlled, became possible.

I propose as a hypothesis that, initially, the hypersensitivity of Tania made the analyst more cautious, waiting for her to become stronger, in order to gradually confront her with her destructive and jealous aspects. And that the prior chronic enactment, in which we both acted out a symbiotic relationship, worked as a collusion to avoid going deeper into these issues. Clearly, it had a purpose of resistance, and was also motivated by countertransferential problems on the part of the analyst. But, given the sensitivity of the patient, the hypothesis that it also represented a "necessary collusion" useful in the analytical process, albeit an unconscious one, cannot be ruled out.

I cannot be absolutely certain, but I believe that this collusion would have been unveiled or would have become noticeable to me, naturally, during the course of the analysis. I suggest that this was violently unveiled, through acute enactment triggered by the office move, because there already existed the conditions to enter into deeper contact with the aspects that emerged, which enabled the alternation and change in the kind of narcissistic defence (thick-skinned <-> thin-skinned). I believe that, if Tania and I, the analyst, had not felt sufficiently strong in our relationship, then perhaps the idealised, fantasised symbiotic relationship would have been maintained, even in the new consulting rooms. One clue that substantiates this possibility is when she said to me, during the violent scene described, that should she know any of the doctors in the building, she would say she was coming, "to study or supervise with me".

The acute, intense enactment caused by the move could also have served as a way of communicating to the analyst that there was no further need for "protection", the patient now feeling sufficiently confident in herself, in the analyst, and in the joint work to dare to confront herself with the truth. For this reason, I considered it a "resource", albeit an unconscious resource. This resource worked in two ways at the same time: first, revealing that there were "blind spots" in the analytical process; second, showing that there was the possibility of "opening one's eyes" (Cassorla, 1993) to the presence of the third, unravelling the symbiotic relationship. It is clear that this "resource" would only be successful if the work of the analytical dyad, on the basis of the perception of the analyst, was followed by comprehensive hypotheses that the patient validated and deepened with her associations and memories. It could be that the analyst was so counter-identified (or disturbed by her conflicts) that the conditions for noticing how "involved" he was did not exist, running the risk of becoming even more "involved".

I would like to make it clear that I do not consider the described enactments as something to be recommended. I merely want to highlight that there is a significant possibility of their occurring with some patients. Ideally, the analyst would have perceived and interpreted this carefully, but it was not possible for me to do so in the prolonged, collusive enactment. However, what struck me was the possibility that this collusion also had another function, in addition to the function of resistance, as I will now explain.

I now speculate that, at least in the patients described, there may be a need for an initial more or less chronic enactment or collusion to take place, which may go unnoticed. In this phase, the analyst and the patient "are preparing" themselves unconsciously to face up to the truth and, when this is possible, a change in the nature of the enactment occurs, which tries to communicate vigorously, in an intense way, what was hidden from the analyst, who will now be able to free himself from the collusion. Perhaps this is a part of the "natural history" of the analytical process with narcissistic and borderline patients: a symbiotic phase (in which unconscious changes also occur, masked by the collusion), which needs time to be worked through, gradually creating the possibility for it to be broken. This sudden break-up (acute enactment) is a sign that the process of working through has now arrived at a point at which it is possible to run the risk of realising that the analyst is a third party, an independent being, no longer a narcissistic extension of the patient. Thus, in the analytical process, the first phases of development are relived, with the possibility that new experiences may substitute archaic negative parental and environmental experiences in order to reach an oedipal situation that can be worked through.

In summary, although acute enactment may be the manifestation of an impasse, it also has a communicative aspect that requires deciphering. Only once the enactment is deciphered can we verify how useful it could be to us. In this text, I also made the speculation that chronic enactment, which takes place more subtly, may occur not only as a resistance but also as a stage of waiting, of maturing, in fragile, extremely sensitive patients. This, then, would be another function of enactments.

As I noted, there are most certainly countertransferential aspects implicit in chronic enactment. An apparent care and prudence on the part of the analyst may thus be hiding insecurity, fear, or a need to remain fused together due to other problems. These countertransferential aspects may facilitate the "coupling" with contents projected by the patient, and it is possible that on some occasions this is inevitable for a certain time. The most important thing is to benefit from this "coupling" in order to understand what is happening and break down blind spots: for this, clearly the analyst needs to remain constantly alert, observing himself, trying to take in what is going on, and not rejecting the help of others. On discussing this material with colleagues, it was mentioned to me that there was a coincidence in the fact that both Tania and myself had experienced many traumatic migrations in our backgrounds, a fact that, curiously, I had not considered before. This fact made even clearer to me the ways in which I, possibly, had contributed to the symbiosis.

And is regular analysis not also a "performance" in which the analyst and patient influence each other mutually through crossed projective and introjective identifications? Certainly. The difference with pathological enactment is that, in the analytical process, the analyst is consciously trying to transform the "enacted" contents of the patient's internal world, and also using the conscious reactions to his unconscious countertransference. In this situation, the analyst tries not to let himself be controlled by the patient. But the analytical situation encourages enactments to occur continually, and the analyst enters into these, intentionally, as co-participant, through the need to be an analyst. His role is to identify early on or to unveil the enactments that occur, at each moment, in the analytical process. I suggest that the majority of enactments (derived from normal projective identifications and which accompany verbal symbolic communication) or a constant series of them, which the analyst unveils through his interventions, can be called *normal enactments*. *Pathological enactments*, derived from massive crossed projective identifications, more difficult to avoid or unveil, could be classified as above: *acute*—when they appear with great intensity, violently mobilising one or both members of the analytical dyad, and lasting only an instant, if understood; and *chronic*—when they are prolonged, in a collusion that takes some time to be identified, or reach a deadlock that is impossible to unveil.

In the following chapters, the hypotheses raised here will be expanded upon and validated using other clinical situations.

CHAPTER SIX

From bastion to enactment: intersubjective models

> Leopards break into the temple and drink to the dregs what is in the sacrificial pitchers; this is repeated over and over again; finally it can be calculated in advance, and it becomes a part of the ceremony.
>
> *Franz Kafka*, 1961, p. 93

This chapter discusses models that refer to what is presumed to occur within the analytic dyad. In this context, situations that hamper the analytic process are examined.

Freudian models

The difficulty in describing what takes place in an analytic session has led to the use of auxiliary models. Freud (1905a) describes the analyst as a sculptor (*via di levare*), revealing the work hidden in the stone. The therapist who makes suggestions, however, would be more like a painter (*via di porre*) who actually puts something on to the canvas.

The model of a sculptor comes close to the archaeological–historical model (Freud, 1930a), where it is as though the analyst were conducting an excavation of mental strata. From the elements discovered, he can also carry out hypothetical reconstructions (Freud, 1937d). It would appear that in this model, the further we proceed with our analytic investigation, the deeper we will get. Strachey (1934) discusses technical difficulties arising from this idea. When Bion (1965) discusses the concept of "catastrophic change", he shows us that the archaeologist–analyst will discover rocks belonging to different "geological strata" all mixed together.

In what I call the "military" model, the analysis aims to reconquer spaces that have been occupied by an invading army that has set up fortresses with troops, fixation points, as it advanced. The analyst attracts the libidinal troops to himself, with the aim of dominating them; the transference will be the battlefield (Freud, 1912b).

Freud also introduced models for describing the analyst's attitude, such as "surgeon" (1912e), "without emotions", and analyst-as-mirror.

In every one of the models so far described, the analyst is active, while the patient seems to submit herself—or at least to resist only passively. But in the model of the chess-game (Freud, 1913c), where the analyst has no idea how the game will be played out, it is fair to assume that the patient does not merely defend herself but can also actively defeat the analyst.

The bastion and the analytic field

The recognition of the countertransference as not merely a pathology of the analyst but as a useful tool for understanding the patient occurred concurrently in Argentina (Racker, 1948, 1953) and England (Heimann, 1950). The analyst, bearing and working through the feelings that arise within himself, picking up his own emotional response, turns it into a valuable tool for investigating the patient's unconscious.

Even though the concept of projective identification was not used in these works, its usefulness for understanding the countertransference quickly became apparent. At first, projective identification was considered an unconscious defensive fantasy, and no more. In the analytic process, aspects split off from the patient are projected into the analyst, who is experienced as containing these expelled elements.

Money-Kyrle (1956) shows that the countertransference can be "normal", a result of the appropriate oscillation in the analyst between projective and introjective identifications. At the same time, in Argentina, Pichon-Rivière (1980) was heading in the same direction. In a way, these authors were anticipating what Bion (1962) would call realistic or normal projective identification, the mechanism that allows the recognition of objects and identification, as a means of achieving communication.

Grinberg (1957) uses the concept of projective counteridentification to show that the patient's projections can reach the analyst, provoking something "real" in him. This would happen independently of any conflicts of his own. At that moment, the projective identification ceases to be merely an unconscious fantasy. The patient doesn't merely defend herself, she also has powerful offensive weapons trained on the analyst. Right away, it becomes clear that the analyst can take advantage of this phenomenon to pick up elements expelled by the patient (Grinberg, 1982).

The ideas provided by Bion (1962b) are similar. The elements that make up the beta-screen (which can't be thought and are expelled through projective identification) are capable of awakening emotions in the analyst, provoking the reaction the patient unconsciously desires. The analyst will attempt to "metabolise" these elements, returning them to the patient once they have been re-signified and can be thought (alpha-elements).

The military model, when associated with the concept of projective identification, is useful for the classic work of Baranger and Baranger (1961–1962), in which they describe the "bastion", an obstacle to the progress of the battle that occurs in the analytic setting. The origin of the word "bastion" suggests fortifications sticking out at an angle from protective walls, making it possible to guard them and fire at enemies.

The idea of a bastion, as a fortification from which analytical work is hindered, might suggest that the analyst is actively advancing while the patient remains withdrawn, defending herself. This impression is inaccurate, however. We can only understand this model within the concept of a *field*. Within this field concept, the current ideas about intersubjectivity are contained.

For the Barangers, the analytic situation involved two people who were taking part in the same dynamic process, one in which neither member of the dyad is intelligible without reference to the other. And in turn, the two people hide multipersonal structures. The *field* is made up of the conjunction of spatial and temporal structures and what is called the "unconscious fantasy of the dyad". This fantasy doesn't have its origins in the sum of the elements of the patient and the analyst, rather "It is something that is created *between* the two of them, within the single unit they make up during the session, something radically different from what each of them is separately" (p. 141). It is important to note that everything that happens in the bipersonal field will not simply be a repetition, in so far as it arises in a new context.

The encounter with bastions brings paralysis back to the field, a feeling that nothing is happening, narratives that are stereotyped. Even though, at times, the Barangers refer to the bastion as belonging to the patient, it remains clear that they mean to consider it as a product of the field. This contradiction is clarified better later on (Baranger et al., 1983), when they consider the bastion as a "precipitate" from the field, which can only occur between this analyst and this analysand, and "arises, in unconsciousness and in silence, out of a complicity between the two protagonists to protect an attachment which must not be uncovered" (p. 2). It is a neo-formation of the field, "around a shared fantasy assembly which implicates important areas of the personal history of both participants and attributes a stereotyped imaginary role to each" (p. 2).

In this way, parts of the patient and parts of the analyst become intertwined, engulfed, in a defensive structure. The bastion may appear as a static foreign body, while the analytic process seems to be continuing to run its course, or it takes over the whole field, becoming pathological. The breaching of the bastion sets off the destruction of the *status quo*, making it possible for the split-off parts to be re-signified, allowing them once again to be part of the emotional world. It is interesting to note the similarity between the Barangers' description and what is discussed in the following as "enactment".

The container–contained relationship, recruiting

The container–contained model (Bion, 1962b) is based on the digestive function; the human mind ought to "digest", "metabolise" crude sensory and affective elements, called beta-elements, which should be contained (taken in and metabolised) by another mind, the appropriate container, making it possible for them to be thought: alpha-elements. The appropriate container, which is capable of carrying out this complex procedure—alpha—will not allow itself to be dominated or destroyed, giving rise to a creatively transforming intersubjective relationship.

It is to be hoped that the analyst will use his alpha-function to help the patient to become capable of using elements that are appropriate for thought, through allowing himself to be sufficiently open to the massive projective identifications of the patient's beta-elements, and capable of transforming them into alpha-elements. The analyst's intuitive understanding leads on to the "intersection" (Bion, 1965) of the evolutions of the patient and those of the analyst.

The alpha-elements make up the mental representation of emotional experience, acquiring the quality of "thinkability" without yet actually taking the form of thoughts. This stimulates the formation of an "apparatus" for thinking them, which causes dream-thoughts, unconscious waking thinking, dreams, memories, ideas, and more complex thoughts. The analyst's mind can also give new meanings to better-developed elements of thought.

I believe the container–contained relationship supports the military model. The patient hurls beta-element projectiles at the apparently containing analyst, and the bond can be destroyed or sterilised. When the analyst has "digested" the mental facts and returned them, metabolised, to the patient, they are introjected together with the analyst's alpha-function itself. It is reasonable to assume that, at this point, "war" is replaced by "diplomacy".

Joseph (1989) explains in detail how the patient's projective identifications can engulf the analyst, causing him to take on complementary roles to those that the patient requires for maintaining the *status quo*, that is, psychic equilibrium. In this way, it is as though the patient were "recruiting" the analyst to take part in pre-established, stereotyped entanglements. The analyst should not allow himself to be recruited, making clear to the patient what it is that he is unconsciously attempting to do. Eventually the analyst, by expanding the projective identifications that are engulfing him, can also recruit the patient. Even certain of the analyst's own elements may come into play. In such situations, the analytic situation will stagnate. The situation comes to resemble the bastions, and the sterile container–contained relationship. It ought not to be forgotten that the word "recruitment" does have unavoidable military connotations.

As we saw above, chronic enactments become manifest in the form of long performances that both members of the analytic dyad participate in without their realising what is happening. In the models studied, they are similar to bastions, sterile relations between container and contained, and effective mutual recruitment. Acute enactments, on the other hand, are conglomerates that include discharges, non-dreams being dreamed, and dreams regressing to non-dreams. They indicate ruptures in former situations.

The clinic

K was twenty when she first came to analysis, and I was just beginning in the profession.

When K first sought me out, and for a long time after that, she complained bitterly of vague and uninterrupted physical symptoms, which for lack of a better word she called "vertigos". Her life had been restricted for many years, her symptoms prevented her from studying, from going out, from having friends. She spent most of her time at home, in bed, her one refuge. Numerous doctors had found "nothing" wrong with her body. Anti-anxiety medication as well as anti-depressants had no effect and just made the symptoms worse. Within a few weeks, to her list of vertigos had been added migraines, diarrhoea, bouts of influenza, fevers, and other symptoms that required medical treatment. K was now also complaining about her analyst, accusing me of incompetence and of being the cause of these symptoms. I was upset, and felt threatened by the patient's complaints and the worsening of her condition.

In time, these symptoms came to be infiltrated by anxiety, psychic discomfort, fear, perceptions that were almost impossible to put into words, but that were different from the physical symptoms. From then on, these began to dominate, replacing the physical body as the site of the suffering.

During this initial phase, I felt useless and impotent, invaded by the patient's complaints. K remained unavailable to any interpretation. I realised that I was struggling to avoid being swamped by her complaints, and felt myself in thrall to feelings that were unusual, confused, and quite uncomfortable. I didn't understand them, and continued to watch myself and K struggling against one another. I had to stop myself from returning to K the attacks I was experiencing from her. On other occasions, I noticed myself trying to become indifferent, but then found myself suffering again, as one of K's assaults hit its mark. I was constantly asking myself whether my analytic skills had been compromised. But it never occurred to me to give up: I felt a strong bond and was sure that in time things would become clear.

K's mother was on anti-psychotic medication, and her late father had been despised by K. She was proud that she experienced no feelings of guilt and located her persecutory objects in her family, perceiving her parents and siblings as dishonest and blackmailing.

In time, the projected objects located in her own body and in her family came to occupy other spaces. This caused the development of intense phobic defences that prevented her from being in many different spaces. However, the analytic situation became a sort of deposit of protective elements, and one of the few places where she felt comfortable.

I have chosen sections from two sessions. We were beginning the third year of analysis, meeting for four sessions a week. In the first section, I will illustrate how K came to involve me in a sadomasochistic collusion; in the second, the "M moment", where I lost control.

The first session took place after a long weekend, during which—despite all her phobias—K had planned to try and go on a journey. She was desperate as the session began, saying she had so much to say about the trip, that the session wouldn't be long enough, she wasn't doing well, not well at all, the trip had been terrible. She then embarked on an uninterrupted litany of complaints, in a tone of voice that emphasised their significance, which tried to convey to me how much she was suffering. She said it was all very tiring, hours of travel, very hot, she'd been unable to get to sleep; she had spent the time before the trip getting anxious, and almost gave it up altogether; the hotel was horrible, the food inedible. And she continued to feel unwell, checking her blood pressure hourly. She doesn't know how she managed—with some considerable effort—to get out a bit; but she felt isolated, and all her travelling companions were extremely unpleasant. She arrived back in the early hours of the morning. She'd had to get up early to come in for her session. She was sleepy. I'll never travel again, and so on …

I felt invaded by her complaints and moans. By then, I'd come to understand that the interpretations of the contained (and she had offered me so much …) did no good. I tried not to become confused with these objects, which were experienced as loathsome, torturing, but I found it hard not to. An image came to my mind, the image of a sort of instrument of torture that blasts everything to powder, to the ashes of the dead. I felt I quickly had to put the brakes on.

I interrupted K's complaining, which she didn't like at all. I pointed out to her that I'd noticed the operation of an "instrument of torture", grinding everything up, transforming everything into shit. I didn't like hearing what I was saying—my tone of voice came out sounding too angry, and I was surprised to hear myself say "shit". It's not how I usually talk …

Responding to my intervention, K complained violently that I wasn't allowing her to speak, that she wasn't being allowed to complain. She shouted at me, and accused me of shouting at her.

I told her that she was shouting at me in order to be able to continue complaining, and that it would be good if we could think together about what function we might ascribe to what was going on. In reply, K said I didn't believe in her suffering, and detailed her complaints yet further, with the aim of convincing me of the reality and intensity of her misfortunes.

I pointed out her mistrust, as well as her difficulty in seeing positive things: the trip, her first in so many years, all the difficulties notwithstanding. (At once, I noticed that I was trying to draw her attention to a "good side", in order to escape from the persecutory anxiety, and this made me feel inadequate.)

It seemed that K didn't hear me, but I was surprised by the appearance of new, and apparently different, material. She recounted how she arrived home in the early hours, and didn't find her mother in her room. She had been alarmed. And without thinking about it consciously, I heard myself say: "And did you think you'd killed her?" Yes, she answered, that's exactly what she had thought. She went to take a bath, then opened the bedroom door and her mother was there asleep. "But she pretended not to hear me."

I asked how she knew that her mother did hear her. She answered that she'd made a lot of noise in the house.

K took up her complaints again, and the session continued.

The M moment

Although there were productive moments during the process, most of it was a write-off, almost completely forgotten. I felt as though I was facing an insurmountable wall, which rejected or sapped the life from every attempt at understanding. It was as though K was using a machine-gun that destroyed anything she came close to, totally indiscriminately.

Even while I was unsettled, I was still aware of these feelings of my own; I imagined that things would become clearer, they would certainly become clearer, given time. I felt that "soft water will wear down hard rock" (a Brazilian saying). At the same time that I felt hit and pained, I also thought that this made me feel more alive, able to recover for the next conversation, the next session. But the more alive I felt, the more intense were the attacks.

Then what I call the M moment happened, four months after the part of the session described above. As had happened before, K transformed one of my interventions, distorting it, feeling persecuted and as a result attacking me. She didn't hear what I had to say and insisted stubbornly that I was accusing her unjustly and was talking nonsense. She shouted at me, and I found myself defending myself awkwardly, wanting to convince her that that wasn't what I was saying ...

At that moment, without thinking, I hit the arm of my chair hard, and at the same time interrupted her, shouting louder than she was. I complained that she wasn't allowing me to speak, and that she wasn't listening to me. At that moment, K stopped shouting and said—quite calmly, and with an air of triumph and in an ironic tone of voice—that I had shouted at her. I replied that, yes, she was right, I had really got quite agitated, I'm only human after all. I added, "It's just as well I am able to get agitated, otherwise you'd just make me agree with everything you say and I'd be afraid of you, dominated, and you wouldn't have an analyst any longer."

After this episode and in the sessions that followed, the amount of complaining and moaning was reduced. The machine-gun stopped for a bit, or at least it seemed less threatening now.

The episode left me worried, and I looked on it as a failure on my part. Thinking about it then, I believed that until that moment I had been a patient analyst, trying not to let myself be contaminated by K's violent projective identifications (not an easy task) and seeking as calmly as possible to digest them and to give them meaning. I attributed the slight effect of my interventions and the persistence of her attacks to destructive aspects that I tried to interpret. When the M moment occurred, I presumed that the violence of the projective identifications had passed my tolerance threshold and I had been engulfed by her psychotic side.

I imagined that the improvement to relations following the M moment were an attempt at avoiding worse damage to the analyst, at saving me. I presumed that K was just waiting for me to recover before she could launch into another attack on me. I felt guilty, certain that my actions had been a result of inadequate mental resources.

But this self-condemning view didn't chime with what I actually observed in the sessions that followed. K wasn't only less violent, she was also closer, more coherent, with a fine ability to observe what was happening to her and what was happening in the analytic setting. And the same applied to me. I soon realised that K wasn't trying to save me; the attacks continued, but my interpretations had been heard and were having an effect. We could both think more clearly now.

So I reformulated my ideas: yes, I had certainly counteridentified with K's objects, and reacted to them because of countertransference problems of my own. But this had been happening *before* the M moment, for quite some time, and I simply hadn't noticed it. I had made myself into a suffering victim, a martyr, who bore the pain masochistically, with no awareness that I was counteridentified with those same aspects of K. In this way, I was submitting (in a way that was unconsciously pleasurable, letting myself take satisfaction in being a patient analyst) to the violence of K's psychotic aspects without even realising it.

My reaction at the M moment was a sort of warning cry, a shout of "Enough!" against identifying with K's masochistic parts. I also became aware of those elements of mine that had become involved. Somehow during the M moment, I was able to put what had been happening until that moment into words, and I think that this was an important factor of change, opening the way to possible reflection in a new area.

Of course, it was only possible for M to occur at just that very moment. Doubtless similar situations had arisen previously, but without my being able to transform them into something useful.[1]

Discussion of the clinical material

Before the M moment, the analysis had been stagnating, with the patient and analyst both implicated in a sort of paralysis, a collusion, tangled up by massive projective identifications. The concept of the bastion, which in this case took up almost the whole field, was very accurate. It is also appropriate to think in terms of beta-elements in search of a transformation, of thinkers, also operating as "projectiles" that attack the analyst's capacity to think, replacing it with a pathological belief in his abilities as an analyst, his "patience" experienced in reversible perspective (Bion, 1963). That is, the analyst has been recruited (Joseph, 1982) to fulfil the predominantly masochistic role in the sadomasochistic conspiracy.

This conspiracy came about as a result of the externalising of internal aspects of the patient coming into contact with those of the analyst, and can be described as enactment. This is all laid bare in the field, or analytic theatre, seeking figurability and thought while at the same time hindering it. The analyst and patient are stripped of each other's projective identifications, and the process feeds on itself, becoming circular.

A hypothetical observer of the analytic scene would describe it as two people mistreating each other, paralysed, with no hope of escape from a world that is tormenting and simultaneously paradoxically pleasurable. He would be unable to tell those elements originating from the patient from those from the analyst, and this discernment would also be damaged in the two massively identified participants. There are indications, therefore, that the interaction of the elements of analyst and patient create other elements, new elements, which make up something other than just the sum of the two of them.

For example, both patient and analyst "visualise"—on some phantasmagorical plane—the mother dead, murdered. This common product is, I think, one of the results of the intersection of the analyst's feeling of not understanding with the patient's of not being understood, and vice versa. Patient and mother–analyst feel like they are dying, they feel murderous. This process was already underway when K abandoned the analyst to go on holiday and he remained behind. The dead analyst was taken, threatening, on the trip, within K, and K remained behind, dying, within the analyst (with him feeling the same way). K's description of her bath, as though she were washing away traces of the crime, can be seen as a counterpart to the "good things", the journey, which the analyst drew her attention to as a way of "cleaning" the battlefield of destructive, murdering elements. Even though they shout at each other and make a lot of noise, mother–analyst and child–patient don't hear one another. We share elements of "pretend".

Until the M moment, we were dealing with an obstructive enactment, operating in a chronic form, as a result of a reversal of the alpha-function (Bion, 1962b). When the M moment occurred, it looked as though the obstructive enactment would take on such force that the devitalised container–contained relationship threatened to explode. The beta-element "projectiles" which were crossing the analytical battlefield might violently demolish the process. *Acute enactment* is the name that I give to the situation where both were shouting and complaining, which culminated in the analyst striking the armchair.

The analytic process was not interrupted, however, and as we have seen the dyad was able to benefit from what took place. I imagine that the beta-elements that violently disrupted the relationship, elements in search of thinkers, somehow managed to find them. It was, then, an enactment with productive results, but which would have been obstructive had it not been understood and interpreted.

Of course, the analyst may also have had his own alpha-function damaged, because it has been hit by the patient's "projectiles", or because the incipient symbolic formation is destroyed as a way of escaping from mental pain (a reversal of the alpha-function), or perhaps even due to aspects originating in the analyst himself. At such a time, the patient's "non-dream" cannot be transformed into a dream by the analyst, and both move into a phase of "non-dreaming"—or rather, of "anti-dreaming". This "non-dreaming" that occurs to the two protagonists makes up the enactment. The material has no meaning, there is no room for links to be made, no emotional resonance for new connections, and the analyst is engulfed by the situation, totally unaware of what is going on. The "non-dreaming" implies a breaking down of the contact barrier that allows the separation of conscious/unconscious.

In the case of K, for example, I not infrequently felt sleepy, not able to sleep nor to stay awake. During chronic enactments, it may happen that the analyst—sleepy or not—imagines that he has "dreamt", but more often than not this supposed dream is a hallucination or something else transformed into hallucinosis. I think this also happened with the supposed dream in which I saw myself as a very patient analyst, convinced that "Soft water will wear down hard rock" would be a productive attitude to take. This "dream" would have been a function of the beta-screen, formed from something resembling the beta-elements and traces of the ego and superego. These traces were evident in the idea that my patience was adequate. Thanks to this belief, it was possible to avoid the possibility of symbolising the sadomasochistic collusion, and maintain the *status quo*.

When the state of sleepiness is accompanied by the potential for productive reverie, then of course the analyst will dream the patient's dream or non-dream, indicating that his analytic function is undamaged or has been recovered.

Looking at the case of patient K, as in others, it can be said that a chronic enactment can be dismantled through an acute enactment. The chronic enactment is made up of a sort of symbiotic interaction, which sets up various stages of evolution: symbiosis necessary as a precondition for the becoming-conscious of individuation; it is possible that the acuity is a result of some unconscious elaboration that is clamouring to be understood. These hypotheses will become clearer in the next chapter.

I would like to reiterate that—contrary to what others have written—the patient and analyst are *not* conscious of what they are doing; if they do realise what is going on (and this is the role of the analyst), if they do understand its function and meaning, the enactment would no longer be necessary, and would instead be replaced by symbolic verbal communication.

As we saw above, I believe the analytic process as a whole can be described as a continuum of normal and pathological enactments. The analyst is trying to transform the contents of the patient's internal world "staged" through interaction with those of the analyst himself, also making use of those derived from his unconscious countertransference. In other words, he willingly engages—as a co-participant—in the enactments that are constantly occurring in the analytic setting, necessarily, simply by virtue of being an analyst. His role is to identify continuous enactments in advance and dismantle them as he goes along. For the majority of these enactments (derived from realistic projective identifications, and occurring in conjunction with symbolic verbal communication), or their development in a continuum, which the analyst uses his interventions to dismantle, I'd suggest that we call these "normal enactments". And then there are what I would call "pathological enactments", which are derived from massive projective identifications, and that are harder to avoid or dismantle; as as been pointed out before, these can be classified as: *acute*—when they appear with great intensity, mobilising the analytical dyad in a violent way, and lasting only moments when they are understood; and *chronic*—which are prolonged in a collusion that takes some time to be identified, or which leads to an impasse that cannot be resolved. Current usage of the term "enactment" refers to those of the pathological type.

Compare the ideas on normal enactments with Baranger et al.: "There is process as long as the bastions are being detected and destroyed" (1983, p. 13). But when the bastions take control of the field, there ceases to be a psychoanalytic process altogether. We can thus consider "bastions" and "chronic enactments" as similar, in so far as the latter demonstrate also the externalising of internal bastions.

Conclusions

The various models described in this work are not mutually exclusive, and there are similarities between many of them. The analyst has to choose which among them it makes the most sense to use. For me, the significance of what is brought onto the stage (or whatever model the analyst chooses to use) depends fundamentally on the model of observation (or "listening", some would say); or, better still, on the analyst's critical capacity, where he is putting himself in the position of a theatre critic watching a performance with certain presuppositions in mind.

That is, as the scenes (or models) take shape, they will be influenced by the analyst–critic's point of view. It is to be hoped that this perspective will emerge from the cohesion of his analytic identity, from where he feels most himself. Ideally what will take place is an alternation between various different perspectives which identify the most significant events, allowing the analyst to enter the scene and experience it in a controlled way: and this "experience" will come about through certain patterns that correspond to the way in which the analyst is living through the analysis as process and the acquisition of knowledge. For this reason, we mustn't despise the influence of "the real person of the analyst" (Cassorla, 1998e)—quite the contrary. Not everything that happens in the analytic setting can be explained by projective identifications, not even in the most normal analyses. There is something within the analyst himself, something that is part of him, which makes him different from every other analyst. I believe that the models we have studied make us take these characteristics into account at every moment of the analytic work. We should bear in mind that it is often the patient who will help us to identify aspects that we as analysts have failed to notice ... And this is only possible if we set aside any sense of superiority towards the patient.

If the analyst felt such a sense of superiority, he would never feel himself to be a co-contributor to the bastions, to the enactments, to the container–contained pathologies, to the non-dreams, to the scenes played out on the analytic stage. And if he refuses to accept the possibility that as director he may lose control of the plot, he may stop being co-author, he may be prevented from exercising his critical skills, he will never be free from this. He would never allow for the possibility of a "second look" (Baranger et al., 1983) and in extreme cases any weakness would be seen as the fault of the patient, or as the fault of the analyst; this would make psychoanalysis into a sort of religion, with its priests who are either infallible or lapsed, rather than an art–science of trial and error, always working with approximations.

Note

1. Joseph (1982) provided a good description of patients like K as "addicted to near-death".

CHAPTER SEVEN

Enactment and implicit alpha-function in the analysis of borderline configurations

The conditions under which psychoanalytic work takes place allow the patient to externalise, in the analytical field, mental states, phantasies, objects, and internal object relationships. This externalisation takes up the form of affects, actions, scenes, plots, and narratives. The manner in which this manifestation occurs discloses features of the mind's functioning. It is for this reason that, during the analytic process, the analyst gets in touch not only with the patient's internal world but also with his own thinking apparatus.

As we saw above, these states consist of extreme hypothetical indications of either the capacity to symbolise (dreams), or incapacity to symbolise (non-dreams), and they are brought into the analytic field through dreams and non-dreams. In practice, we are dealing with intermediate or mixed situations since psychotic functioning oscillates and coexists with non-psychotic functioning, as well as with PS<=>D (Bion, 1963). For example, there are non-dreams that seek to become dreams, quasi-dreams, dreams that resist being broadened in their meaning, dreams into non-dreams, interrupted dreams (Ogden, 2005), and confused states that mix non-dreams with dreams. In this continuum, we see varying degrees of symbolisation, such as non-symbols (raw elements), precarious symbols with limited capacity for connection, symbolic equations

(Segal, 1957), obstructed or sophisticated symbolic networks, and so on. In borderline patients, non-dreams alternate, sometimes rapidly, with dreams that are more or less elaborate.

In earlier chapters, we raised the hypothesis that during chronic enactment, which occurs mainly in borderline configurations, vaguely perceptible psychic change may be taking place, and this change will be a factor in the undoing of the enactment. In this chapter, we will go more deeply into our study of these situations.

To facilitate the study of those situations, I shall divide them into stages:

Phase 1: The analyst believes the analytical process to be going fine, evincing a progress in the work of the analytical dyad.

M moment: On a given moment, the analyst loses control of himself and releases a discharge, an unthought-of action. At once, he realises his mistake and feels upset and guilty.

Phase 2: Concerned with assessing the consequences of his behaviour, the analyst surveys the progression of the analytical process and is surprised at his finding that: a) no harm has been done; b) the analytical process has become more productive.

Next, perusing the situation retrospectively, the analyst confirms that his initial impression, that the analytical process was progressing well (phase 1), was wrong. Actually, it had been coming to a standstill, and the analyst had been unable to discern it.

Presently, I shall examine the origins of inadequate discharges (M moment), the factors that turn the analyst blind to the stagnation of the process (phase 1), and those that occur after the M moment and render the analytical process productive (phase 2).

The clinic

Phase 1: The undetectable paralysis of the analytical process (chronic enactment)

This occurs generally with patients with obvious destructive components who waste no time in displaying themselves transferentially. The analyst at once intuits borderline configurations, but he believes that the difficulties at hand are inherent in the analytical process and that the attacks, blocks, and resistances will gradually be understood.

However, an observer external to the work of the analytical dyad (a colleague, a supervisor) will have a different view on the matter. His impression will be that the analytical process is stagnated in an important area, and that the analytical dyad is entangled in an obstructive collusion, a chronic enactment. Later on, the analyst will agree with the observer and realise that he was blind to what was going on.

The obstructive collusion (phase 1), undetectable, usually assumes two shapes:

1. The patient complains, protests, shows dissatisfaction, and sometimes challenges the analyst directly. The analyst acknowledges the attacks and tries to understand them and interpret them, positive that if he does not lose his patience, he will obtain good results.

    And yet, as has already been mentioned, the external observer thinks that the members of the dyad are not really interested in doing something to stop the violence and the suffering. It appears to him, moreover, that there could even be a certain amount of pleasure in maintaining the situation, that is, he suspects the existence of a sadomasochistic conspiracy. The analyst's apparent patience would then be a cover-up for his role of suffering victim. That way, the analyst himself attacks the analytical process, although he has no awareness of it.

2. Just as in the previous situation, there is an obvious destructive component here as well, but one that oscillates with moments of mutual idealisation. In those moments, the analytical process seems gratifying to both members of the dyad, who understand one another effortlessly. The analyst believes that the analytical process is being fruitful. The external observer, however, realises that analyst and patient are seducing each other and assumes that the aim of the seduction is to cover up the destructiveness.

    As mentioned above, in both cases the analyst is blind to those conspiracies (chronic enactments), despite feeling somewhat troubled. Not troubled enough to "open his eyes", however.

M moment: acute enactment

At a certain point, a discharge occurs. An unthought-of action, an intense, violent, and usually instantaneous fact that seizes the analytical field and appears to be about to blow it to pieces. Let's go back to the situations presented in the previous chapters.

Patient K complains of unclear bodily symptoms that motivate her to see a variety of doctors, with no organic disease being found. She lives with many restrictions, afraid to leave the house, unable to attend classes and to have friends. During the analytic sessions, she discharges all those complaints and moans, unable to think them. The analyst's interventions are of little use and are on the whole ignored.

Despite being aware of the sterile and persecutory atmosphere, which has lasted for as long as several weeks, the analyst keeps confident. His awareness of what is happening assures him that, if he carries on his analytical work, the hindrances will be understood and dissolved.

In a given session, K accuses her analyst of not understanding her suffering, of underrating her symptoms and of underestimating the meanness of her family and friends, who mistreat her. On a given moment, she complains of one of the analyst's observations (which she had deformed), thus justifying her belief that he is being unfair to her. The analyst knows that K's projections are common and attempts to find a way to show them to her, but K will not listen and keeps protesting, now almost shouting. He is not able to find a break to make himself heard while K's moaning goes on. Suddenly, and without premeditation, the analyst lets his hand down hard on the arm of the easy chair, and that makes a loud noise. Speaking over her, and louder than her, the analyst interrupts her wailings. He tells her that she is not listening and won't let him have his say.

At that point, she quietens down. Then, very calmly and with an ironic tone of voice, she observes that the analyst became agitated and yelled at her. Still tense, he admits that yes, she is right, that he reacted that way because he is human. He adds, a little cooler: "It is a good thing that I can get agitated, otherwise you would make me agree with everything you say, and in that case I would be frightened of you, and you would no longer have an analyst."

The episode left the analyst feeling worried, guilty at what he considered had been a failure. He assumed he had been unable to endure the intensity of K's attacks, losing his patience, and he was scared of the possibility of having discharged internal aspects of his own due to unsolved personal conflicts. He had no doubts that the event would damage the analytical process, and he expected K to pay him back in the following sessions. He also feared that K would quit the analysis.

We might recall the patient Tania, whose analysis oscillated between phases when she behaved in a violent, destructive way, attacking the analyst, and phases when she was cooperative, bringing forth rich material that allowed for fruitful work and amplification of the mental universe. The analyst identified at once a certain pattern: following phases of creative evolution, there would be a surge of attacks that endeavoured to ruin the achieved progress. During those phases, Tania would try to show that she did not need analysis. The analyst did not feel knocked down by her destructiveness and understood those displays as evidence of borderline functioning. Work appeared to proceed in a productive fashion, with forwards and backwards movements understandable within the transferential context. Sometimes the analyst would surprise himself, waiting for Tania's arrival with expectation, regarding her as an interesting patient. That caused him to wonder occasionally whether the analytical process might not be going "too well", and whether he might be in a state of blindness to certain aspects of it.

At a certain point, the analyst moves his consulting room from his house into a building occupied exclusively by medical offices.

In the first session at the new consulting room, Tania arrives with an upset countenance. The analyst feels beleaguered and frightened. Standing, she says in an aggressive manner that she is quitting the analysis. Her confused and repetitive speech is jagged and impervious to all questioning. The analyst is feeling very uncomfortable, flabbergasted, and with no idea of what may be going on. Automatically, he steps back toward a couple of chairs he uses for interviews, and he sits in one of them. Tania still stands next to the door she has not bothered closing, protesting in challenging tones and threatening to leave.

At one point, the analyst is able to seize a momentary break in her flow of words, and he manages to tell her that he does not understand why she is in such a state and asks her to explain her accusations. He has to raise his voice so that she really listens to him.

Gradually, he begins to understand that she complains of having been misled because she was not told that the new consulting room was in a medical building. She argues that she is disgusted by the horrible and filthy building and by the sick children that amble through the hallways and her belief that all the occupants were there to "make money".

When the analyst asks her if she is afraid of feeling very ill, Tania says it is not that. That luckily she does not know any of the doctors in the premises, and even if she did know them, she could always tell them that she came to talk to the analyst about study groups.

Introspectively, after the session, the analyst realises that he is feeling strained and guilty, with an impression of having made some mistake. His first notion is that he had failed regarding the communication of the change of address by having missed something important. He believed that his mistake had made the patient suffer unnecessarily. He also feared that he was missing some blind spot, due to countertransferential problems. He also grasped fleetingly that he was bothered at having left his analyst's chair, behind the couch, for the interview chair. Finally, he was certain that he had made a number of mistakes, though what they were was not totally clear to him.

In the situations described above, the analyst has the impression that the analytic relationship has blown up, that the analytical field has been damaged, if not altogether destroyed. That impression leads him to the notion of trauma.

Phase 2: after the acute enactment

As pointed out above, after the M moment the analyst is worried, afraid that the analytical process has been harmed. In his anxiety and reparatory wish, he seeks to examine meticulously what happened after the explosions and during the following sessions.

Contrarily to what he expected, he is surprised by the emergence of something new and productive in the analytical field, and a greater proximity between the members of the dyad is quite perceptible. The patients bring reports, recollections, daydreams, and night-dreams filled with rich symbolic content, whose interpretation brings about fresh associations and precipitates the expansion of the mental universe.

Patient K

After the M moment, in the following sessions, the symptoms and complaints give way to accounts, memories, and dreams. These turn into impressive recollections and revivals of situations of abandonment, for instance, forgotten memories relating to her mother's psychiatric internments and suicide attempts, as well as separation threats from her parents, situations that were retrieved in the relationship with the analyst. In a traumatic childhood episode that she had not told before, she arrives home and, after searching the whole house, cannot find her mother anywhere. She then imagines her mother has died, and she panics. She begins to asphyxiate and requests medical assistance. Phantasies of being abandoned and of abandoning the analyst allowed associating such primitive traumatic episodes with terrors of losing him.

Patient Tania

In the sessions following the acute enactment, Tania brings rich symbolic material, particularly dreams followed by fruitful associations. Contact is made with phantasies, memories, and plots concerning abandonment, separation, disappointment, and intrusion, facts that had not emerged with such abundance until then. Tania remembered home moves that her family had been forced to make, due to her parent's job, and which entailed a constant separation from childhood friends. Behind each move was always her mother's ambition to make more money, and nobody was allowed to question her decisions. Those circumstances were revived in the analytical field due to the analyst's change of address. Tania felt forced to leave the analyst's home, where she imagined herself part of his family, for a place that was felt as being unpleasant and hostile. There arose also childhood memories, facts or phantasies, related to threats of sexual intrusion. It became possible, little by little, to reassign a meaning to these aspects, which then became part of the symbolic web of thought.

The observation of what happened after the M moments (acute enactments) shows, therefore, that the analytical process develops into something much more potent and thought-oriented than before the explosion (phase 1). The analyst is thus obliged to conclude that his earlier perception of that phase was erroneous. What had appeared to him to be productive was, in fact, stagnant. Only now is he aware of the collusions: a sadomasochistic one with K and one of mutual seduction with Tania. In other words, the analytical field was already paralysed, in some aspects, *before* the M moment, but the analyst could not see it. The acute enactment (M moment) *opens his eyes*, as it were.

Reversed perspectives and the analyst's thinking capacity

Reflecting on what had occurred, the analyst realises how his capacity for thinking had been attacked. Two reversed perspectives took place (Bion, 1963)[1] of which the analyst is at once aware.

The *first reversed perspective* referred to the perception that analyst and patient are engaged in productive work (phase 1) before the M moment. That was a false perception—in some areas the exact opposite occurred: the process had been coming to a standstill because patient and analyst identified with each other, forming an obstructive collusion, a chronic enactment. What the analyst imagined were *dreams*, or *non-dreams* being dreamed, were actually *non-dreams-for-two*.

Thus, with K, the analyst becomes aware that his supposed *patience* when facing the violence in the analytical field was in reality part of a sadomasochistic collusion. His blow to the arm of the chair was a cry of "Enough!" to his masochistic subjection, along the lines of what Symington (1983) calls an analyst's act of freedom. The analyst was also ridding himself of his former belief (similar to a transformation in hallucinosis) that his patience was beneficial. He is thereby disentangled from the collusion with K, indicating that he is a separate person.

With Tania, the analyst grasps the seductive collusion that made the analysis so *rewarding*. The *reward*, a belief, masked its opposite—a stagnation in certain areas. The liberation from the collusion was encouraged by the shift of address, stressing that the analyst and Tania were two distinct persons.

The *second reversed perspective* referred to the perception of acute enactments. The analyst's former viewpoint was that these enactments were the outcome of faults in his own thinking capacity. Observing the chain of events forces a different perspective on him: the M moments disclosed, in fact, a disruption in the obstructive collusions of phase 1 and a repossession of the thinking capacity.

When the two reversed perspectives are undone, the analyst realises that, even when constrained by the M moments, he had been able to somehow describe and interpret what had happened. He had not been able to value that fact because he was feeling guilty.

Thus, when the analyst had been shown, with K, to be a person who could get agitated, he also disclosed that his patience was not omnipotent (as it appeared to be). When the patient realised that his analyst could take care of himself and not be destroyed, he was more at ease with the violence of his destructiveness.

The seductive collusion with Tania is undone when the analyst is able to discuss the phantasies relating to the change of address. Tania imagined herself as part of the analyst's family, living symbiotically in his idealised home. By that, she managed to deny separation, exclusion, envy. The change of address was experienced as an abrupt desymbiotisation.

Preliminary theoretical hypotheses

The above-mentioned facts help the analyst to understand that the acute enactments, indicators of the explosion in the analytical field, encouraged useful interpretations. In other words, the analyst was, to begin with, surprised at the acute and intense manifestation of the *non-dreams*. And yet, upon pulling himself together, he was able to somehow dream them and integrate them in the symbolic net of thought.

The analyst might feel content with confirming a known fact—that enactments become useful *after* their grasping and interpretation. However, the analyst does not yet know why he failed to identify the collusion in phase 1, spotting it only after the M moment. Nor does he know what caused the chronic enactment to become acute.

One other fact that drew the analyst's attention is that, after understanding the M moments, the patients' associations led to the identification of real or imaginary situations of a traumatic character. Both K and Tania show that, during the M moments, they revived such situations: exclusion, disappointment, violence, separation, intrusion.

Based on this and the acutisation of the chronic enactment, the analyst formulates a hypothesis, which now he shall have to investigate: if during the M moment there emerged a traumatic fact, might not this fact have been present already in the previous chronic collusion (phase 1)?[2]

Chronic enactment and traumatic dream

Thinking over the characteristics of chronic enactments, the analyst finds that it would not be unwise to compare them to traumatic dreams. In both, one comes across the endless repetition of a scene, with no amplification of meaning—a non-dream. The difference is that in traumatic dreams there is a manifestation of extreme anxiety, which does not occur during chronic enactments.

However, as has been pointed out, there is anxiety underlying the chronic enactment, although it does not manifest itself and goes unnoticed by both members of the analytical dyad. Could it be, then, a function of chronic enactment to plug up anxiety?

We know that one of the functions of the traumatic dream is the frustrated search for the signal anxiety (Freud, 1926d), a function that would, had not it been harmed by the traumatic situation, activate defences against it. In fact, trauma (the intensity of internal and/or external stimuli) constitutes itself as trauma precisely because the mind was injured to such an extent that it was rendered unable to set off the protective sign-anxiety. The mind is therefore experienced as being destroyed and the patient suffers annihilation anxiety.

That injured mind loses its capacity for representation and symbolisation. A hole sets in, a terrifying non-mental void. Mental pain is experienced that mirrors the menace of *nothingness*, of the unnameable—the *nameless dread*. The traumatic non-dream encompasses the repetition of the traumatic situation, in a frustrated attempt to dream it. As the patient's mind is injured, one would expect the analyst to be able to dream that non-dream.

Thus we may regard chronic enactment as a non-dream-for-two with plugged-up anxiety, in which the traumatic situation is frozen and unable to manifest itself openly.

At some (M) moment, the chronic enactment explodes and gives way to acute enactment. This shift indicates a revival of the trauma, which had been frozen, and release of the plugged anxiety, with both seizing abruptly the analytical field.

In short: the observation of the consequences of acute enactments allows us to understand that, thanks to them, the analyst opens his eyes and realises that he was involved in an obstructive collusion, a chronic enactment. This collusion encloses a concentrate of frozen phenomena related to traumas, such as terrifying affects born of annihilation anxiety, mnemonic traces of impact, samples of injured mental functions, and defences against the perception of these aspects.[3]

Acute enactment signals a thawing of the concentrate and dissolution of the former block. The trauma is revived in an acute manner. The analytical field is seized, in an intense and violent way, by affective explosions involving detachment, abandonment, intrusion, separation, annihilation. In other words, acute enactment is the trauma revived in the analytical field.

This revival, however, will *not* be traumatic, partly in so far as the analyst, following the M moment, is able to understand, interpret, and reassign a meaning to the trauma, even when this is not an altogether conscious effort at first. Phase 2, with plots that allow being thought, signals that part of the injured mind has recovered, repossessing the symbolic function and the amplification of the mental universe.[4]

Now it is possible to understand more clearly why the analyst feels guilty following acute enactments. He fears that his presumed faults have contributed to *re-traumatising the patient*. Even if not perfectly patent to him, the analyst intuits that the acute enactment is now a result of the felling of defences against the trauma which was frozen in the chronic enactment.

Implicit alpha-function during chronic enactment

According to the proposed model, in order to avoid being re-traumatised, the traumatised patient "clings" to the analyst, encouraging him to take part in the chronic enactment. This *grip* is similar to that of a drowning person on his rescuer—so fierce that both are paralysed.

The immobilised analyst must not be intrusive nor give up the patient either, the two traumatic situations *par excellence*. And, when the patient paralyses the analyst (and the latter allows himself to be paralysed), the analytical process comes to a standstill.

The questions deserving more investigation at this point are the following:

1. Which factors are responsible for patient and analyst, all of a sudden, relinquishing their hold and trusting the possibility of reviving the trauma?
2. Why does trauma remain frozen as chronic enactment?

I believe that the emergence of trauma, by means of the chronic enactment, occurs at a given moment (not before and not after) when the analytical dyad unconsciously understands that sufficient mental functions have been restored to bear and handle the revived trauma.

To advance hypotheses on *how* that recovery of the mental functioning in traumatic areas occurs, we must examine in detail aspects of the analyst's work during chronic enactments. That examination shows us that, despite being blind to his involvement in the obstructive collusion, he nonetheless suspects that something is wrong and tries to grasp it.

Thus, in K's case, the analyst was aware of the violence, the envy, and the attacks on thinking capacity, which he attempted to describe and interpret. These interpretations were correct as regards form and even timing. Meanwhile, the patient would attack them or quickly devitalise them. The analyst believed he understood what was going on and that he should continue patiently interpreting, without giving in. He was reminded of the Brazilian saying: "Soft water will wear down hard rock".

With Tania, the analyst sometimes wondered if the analytical process was not going too smoothly. He even entertained the idea of discussing the material with his colleagues, but never actually did. During the phase in analysis that has been described, Tania would readily agree with transferential interpretations concerning separation and exclusion. Only after the M moment did the analyst realise that the easy concurrence was just a way of devitalising the process and thus hindering a deeper probe.

In other words, one finds in these cases that part of the analyst's mind grasps the defences against trauma and seeks to interpret them. But these interpretations do not work or are devitalised, and obstructive collusion remains. This is not clear to the analyst. That is, during the chronic enactment, despite analyst and patient being, as it were, interwoven, the former keeps, to a certain extent and in some regards, a capacity for discrimination. That is, he is able to use implicitly his alpha-function in some channels running parallel to the obstruction.[5]

I suggest that this implicit alpha-function gradually restores the patient's mental functions. At some time, there is the unconscious intuition that there has been sufficient restoration for the patient to be able to face, with diminished peril, the revival of the trauma. That confrontation is crucial to the reassignment of meaning. Defences are relinquished and the trauma is revived as acute enactment.[6]

The hypothesis raised above, concerning the implicit alpha-function, makes us presume the existence of deep unconscious communication between the members of the analytic dyad. Could it be still another function of chronic enactment—to facilitate this unconscious communication?

During chronic enactment, when the patient clings to the analyst, plugging up the traumatic injury, this assumes the role of *protective shield* (Freud, 1920g), the same protective shield that was missing in the traumatic situation.

It is usual for the baby to constantly test the mother's capacity for acting as a protective shield, since all of life's situations are potentially traumatic. In order to do so, he needs to grasp the mother's emotional states. Possibly, the more sensitive and vulnerable the baby is, the sharper this ability gets. I believe the patient will do the same with his *analyst protective shield*. The analyst, in his turn, also assesses unconsciously the mental functioning of his patient, while at the same time injecting in him implicit alpha-function. This process would thus bear a relation with what Stern et al. (1998) call *shared implicit relationship*, an intersubjective rapport prior to symbolisation.

During chronic enactment, even if the analyst seems unable to understand, incompetent, or even aggressive, the patient still feels that the re-traumatisation is less upsetting than the trauma of the past. The reason for this is twofold:

1. the patient phantasises that he controls the analyst;
2. the analyst, should he fail, goes on working in other areas of his mind, trying to observe, investigate, and discriminate, never renouncing the wish to understand further.

These facts are part of the implicit alpha-function. The patient perceives this interest. In other words, even when some areas of the analytical process appear to have stagnated, an implicit progress takes place concomitantly in others.

So we will have to re-examine the contents of acute enactment. Not only is the trauma revived, involving discharges, but non-dreams are occurring and being dreamed, and dreams are reverting to non-dreams.

Unconscious communication during chronic enactment

The observations and the hypotheses raised lead us into presuming that, underlying the paralysis of chronic enactment, movements are taking place that retrieve early episodes of the mind's development, with its possibilities and hindrances.

The patient unconsciously scrutinises her *analyst protective shield*, through projective identifications, assessing his containing capacity. The analyst, on the other hand, microscopically examines the traumatic fabric and the defences that strive to protect it. Accordingly, he measures the amount of reality that he is injecting into the patient, careful to avoid re-traumatising her. The introjection, by the patient, of thought functions, is processed little by little. Elements of the traumatic situation thus gradually acquire conditions for being thought.

Using the model of trauma as wound, one might say that it heals from the symbolic periphery extending towards the centre of the traumatic nucleus (Levy, 2012).

The analyst follows his patient's movements—his difficulties, blocks, obstructions, and relapses. When the patient refuses to give the analyst's hypotheses thought or devitalises them, the latter assumes unconsciously that the injured area has not recovered enough to tolerate reality and that his work must go on. On the other hand, by not recognising clearly the devitalisation of the process and his recruitment by the obstructive aspects of the patient, the analyst also contributes to the paralysing collusion.

It is a part of the analyst's implicit alpha-function to have the capacity to tolerate patiently the obstructive movements brought about by the traumatic injury and the hindrances to the recovery from it, without giving up the search for new approaches to what is taking place. I believe that patience to be necessary and closer to what we might call normal masochism.[7]

Chronic enactment ceases when, at some point, it is intuited that the traumatic fabric has recovered enough for the defences to be surrendered. The analyst no longer needs to act as a protective shield. The traumatic situation is then revived as acute enactment.

Should the recovery of the traumatic fabric be insufficient, the revival of the trauma would be aborted and the defences raised again. This is probably a frequent event with chronic enactments.

The described process may be regarded as a work of working through of the trauma, similar to the work of mourning, in which each aspect of the trauma has to be meticulously worked through.

And yet, is not the above description at odds with the observation of the analyst paralysed by the obstructive collusion, in the chronic enactment? As has been pointed out, the analyst's mind works simultaneously along two channels: in one of them, he contributes to the paralysis, his alpha-function is obstructed, and he exists in pathological masochism or using manic defences; in the other, he surrenders, and that surrender takes the form of normal masochism, necessary for the obstructive collusion. The analyst becomes involved in the process by his need to reach deeply into the traumatic injured area. He must live it, put its vulnerability to the test, adding carefully to its recovery, bearing pain and suffering.

In short, the analyst will experience inside himself the same as the patient, having to deal with the traumatic area so he can return it to the patient in a better half-way-recovered shape. Obviously that takes time, sometimes a very long time, and that will be the duration of the chronic enactment, time enough for the working through of the trauma.

Borderline in clinical practice

The patients referred to above cannot stand reality, which they feel as traumatic due to their lack of mental conditions to think it. This deficit may ensue both from internal factors and from the intensity and quality of the traumatic stimulus.

These patients cling to the analyst (sometimes through chronic enactment) in the analytical process as much to avoid trauma as to restore mental functions through the introjection of the analyst's alpha-function. These facts are part of the borderline patient clinical practice.

The borderline patient is described as inhabiting an empty world, lacking cohesion in his self, split and projected into objects from which he at once desperately depends and feels as intrusively threatening. His basic anguishes are of separation and intrusion, and they hark back to the terror of not-being, of non-existence, of annihilation (Figueiredo, 2003, 2006; Fonagy, 1991; Green, 1986; Grotstein, 1984; Kernberg, 1980).

It is nonetheless possible that, at the same time, other split-off parts of the patient work relatively well. The ego's instability is an outcome of a faulty introjection of the object, experienced as persecutory for the reason that into it were projected destructive and envious aspects. The cohesion of his identity is ultimately dependent on how he experiences the external objects inside which he lives projectively. Rey (1994) describes these patients as persons living in a shell, persons who have an outer carapace but no spine. By living as parasites in that shell, which they seem to have borrowed or stolen, they are constantly feeling unsafe.

Archaic anguishes, an offspring of early traumas, make the patient cling to the analyst in order to avoid both separation and intrusion from the environment. The chronic enactment discloses life inside the shell, into which the analyst is lured. Movements of attack and closing in take place inside the shell, with no risk of trauma since the object is kept under control. This is why the analyst feels constantly provoked, attacked, or seduced, and yet immobilised as regards the productive use of those feelings.

The patient's provocation of the analyst may seem like a way of testing reality; but as the initial traumas took place when the relationship was dyadic, a triangular space allowing for thought has not been formed (Britton, 1998). That is why the supposed reality tests fail. In other words, there is no space for dream, and the chronic enactment going on inside the shell replicates the dyadic situation.

A vicious circle is then formed—the patient feels traumatised by reality because he lacks a triangular space to think. The lack of such a space ensues from a failure in working out the oedipal situation, which prevents the employment of resources from the depressive position whose attainment fails to occur. Concomitantly, the contact with the triangular situation is experienced as traumatic because no resources are available to symbolise it, and the dyadic situation is maintained or returned to. The latter, in its turn, is unstable, threatened by the contact with the third, with reality, and so on.

As already seen, during the non-dreams of chronic enactments in the analytical situation, the patient clings to the analyst in an effort to avoid reviving the traumatic circumstances. The analyst should realise this for what it is, but he doesn't—he is paralysed by massive projective identifications. However, along channels running parallel to the paralysis, he is unconsciously injecting implicit alpha-function.

The alpha-function allows dreaming, symbolisation, and thought. These processes bear on the activation, *at the same time*, of other mechanisms: contact with reality, self–object separation, recovery of parts of the self that the patient placed into the analyst. For this to take place, the patient must mourn the lost object, discerning what belongs to the self and what belongs to the object. The latter is now seen from a more realistic viewpoint. Steiner (1996) argues that it is not known how the parts of the self are restored and believes that perhaps a change occurs in the perception of the object. We may suppose that that shift in perception follows precisely the injection of the analyst's alpha-function. In other words, the alpha-function promotes the capacity for symbolisation, which is the same as dreaming and thinking, which is the same as working through the mourning for the object and for the lost parts of the self, which is the same as taking responsibility for the self and the object, which is the same as getting in touch with reality, which is the same as creating a triangular space, which is part of the depressive position, in which frustration can be tolerated, and thought is allowed, and the oedipal situation worked out, which allows an experience of reality, and so on and so forth.

For these highly complex and entwined processes to take place, it is necessary, besides the presence of a living person with an available alpha-function, to consent to the passage of the necessary time, the time of mourning, the time of the process of working through of traumas, the time of chronic enactment.

Final considerations

Surely a professional may become blind to the patient's material due to personal countertransferential difficulties, the result of unsolved conflicts. In such a case, he is responsible for a possible enactment. In the present work, however, I am concerned with discussing situations in which the professional is involved in the enactment not only due to personal faults but also as a way of reaching deeply into traumatised areas.

At least seven simultaneous functions can be identified in these chronic enactments:

1. avoidance of trauma revival, by freezing it and plugging up anxiety;
2. immobilisation of the analyst so that he is not able to re-traumatise;
3. use of the analyst as a protective shield against trauma;
4. allowing profound unconscious contact between patient and analyst, making it possible to examine the traumatised areas;
5. employment of the analyst's alpha-function;
6. restoring of functions and injured parts of the mind and working through of the trauma;
7. abiding the necessary and adequate time for that cooperative work to take place.

It is not known exactly how the alpha-function works (Bion, 1962b). In this work, I have laid emphasis on its implicit action and associated it to the profound unconscious communication between the members of the analytical dyad. It would appear that the analyst's unconscious dream is grasped by the patient, outside all explicit communication, and this fact deserves further research. Stern et al. (1998) have brought forward a number of creative hypotheses concerning implicit intersubjective movements, co-existing with the explicit understanding of the transferential relationship. These movements result in what these authors call *moments of meeting*, which occur when each participant (particularly the analyst) manifests "something unique and authentic of his or herself as an individual" (p. 192) beyond his or her routine therapeutic role. These moments of meeting alter the intersubjective context, opening up a new space for re-arranging the defensive processes. These ideas are very close to what I presume occurs during chronic enactment and which results in acute enactment.

We are still struggling, however, with an unsolved problem. Even if one acknowledges the importance of the shared implicit relationship, why must the analyst remain unconsciously involved in the chronic enactment? Would it not be more useful for the analytical process if the analyst were to free himself from the collusion, and retain the required patience while injecting more explicit alpha-function? In order to try to provide an answer for these questions, I will once more evoke the analogy with the maternal function.

An adequate mother endeavours *to be* her baby, experiencing his suffering and traumatic situations so she can dream them in his stead. For this to occur, she partially shuts her eyes to her own needs, allowing her normal masochism to occur. Something akin to an enactment is then formed, the mother suffering along with her baby and yet not fully aware of it. Thus, mostly unaware of the unrealism of her masochism, she is able to maintain it for as long as necessary. If that negation is prematurely shattered, there is the risk of the mother not being able to bear her identification with the baby's suffering and detaching herself from him in a traumatic way.

In extreme situations, parents will be willing to get killed in order to save their children's lives. This is possible only when there is a deep identification with them, whereby they are felt as a part of themselves, beyond explicit reason.

As such, the enactment is necessary not only by virtue of the seven functions above described, but also because the analyst must deny temporarily the unrealism of his masochism—as is the case with the baby's mother—in order to suffer at-one-ment with his patient.

Notes

1. The reversion of perspective describes how contact with reality can be blocked, the figure being taken as background (or vice versa), as occurs

in the classical experiment of the psychology of form, where one can see sometimes two faces, at other times a vase.
2. Later on, the analyst will verify that he had intuited invariants already present in the pre-catastrophic phase which remained after the violent catastrophic change (Bion, 1965, 1970) manifested as acute enactment.
3. Despite the fact that in trauma the records of experience are not part of the symbolic network, some memories of traumatic situations may by inscribed as fear, guilt, shame, humiliation, dissociated but perhaps precariously symbolised (Person & Klar, 1994). However, the connection with other symbols does not take place and the trauma remains split from the symbolic network that makes up thought.
4. Obviously, these sporadic recoveries will be followed by new relapses, the analytical process evolving like a spiral of forward and backward movements.
5. Baranger et al. (1983) show that the bastion—which I believe to bear a resemblance to enactment—can be made up as a static foreign body, while the analytical process runs its course in other areas.
6. In the example of the drowning person, it is as if the rescuer (by keeping alive and striving to think) is able to persuade the traumatised person to trust the resources of the dyad to survive, even if they cannot avoid swallowing a lot of water when they let go of one another. That way they can separate and help (think) each other.
7. This normal masochism is similar to the mother's patience and capacity to tolerate suffering without discouragement. This subject was approached, in a creative way, by Galvez (2004). Bion (1970) also uses the term "patience" to designate the suffering and the tolerance to frustration that the analyst must bear while waiting for the selected fact.

CHAPTER EIGHT

Dreaming bizarre objects and early traumas: the continuum dream <-> non-dream

We might say that there exists a continuum extending from dream areas to non-dream areas, something like a spectrum of colours. This continuum illustrates how one can locate mental functioning in terms of the capacity for mentalization and symbolisation. Oscillations in the continuum indicate how this capacity is broadened and how it is attacked, and also shows movements between beta-elements <-> alpha-elements and PS <-> D.[1] At one extreme are ideal areas of whole symbolisation. Next, one can see areas where symbols have less capacity for meaning and connection. Then come symbols that have degenerated in varying degrees. Finally, fragile connections under constant attack lead on to areas where the symbolisation is precarious or non-existent, with the predominance of non-symbolised areas. Permeating this continuum are areas with symbolic equations (Segal, 1957), where symbol and symbolised run together, and areas with apparent symbolisation, but where the patient's capacity for abstraction is limited. Rigid organisations (Brown, 2005) with apparently intelligible beta-elements (Sandler, 1997) may simulate dreams, but they are *false dreams* (Cassorla, 2009a) that mask non-dreams. Deformed or fractured symbols mix in with split mental functions and are described as bizarre situations, as we will see in the clinical case of Paul. Discharges into acts should not be confused with acts that are thought about. All elements in this continuum may be expressed at the same time. We therefore move from more or less symbolic areas to areas that are psychotic and traumatised in varying degrees with representation through images that is deficient. In traumatised patients and those with borderline conditions and confused functioning, dreams and different types of non-dreams may alternate rapidly or appear mixed, thus confusing the analyst.[2]

With so many possibilities to discuss and to work with, I will now face the difficult task of highlighting some of the facts in this continuum. We have non-dreams that seek to become dreams, as well as dreams that are reluctant to expand their meaning, dreams being transformed into non-dreams, quasi-dreams (Rezze, 2001), states of confusion that mix non-dreams with dreams, concrete non-dreams that simulate dreams, non-dreams that surface as nightmares and the like. Illustrative situations of the function of dreaming take place when patients in recovery can remember and retell non-dreams (from childhood, for example), with emotion. Such dreams are symbolised retroactively in that they hardly seemed alive and have inhabited a meaningless world, as we saw in Helen Keller's case and will see in the material about Paul.

Dreams can be defined as productions that symbolise situations that move flexibly and creatively throughout the symbolic network of thinking. Defences are always found in this type of movement, but they can be described as non-psychotic. During a dream, dangerous areas may be approached and nocturnal dreams can be interrupted as nightmares (Ogden, 2005). They are non-dreams that wake the dreamer up, perhaps to provide the person with some physical movement that will discharge them.[3]

During a waking dream, the analyst can note when the patient is unable to perceive reality (either internal or external) by transforming symbolic thinking into non-dream discharges or behaviour. The analyst observes the attack on thinking and the retreat of the mental universe. The opposite indicates its expansion.

An analyst may sometimes perceive that certain dreams cover up areas of potential non-dreams in order to keep these areas from becoming manifest. Dreams and non-dreams may run together or quickly become their own opposites, leaving the analyst confused. Discharges, on the other hand, may or may not be accompanied by images. The images have varying degrees of clarity, bizarreness, strangeness, permanence, rigidity, or connection, and may be experienced as part of the patient's internal world, the outside world (as hallucinations), or both. In addition, non-dreams can become evident through *nothing*, through a void. The analyst is unable to grasp them. Sometimes outlines of dreams occur to him in the form of images that seem like deserts or empty spaces, as we will see below in the section on Susan.

If we take a clinical vertex, we can imagine, at one extreme, an autistic or catatonic patient who is completely unable to express himself, or even to think thoughts. Within our spectrum, near this extreme, we may encounter a somatising patient whose non-dreams become manifest through repetitious physical complaints. Another may bring in such fragmented non-dreams that they are like a stream of urine, for example (Segal, 1981). In these cases, nothing usually occurs to the analyst and, if he is lucky, his work often begins by dreaming elements from other, more accessible, areas. Another patient may spew out words without meaning, or eject mental debris, and the analyst may have outlines of images that escape him or are difficult to retain. Next along the spectrum are patients who can call up images or scenes, but they are static and without emotional resonance. The analyst might be able to use them as material for his own dreams. Oneiric flashes of daydreams (Ferro, 1996), night dreams, stories, and symbolic narratives indicate the other extreme, where alpha-elements become evident, worked through in a more, or less, adequate manner by the dreaming and thinking apparatuses.

Non-dreams can become evident through behaviour or through mental gestures, and they resemble pantomimic wordless theatrical performances (Sapisochin, 2007, 2012, 2013) that involve the analyst. When the analyst realises her countertransferential involvement, she is already transforming the gestural representation into verbal representation based on images. Non-identified psychic gestures may be chronic enactments.

If our vertex of observation is the capacity to symbolise, we may come across other aspects in the continuum, such as discharges of non-symbols, signs and quasi-symbols, symbolic equations (Segal, 1957), static symbols (images, symptoms, acts, etc.) that are difficult to connect, symbols with a certain degree of connection but that have lost their capacity of expression (Barros, 2011), attempts at symbolisation through mental gestures, and symbols that are linked together in varying degrees of creativity. This expanding spectrum, which ranges from non-symbol to symbolic network, is a two-way street, and there are both advances and setbacks. Some categories can cover up others, or several may become manifest simultaneously.[4]

By reducing our vertex of observation of areas of mental functioning, we will see that non-dreams of the psychotic part of the personality involve beta-elements that have resulted from a reversion of the alpha-function. That is, the non-dream contains debris of objects and parts of the mind that can become manifest as closed-off, inconsistent, and usually bizarre scenes. The analyst dreams on the basis of her experience of this debris.

Such dreams contain traumatic areas that may sometimes emerge in more or less explicit forms. The consequences of the trauma, identifiable in the analytic relationship, are varied, and cover a range resulting from the "intensity" and the "extension". At one extreme of the spectrum, we see areas of non-image-based representation, of empty representational spaces. There is a fracture, or breakage, in this interplay, resulting in a zone of psychic pain that is not figurable. What might be noted are debris from areas adjacent to the trauma that seek to be relived both to control the trauma and to try to work it through. There would seem to be a sort of symbolic framework around the empty space that can, *a posteriori* (*après-coup*), give it some meaning (Levy, 2012) or that may form a rigid beta-screen with this same function (Brown, 2005). The traumatic core reveals nothing or, better said, indicates the existence of a void (Lutenberg, 2007; Winnicott, 1974), a blank (Green, 1983), or a black hole (Grotstein, 1990; Guignard, 1997; Imbasciati, 2006). The analyst has to dream this void, which is more difficult than the previous situation. She will usually have to use patches as *constructions* of her "raw material" (Freud, 1937d), which demand more *drive wager* from her (Marucco, 2007).

Following that, along this spectrum, there may be areas of precarious symbolisation. Another intermediary area may correspond to what Khan (1963) called "cumulative trauma", in which situations of rupture of the protective shield that were not acute or intense accumulate in a silent manner. However, there is no possibilty of the occurrence of adequate symbolisation, that is, the transformation of raw elements into potentially thinkable elements, alpha-elements.

In certain traumatic areas, symbols, in their representative aspect, can be formed, but they lose their plasticity as representatives and expressions of things, weakened in their denotative and expressive character (Barros, 2005). Apparently intelligible beta-elements (Sandler, 1997) and balpha-elements (Ferro, 1996) are repercussions of this type of situation.

Areas from before the formation of the mental apparatus can appear in the analytic field, bringing about discouragement in the analyst. These areas that simulate non-existence can be covered over by autistic barriers (Korbivcher, 2013). The analyst, when identified with these areas, has to bear her condition of non-existence. We would be in an area before the existence of beta-elements (Korbivcher, 2013; Meltzer, 1975). The analyst's capacity for reverie is challenged to dream suppressions, voids, and the remains of marks that are a part of the most primordial mind (Green, 1998). The *drive wager* would seem to be greater and the analyst must create images in her mind that give meaning to the void. When they emerge, it can be seen that they not are the product of identifications, nor are they constructions. The analyst is surprised to see that she used aspects of her own mind, some of which she was not even aware about. These aspects will be illustrated in the section about Susan. This work of *figurability* involves strong identification of the analyst with her patient and a process of regression that is therefore also intense. The analyst feels obliged to represent in view of the consequent dread towards non-representation (Botella & Botella, 2005).[5]

It is not always possible to differentiate between psychotic or traumatic areas and areas from the primordial mind. Continuous microtraumas can add to, or be aggravated by, other traumas that occurred at different stages of mental development. It is certain that the psychotic area always includes elements of trauma, and that areas adjacent to the trauma behave as psychotic. At the same time, very early areas permeate these manifestations and nothing prevents traumatisms, that is, traumas that could be dreamed in some way (Bokanowsky, 2005), from appearing at the same time.[6]

Dreams and non-dreams are part of an epistemological continuum, but they emerge in the clinical analytic field, alternate with one another, and interpenetrate one another in a parallel way by running together. Decades ago, Grinberg (1967) called attention to dreams and mixed discharges, which he called mixed dreams.

Non-dreams that involve representational deficits or voids may try to "hitch rides" from traumatic or psychotic non-dreams or from non-psychotic dreams. One of the analyst's tasks is to avoid being deceived by non-dreams or by manifest dreams that cover up the void.

I therefore present as a hypothesis that non-dreams of psychotic areas always include elements that correspond to the traumatic void and to unrepresented areas of the primordial mind. They hide and become evident among the psychotic debris and through breaks experienced countertransferentially. Possibly, when the analyst transforms such psychotic non-dreams into dreams, she is also implicitly doing the same thing with the other non-dreams and void. Therefore, she does not dream only on the basis of projective identification resulting from beta-elements of psychotic non-dreams, but also on the basis of other types of more primitive identification (some of which have been proposed by Sandler (1993) and Franco Filho (2000)) which are hard to conceptualise. The analyst's dreams might also include, in some way, outlines of constructions and work of non-explicit figurability referring to areas that are likewise not explicit.

The palimpsest model may be of help here. Dreams cover over areas of non-dreams, dreamed traumas cover over other traumas, which cover over others, that are transmitted inter-generationally...

If these hypotheses prove to be correct, we could certainly expand our reasoning to include symbolic dreams, and we would see that an analyst who re-dreams a dream of her patient, in a *dream-for-two*, is also implicitly dreaming in non-symbolic or empty areas. In other words, the analyst's alpha-function explicitly or implicitly works concurrently in all areas of mental functioning or non-functioning, even those that do not emerge explicitly in the analytic field. These facts challenge us to delve deeper into the functioning of reverie and figurability, of containing and negative capacity, patience and normal masochism, counter-identifications and identifications with voids, and so forth. All these are considered factors of the alpha-function, which also involves deep unconscious communication, which is still insufficiently understood.

Now, I will present short descriptions that illustrate the dream work of the analyst when listening to bizarre non-dreams and non-dreams with voids resulting from early traumas. In these latter, communication is carried out through sensorial aspects.

Paul and the analyst's bizarre pen

Paul, aged thirty-five, says that he has always lived in a terrifying world, in the sense that he always felt that something undefined but terrible was about to happen. But he had not the slightest awareness that he was living in this world because, for him, life was supposed to be like that and he was sure that everyone felt the same way. Today, he uses the term "panic" when referring to this dread without a name.

In recent years, he has developed a better capacity to take a distance from things and observe the world, but he nonetheless maintains a considerably psychotic way of functioning in general.

During one session, as he sat facing the analyst, he mentioned that he had received a prize in the mail, a pen, together with a letter asking for a financial contribution for a religious organisation. He kept the pen but threw the letter away because the organisation belonged to a religion different from his own.

But the pen soon became threatening for him, and he knew he had to get rid of it somehow. He obsessively mulled over in his mind a list of people he could give the pen to, including a neighbour, a cousin, his housemaid, and a co-worker. He said that these are all envious people. They envied him, and he imagined that if he gave the pen to one of them, the envy could be appeased. But he could not decide whether to give the pen away or not and, if he gave it away, who to? These thoughts hurt his head, which felt like it was going to explode, and he imagined his skull opening up and his brains spilling out, like he saw in a recent movie, where a criminal was shot in the eye.

Hearing this account, the analyst imagines the scene of the brains spilling out and realises that he feels a mixture of disgust and pleasure. The analyst also notes that Paul's envy bothers him and stirs up his anger. He thinks that the pen might be a present loaded with envy. But he knows that saying this to Paul now would serve no purpose except to vent his own wish to retaliate.

The analyst surprises himself by asking Paul if he had not thought of getting rid of the pen by leaving it with him, the analyst. Paul answers that he had not considered that possibility because the analyst might leave the pen on the table and this would make him, Paul, feel threatened. At this moment in the conversation, Paul is looking at another pen, the analyst's, which is on the table. Paul looks at it suspiciously. The analyst asks him what he sees, and Paul answers that this pen has taken on a different consistency and he can see it grow. It is growing very large and filling his entire field of vision and this makes him feel very frightened. He moves his chair away from the table and asks the analyst to put the pen away, which the analyst does.

The analyst tells Paul that the pen on the table has become emotionally similar to the one he received as a prize. The climate seems dangerous and the analyst keeps on talking, carefully, looking at Paul in order to appraise how he is taking the analyst's words. The analyst says that both pens were contaminated by negative emotions and that this is why they became dangerous and why Paul feels threatened.

Paul says it is very good to hear the analyst's comments, which indicate the analyst understands him. But he wonders why the pen seems dangerous to him. The analyst feels satisfied at having encouraged some responsibility and curiosity in Paul. But at the same time, the analyst mistrusts his own reaction. He fears that Paul might simply be trying to please him.

The situation described above shows how internal reality is linked to external reality in order to constitute clusters that are seen as bizarre objects. In this sense, through deteriorated remains of symbols and symbolic equations, the pen may have represented a complex set of emotional experiences related to guilt, hatred, envy, voracity, sex, and the like. These experiences, visually brought together, are shattered along with parts of the mind, and these clusters are connected to objects, people, body parts, and to the analyst. Bizarre objects seek discharge and, at the same time, seek dreamers who will symbolise them.

Most of the interpretations that came to the analyst's mind at that point seemed intellectualised to him, and involved theoretical explanations about what had occurred. This led the analyst to the conclusion that his capacity to dream was impaired. So he kept quiet.

Paul then said that other students at the school where he studied as a child were envious of him because his family was better off financially and lived in a better home. On the basis of earlier statements, however, the analyst had created in his mind an image of Paul's house as being very poor and dirty, located on a lower level than the other houses nearby. This image, barely conscious to the analyst, was the result of his attempt to represent in images, emotional experiences related to deterioration, destructiveness, and inferiority, in other words, life in an impoverished and decadent world. This image was the opposite of that which Paul was describing now, but it indicated what Paul had concealed. The analyst was also aware that these images were related to experiences in his own life, even to the neighbourhood where he grew up.

Paul's memories and associations seemed to indicate a certain amount of dream work. At this moment, the analyst communicated to Paul the hypothesis that Paul had thrown away the letter that came with the pen because it reminded him of this situation—the envy of poorer people who needed donations and whom he considered different from himself. But the analyst did not feel it would be convenient to point out the feelings of envy inside Paul or between Paul and the analyst.

Then Paul said he was afraid of dying. The analyst told him that he, Paul, felt threatened when he heard the analyst talking about feelings of envy. Paul answered that "we are all going to die sooner or later". The analyst felt that this remark "killed off" his intervention and reminded Paul that he, the analyst, was also going to die.

At this point, Paul was looking at the analyst and smiling, and he ironically stated that the analyst would die before him, Paul, because the analyst is older. The analyst felt a shiver go through him.

Before the analyst could recover, Paul announced that it was time to end the session, and stood up. The analyst said there were still five minutes to go because they had started late. Paul answered that he was used to having people take advantage of him and that he always came out on the losing end. So he decided to leave before the analyst told him to go. The analyst told him that if he stayed the five minutes, it would be to the advantage of both and no one would have to come out the loser. Paul looked surprised and said that this had never occurred to him.

The analyst felt that some progress had been made up till that point, but he feared that things could unravel easily. He also realised that he had been reticent to show Paul how he had attacked the analyst and Paul's fear of retaliation, and this may have encouraged Paul to try to end the session. The analyst had some doubts as to whether his "cowardice" reflected control by Paul of his massive projective identification (non-dream-for-two) or if it indicated the need to give the analytic pair enough time to digest the facts in a way that would not traumatise them (time for the dream work). He hoped that the dream work would become the rule.

During the next session, Paul said that, the day before, he had caught himself looking at his wife in a different way. He got home from the session and his wife greeted him like she always does, but he had never noticed how kind and gentle she was with him and how she took care of him. He remembered that he had always felt that his wife stayed with him out of some sort of interest and that he never really felt loved until yesterday. He added by saying that he never knew what love was. At this moment, Paul was moved. The analyst felt that his emotion was genuine, but he also noted that, in a parallel area, something suspicious was still going on. Then Paul described traumatic situations he had experienced in childhood, which he associated with his incapacity to trust and to love. The analyst listened and even included himself in the plot. The session developed mainly as dreams-for-two, and at the end of the session Paul looked at the pen still on the table and said that today, "It's just a pen."

This short case description shows how a terrifying world replete with bizarre objects can become manifest in the analytical field. Since, in this area, Paul was mistaking an object for his self, he too was a terrorist. The analyst was included in this world; he also experienced the dread, and he had to give it meaning. Then at a certain point, Paul was able to see the world as different from himself. The mechanisms of the depressive position became visible, and we saw Paul trying to carry out some type of reparation, but going backwards was always a threat.[7]

The moment described above was certainly the result of a great deal of mental effort, and the analyst was doubtful about its permanence because he had already seen other similar situations that were later reversed. He would have to dream and re-dream the various traumatic situations many times over. In other words, there was need for a great deal of working through, which always involves a gradual process. A supplementary working through takes place at the same time, inside the analyst's mind, and this is how clusters are undone so that traumatised areas can take on meaning.

Dreaming voids and early traumas

> The analyst wakes up feeling out of sorts, but he cannot clearly locate this feeling. He has the impression that it is not related to anything physical, but to something in the emotional sphere. He probes around for verbal symbols that might represent what he thinks he is feeling, but he cannot find any. Even if he tries to name the feelings, such as "tiredness", "fatigue", or "boredom", the words do not fit and lead him to be concerned with the vitality of his analytic function, which he will have to use all day long.

The analyst becomes aware of the shortcomings of verbal symbols when used to describe affective states that cannot yet be connected to the symbolic network of thought. These states, even though inadequately named, serve as an alarm indicating that the analyst should pay attention to himself.

> Now the analyst is with his first patient and realises that his uneasiness has disappeared. He is operating satisfactorily. He continues to work normally until mid-morning and during a longer break he remembers Susan, who will be his last patient this morning. He realises he is concerned with her.

As he has a cup of coffee, memories about Susan's analysis come to mind. After the first phase of her analysis, which was apparently productive, she started complaining about physical symptoms that were very hard to describe. They were about undefined fears, great concern over fatal diseases, frantic searches for doctors, and somatic treatments of all types. The analyst tried to put these fears into words and give them meaning, but he had felt that his efforts were useless and that his interventions had not really made sense to her. The contact with this challenging area encouraged the analyst, but Susan continued to complain incessantly.

Little by little, the analyst became discouraged and struggled to give meaning to his own lack of competence. Working with Susan had become unpleasant. He remembered that, little by little, he was feeling sleepier than usual, made drowsy by her repetitive ramblings on. It was an effort to stay awake, and he began feeling that his attention and concentration were on the decline. He was aware that his analytic capacity had weakened, and he tried to examine his own feelings in the hopes that this would give him some hint as to how to understand what was going on in the work of this analytic pair.

The above description is similar to the one before it, but it includes a patient, Susan. The analyst *feels* the emotional experience. Since the experience does not yet have meaning, he cannot *suffer* it. The analyst continues to search for verbal symbols in order to take a distance and give meaning to his exasperation and feeling of hopelessness. The memories that come to his mind indicate some type of opening in this search.

During this same coffee break, the analyst continues to review his work with Susan. He feels uncomfortable about the strange taste of the coffee, to the point of having to put more sugar in it if he is going to drink it. Later on, he will pour it down the drain.

He realises that is he intrigued about the change that has been taking place during the last few sessions. For a while, he had felt sleepy and had to struggle to stay awake, but now he feels overcome by a certain growing sense of fear. Susan has seemed more distant than before and her way of crying was different, even frightening. As he tries to visualise what he is thinking about, the analyst realises that he has even gone through moments of dread. He supposes that this is why his sleepiness has disappeared. He now has to stay on the alert and feel preoccupied, and it has become hard to daydream and to dream. Outlines of daydreams were terrifying, as they have involved death, suicide, and something else that he cannot find words for. But only now, during his coffee break, has he become aware of these outlines of images. He realises that his mind cannot bear them.

The analyst feels frustrated because he is unable to dream the beta-elements that invade him. Only later will he perceive that the bitter taste of the coffee was a sensorial attempt to give meaning to "bitter" emotional experiences. The coffee thrown out represents, in an act, the expulsion of unbearable facts. This act has a symbolic component, but access will be given to it only when it is dreamed and thought.

The author feels the need to broaden his capacity for representation and seeks help from the theoretical model of trauma. The beta-elements cannot be signified by Susan's mind because this mind has been deficiently constituted and/or because the intensity and quality of the elements is greater than her mind's capacity to dream. In this model, something happens at the beginning of the constitution of the mind which traumatises it to the point that it is unable to dream in certain areas. Later, internal and external factors that mobilise these areas cause them to be experienced as traumatic facts.

However, there is something new here: there is an analyst, and it is hoped that he can dream the elements that Susan cannot. It is as though the analyst lends her his alpha-function. But the analyst's mind seems to be as traumatised as Susan's. We know that expelled beta-elements enter into the analyst through projective identification in order for him to dream them. At the same time, however, they seek to control him in order to maintain the *status quo*. But we might ask which traumatic areas of the analyst himself were also activated.

> As he daydreams, the analyst suddenly becomes aware of "something else" that has terrorised and accompanied the outlines of the frightening images. In a flash, he sees himself dead. Maybe he even saw his own dead body and feels a dread he had never before experienced. He feels that he has lived through post-death nothingness, non-existence. To escape, he has tried desperately to replace this feeling with another. He can only calm down when he remembers the image of his children playing with him when they were small. But he only realises this later on.

Observing the work of the analytic dyad, we can say that things were at a standstill. In part, the patient and analyst are joined together through mutual massive projective identifications of beta-elements. Discouragement and sleepiness were replaced by concern, alertness, and dread, but without being signified. An external observer would describe this situation as affective states and sketches of scenes that are constantly repeated but that continue without solution.

The names *non-dreams-for-two* and *chronic enactment* could be applied to the clinical facts described above since both members of the analytic dyad, somewhat paralysed, are unable to dream. But the fact that the analyst is conscious of this fact makes the term "chronic enactment" partially inappropriate. By definition, during a chronic enactment the analyst is not aware that he is involved in an obstructive collusion. But it is quite probable that, in split-off areas, non-dreams-for-two, unperceived by the analyst, are also taking place.

The visual image of the dead analyst can be considered an alpha-element, but this unbearable image was instantly reversed. It was followed by other unbearable images, including thinking about the analyst's children without their father, therefore orphans, and this image gave rise to the image of the analyst as a child seeing his own dead father. This traumatic plot could only be revisited *après-coup*, as usually happens with traumatic facts. Intelligently, the analyst forged a different and substitute plot, seeing himself alive and healthy and taking care of his happy children.

The non-dream-for-two is a mixture of discharges and behaviours that evidence the attack on the dyad's capacity to dream. That is, face to face with emotional experience, the mind should activate a mechanism that will give it meaning, but this mechanism is unable to deal with the experience, and is attacked and destroyed.

> As we saw above, the analyst has treated his first morning patients adequately, before Susan's appointment. But now, after the coffee break, he is amazed at the memories and images he had during the period. He knows that exaggerated attention to these facts can block his intuitive ability, and he tries to maintain a dreamlike state of mind that will let him experience what takes place. Even though he knows how difficult this is, he tries to obey the technical recommendations he regularly follows, which are to try to be present without desire, without memory, without the intention to understand, in order to be able to be surprised with anything new.
>
> As the analyst opens the door for Susan, he realises that his pulse is accelerated. He feels relieved to see her alive in the waiting room. As he looks at her, he sees a prisoner in a concentration camp, waiting for death and not yet having killed herself for lack of strength.

Susan goes to the couch with great difficulty. The analyst notices that his concern has turned to discouragement and he now feels overcome by desperation. He sees himself questioning the psychiatric treatment Susan is receiving concurrently with analysis. Later, he will see himself trying to throw his helplessness, guilt, and desperation out of the window, out to psychiatry.

Susan drags herself to the couch and the analyst follows her as he feels his own analytic capacity dragging along behind. The account could continue on like this and would not be very different from those of earlier sessions. But this time something happens that surprises both patient and analyst. Before Susan gets to the couch, the analyst, without knowing why, says he would like her not to lie down today. It would be better for her to sit in the chair.

Susan stops, looks at the analyst, and hesitates. She then turns and reluctantly goes over to the chair and sits down, and the analyst sits down in his chair opposite her. Both analyst and patient know that something different is going on, but they do not know just what.

The episode described above recounts an action by the analyst that, apparently, had not been well thought out. In other words, he was acting out. Let us try to discover the origin of this process by examining what had happened before.

If we remember the analyst's state in the morning when he woke up, we could easily suppose that, during the night, his dreams had sought to symbolise aspects searching for representation. But the dream work was not sufficient and the dream was interrupted, leaving in the analyst the feeling of something bad—note the opening phrase of this text: "The analyst wakes up feeling out of sorts". This "bad feeling", consisting of beta-elements that had not been transformed, evacuated, from his mind, showed up as symptoms.

This same dream, however, continued unconsciously during the day (while he was awake) and the analyst managed to find approximate words for what he was feeling, such as discouragement and boredom, which functioned as signals. At the same time, in parallel areas, the analyst's function remained intact and the analyst was able to dream what was going on with the patients who came in before Susan.

In the interval between patients, the analyst realised that his unconscious dream was related to Susan and that he was even trying to dream terrifying losses and mourning of his own. Later, he would confirm that they were complementary to Susan's dreams. He was also convinced that this had been occurring in nighttime dreams.

Therefore, when the analyst opened the door to let Susan in, he felt taken over by beta-elements, but they had already been trying to be dreamed unconsciously for quite some time. The image of the field of concentration provides some hints as to meaning. At the same time, the analyst unsuccessfully projects feelings of guilt and impotence into the profession of psychiatry.

The analyst's invitation for Susan to sit down might have been the consequence of his desperation in trying to change the stalled plot of the dyad, due to the change in the analytic situation. He wondered if it might be better to stop being a psychoanalyst and to speak socially with Susan by consoling or otherwise helping her. Or he could simply tell her, face to face, that it is no longer possible to analyse her and that the contract would have to be breached. These are hypotheses that went through the analyst's mind later on when he was thinking about the session, but these would have been actions that were not thought out and aimed at removing psychoanalysis from the relationship, turning it into something else.

If, on the one hand, this analytic self-criticism suggests a careful evaluation of the analyst's responsibility, it could also have to do with the reaction of a moralistic superego that often operates with attacks against his own capacity to think (Bion, 1962a). To replace it with an ego in contact with reality, it would be important to carefully note what happened next.

> Susan and the analyst are seated and facing one another. The analyst looks at Susan but he can hardly see her expressions, which she hides by turning to one side and looking down. But this attempt to hide is what most stands out for the analyst, and he can also see how she wrings and twists her hands and feet.
>
> Without knowing why, the analyst fixes his gaze on Susan's semi-hidden face, but he sits in silence, since he has no idea what to say. At the same time, he wonders whether he has made a mistake in asking her to sit in the chair, and he still does not know why he did so.
>
> After a few moments, Susan begins to cry. Gradually her face becomes more visible and the analyst is moved by seeing tears roll down her face. She had never cried like this during a session. The analyst realises that he is no longer afraid, and senses an immense sadness that makes him feel relieved, as if the tears were washing his soul.

After a few moments, the analyst realises that Susan is looking for words in the midst of her sobs. Now she looks intensely into his eyes and says: "This is the first time anyone has ever looked at me … . It's the first time anybody has ever looked at me", she repeats as she continues to sob. Looking at the analyst and then looking away, she describes moments from her past with her mother, and says that her mother never paid attention to her, never listened to her, but especially, never looked at her. She had longed for her mother's glance so she could feel she was alive and real, but she only found a "non-look" that annihilated her.

The gridlocked plot is shaken loose and the emotional experience of the here and now takes on meaning at the same time that it opens up to Susan's symbolic network and stirs up affects, memories, and thoughts that broaden the meaning even further. The terror of not existing, which, some time earlier, could not be represented, is related to emotional experiences from the present and the past, condensed especially in the annihilating non-look.

This view of the facts leads us to conjecture that the analyst's act proved to be more complex than a simple discharge. It involved unconscious dream work that resulted in action that in some way represented Susan's need to be seen and to feel herself as existing.

We can classify this act as an acute enactment, as it involves a mixture of discharges, beta-elements being dreamed, alpha-elements being formed, and outlines of thought in search of development. The mixture, abruptly introduced into the analytic field, continues to be dreamed by the dyad, and it undoes the earlier chronic enactment. Of course, areas where there was differentiation between this and non-enactment were also part of the process.

I suppose that the trauma of non-existence initially made Susan grab onto her analyst in a type of fusion, where she avoided becoming aware of the separation between self and object. The analyst also became involved in the situation and there are indications that factors of his own contributed to this. This was the origin of the chronic enactment, namely, a way to keep the trauma in a frozen state. This fusion consequently made it impossible for there to be a space to symbolise, thus blocking the development of the capacity to think.

This fusion, as fantasy, could protect Susan from coming into contact with her feelings of non-existence. At the same time, however, the constant threat of separation, of discrimination between self and object, kept her in a state of terror. Worse yet, the fusion was also felt as deadly because the object, confused with the self, had also become deadly.

It would seem that when the analyst invited Susan to sit down and face him, he felt uncomfortable not only because he knew that his analytic function was unstable, but also because he intuited that he was stimulating a perception of separation between self and object. He felt hesitant and guilty for the possibility of having traumatised Susan by confronting her with reality. But his attempt to change the analytic setting also involved care on his part, and it indicated a loving link that made Susan feel considered and, especially, seen.

The fact of having opened up a space for symbolisation and thought confirms what was predominating in the episode, namely, the loving discrimination between self and object. On the other hand, we must also suppose that this discrimination took place as a result of symbolisation, through which the trauma was attenuated. The paradoxical question that comes up is: can we only experience a triangular relation if it is thought about, and can we only think about it if we are going through it? In our model, this emotional virtuous circle is unlocked by an object with an available alpha-function. But this alpha-function can only be available if the object is able to move between triangular situations and the chaos that leads to dual situations.

In other words, it seems that this abrupt separation between Susan and her analyst (the acute enactment) occurred only because some type of implicit symbolisation was already taking place. That is, Susan's despair and her traumatic dread of something like death were being unconsciously worked through by the analyst's dream through an *implicit alpha-function*, with repercussions in the dyad's dream. Although the work seemed to be partially paralysed, in parallel areas the analyst continued to try to dream, but Susan constantly devitalised and inverted the analyst's dream by transforming it into a non-dream. The analyst continued to insist, struggling against his own discouragement and fear, but he also contributed to the inversion. Both members of the dyad were afraid to relive their traumas.

We can visualise part of this work in the images of the dead bodies, concentration camps, dead parents, and living parents with happy children. Characters seek thinkers, and thoughts seek characters. Destructive affects and deadly non-looks struggle against several facets, such as the capacity for acceptance, attempts at forming symbols, and loving glances, that are the products of both members of the dyad, being worked through unconsciously. The acute enactment that emerges shows that the trauma of distinguishing between self and object can be experienced in an attenuated form thanks to the implicit alpha-function that was occurring and that culminated in a re-signification of the look.

If the capacity to dream the trauma had not been sufficient, the earlier plot would have returned. That is, the alpha-function would have been reverted and Susan would have felt traumatised by the acts of the analyst, and/or the dyad would have returned to its fusional relationship. Situations like this must have occurred often during the previous process.

The episode described above allowed the analyst to become aware of aspects of his own. He could also begin thinking about his difficulties in seeing Susan in other ways and making her feel seen. Susan, with steps forward and steps back, was gradually developing her capacity to see herself and her analyst from different perspectives. Her capacity to live in a triangular situation and her capacity to think developed concurrently.

The analyst also realised that the first phase of the analytic process, which had seemed productive, involved phenomena in the non-psychotic area, specifically, in dreams-for-two between Susan and her analyst. But these dreams also shrouded over the functioning of primitive areas. During the treatment, it was seen that the primordial function of the supposed dreams-for-two often served as this shroud. For this reason, they functioned as false dreams.

The analyst's dream

In the clinical situations described above, we saw how analysts must become deeply involved with their patients in order to live through situations the patients are unable to symbolise. At the same time, they must take a distance from such experiences in order to transform them into dreams.

When we experience this unsymbolised world with our patients, we can come into contact with annihilation and non-existence. When the analyst is unable to bear these facts, he may return them to the patient and/or turn himself off. He may simply "go away", although this "going away" can be momentary and aimed at recovery. Often, the analyst perceives the fact because the patient complains about it in some way.

But if the "absence" is prolonged, the patient will feel left alone and will literally go away herself through madness or suicide or, at best, go to another professional.

The analyst's blockage in symbolising, which is equivalent to the patient's despondency, can cause the analyst to feel frustrated with his answers and, even though they may not be aggressive rebuttals, he can see that they are inappropriate, such as support, rational explanations, unnecessary questions, acts of compassion, and so forth. The impotent analyst can complain about the patient's supposed lack of cooperation. Such interventions are non-dreams aimed at filling in the apparently empty terrifying spaces.

Even though such interventions are not recommended, it is nonetheless curious that they might not be prejudicial under certain circumstances. I feel that their contents are often interpreted by the patient as less important than the perception that the analyst is alive and interested. That is, the patient realises that the analyst, even though frightened and not very strong, continues to seek, by trial and error, to give meaning to what is happening. As a result, the patient also feels her own existence.

These facts are part of what I have called implicit alpha-function. In areas parallel to non-dreams and chronic enactments, the analyst seeks to dream unconsciously what is happening and, through trial and error, successes and reversals, gradually gives meaning to traumatic situations. This outline of meaning becomes evident only after a great deal of work of implicit dreaming and can even emerge as acute enactment.

The facts described clearly show that supposed failures of the analytic function should be examined in detail. Understanding them can give us important leads as to what is happening in the work of the dyad and we will not be surprised to discover that certain interventions by the analyst are aimed solely at reinforcing emotional links while the work of symbolisation tends to be developed or is taking place implicitly. However, I do not believe that mere emotional support without the effort to look for meanings is sufficient. This fact differentiates psychoanalytic work from that of other approaches.

I think that the analyst works simultaneously in all mental areas. Interpretations in the symbolic area also benefit the psychotic and traumatic areas of the mind. Moreover, when the analyst works in an area of the mind where the capacity to symbolise is impaired, he is also stimulating the symbolic network which exists in a non-psychotic area of the mind. For instance, traumas could be *re-dreamed and remembered* (those traumas that had been symbolised but repressed), *dreamed and re-constructed* (those that had been transformed into psychotic non-dreams), and *dreamed and constructed* (that part of the primordial mind that can never be remembered). These processes might all occur concurrently.

Notes

1. Grotstein (2007) used the term "mentalization" to refer to the passage from sensorial reality to image and from there to thinking about the next step. This occurs when alpha-elements placed in sequence give rise to narratives.
2. This question, very pertinent today, about representation and symbolisation in psychoanalysis, is treated by numerous authors, including Botella and Botella (2013), Marucco (1998, 2007), Green (1983, 1986, 1993, 2002a, 2002b), Barros (2002, 2011, 2013), Ogden (1989b), Melsohn (2001), Ferro (1986, 2002b), Cassorla (2009c, 2012c, 2013a, 2013e), Rosas de Salas (2010), Minerbo (2011), Levy (2012), Levine (2012), Scarfone (2013), Reed (2013), as well as in chapters of books edited by Azvaradel (2005), Rose (2007), and Levine, Reed, and Scarfone (2013).
3. Bianco (2009) observed that patients with sleep apnoea wake up just when their dream has been transformed into nightmare.
4. Segal (1981) has described predictive dreams that involve symbolisation and evacuation at the same time.
5. Botella and Botella (2005) also discuss trauma as negativeness that tends to be present under the form of normality of the affects but absent in the associations, transference, and countertransference. Its existence appears through certain disorders, or "accidents" in thinking.
6. Bokanowsky (2005) distinguishes trauma, where destruction of the mind occurs, from traumatism, which reveals itself in non-psychotic areas.
7. But we should not confuse defensive reversion, involving a rigid PS, with adequate oscillation between PS <-> D, which is part of the thinking process (Bion, 1962b).

CHAPTER NINE

What happens before and after acute enactment: the validation of clinical facts

In previous chapters, clinical configurations that were linked to acute and chronic enactments were described and theoretical hypotheses about their origins, functions, and consequences were proposed. These configurations and hypotheses will be validated in this work. The various steps of this project's early development can be found in Cassorla (2001, 2003, 2004, 2005a, 2005b, 2007, 2008a, 2008c) and its more recent developments in Cassorla (2009a, 2009c, 2013b, 2013c, 2014b, 2015, 2016a, 2016b). The clinical work and theoretical formulations will be summarised and clarified through this validation process.

We know that it is impossible to separate totally the clinical fact from the explicit or implicit theory of observation being used. Taking this into account, and in tune with the clinical observation of situations similar to the one I have described, I have hypothesised that during chronic enactment, the analytic dyad is set up in such a way that traumatic situations become congealed so as to avoid contact with reality. This happens owing to massive mutual projective identifications that foster a dual relationship, which in turn defends against the triangular relationship. Configurations such as these, described as borderline, obstruct symbol formation and the capacity for dreaming. They close off access to reality.

Chronic enactment ceases in two situations:

1. when analysts take a "second look" (Baranger et al., 1983) at the material, listening once more to what they have listened to (Faimberg, 1996), either on their own or with the help of a colleague;
2. when there is an acute enactment.

An acute enactment's intensity makes an analyst realise that things have become abnormal in the treatment. When analysts realise that something out of the ordinary has happened, they can reclaim their analytic capacity and once more become able to dream, to provide meaning, and to think about what is going on. Then they can accept that without knowing it they were involved in a chronic enactment that preceded the acute enactment. Once they are conscious of these facts, analysts can strengthen the analytic process.

There is, of course, the risk that the dyad will neither perceive nor profit from the acute enactment, and this will create impasses or will bring back the chronic enactment.

The validation process

Psychoanalysts are clinicians, researchers, and psychoanalytic thinkers all at once. In their work, they dream, think, and display their thinking or make their thinking public—if only to themselves and to their patients. At the same time, analysts are always seeking validation concerning what they perceive to be happening. To validate is to test whether the "facts" are what they seem to be. To validate is to find the degree of truth behind what one sees and thinks. In judging whether a particular perception is true or not, human beings intuitively use their common sense to confirm that their observational senses come together and agree with one another (Bion, 1963; Sandler, 2005). And this can be broadened when people want to know if other people's way of seeing is similar to theirs, or at least not contradictory to their own. This is the basic validation process in experimental science: findings are evaluated through several different researchers' experimentation.

In psychoanalysis, we are confronted with rebellious variables that, beyond their never being repeated in exactly the same form, are in constant transformation. On the other hand, the instruments of observation and the mental processes are part of what is being observed. We thus have to make our subjectivity objective (Cavell, 1998; Renik, 1998).

Clinical investigation, that is, the observation of what happens between both members of the dyad in the analytic field, has given rise to psychoanalysis' main discoveries. For clinicians, the most important validations concern whether or not their work is creative and useful for their patients' development. In this model, no validation is possible when an analyst has no idea what would constitute "creative and useful work towards their patients' development". This concept must be present before any validation can take place, and this concept is peculiar to a specific theoretical framework.[1]

In this work, I shall use three types of validation:

1. *Micro-validation*: that is, an evaluation of what happens during a session's movements. In this model, such an evaluation comes about by observing the emergence (or lack thereof) of ideas, affects, memories, and associations in the analytic field. Such factors tell us that the network of symbolic thought is being extended, that dreams-for-two are alive and operant. This is what I call "creative work and development". An intrinsic part of the analytic process is the observation of the emotional states that arise in the analytic field—especially the analyst's ideas, feelings, and daydreams. Patients are important members in the validation process ("the analyst's best colleague", Bion, 1980) since their responses are instructive in evaluating our interpretations. It is this micro-validation that has made it possible for me to affirm, as I did above, that once an acute enactment is perceived, "the analytic process is strengthened".

2. *Macro-validation*: that is, the observation of what goes on during "second moments" outside a patient's sessions—one might call this a "second look". Practising psychoanalysts routinely use this resource when they take notes on what they went on in a session so as to consult them later on. When they write out these process notes, they often acquire a better understanding of the session. Psychoanalysts often present their observations to their colleagues, either one on one or at scientific meetings. Their colleagues must be psychoanalysts, which implies that there is a shared (or at least non-contradictory) theory of observation among the profession's members.

In the model I propose, the best way to check our sense of what went on in a session is to tell it to a perceptive colleague as if it were a dream. Such a colleague will dream the facts as they are told using vertices that complement the analytic dyad's dream presented by the analyst. In the event the colleague dreams similar or complementary dreams, the experience the analyst has had is held to be valid. Even before this can happen, however, there must be a reasonable consensus among researchers concerning:

3. *Peer macro-validation*: that is, when clinical material is presented several times—at scientific meetings and in psychoanalytic publications—researchers hope to verify that the clinical facts they observed were also observed by the psychoanalytic community. And, in the event they are, researchers also want to know to what extent their theoretical hypotheses are understood, accepted, modified, or refuted.

This process is especially complex in psychoanalysis because there are many different theoretical frames of reference that, as we have seen, affect observation, evaluation, and the formation of hypotheses. On the other hand, the system of peer validation is not really systematic. It is almost random and can depend on ideologies, politics, language, and culture. In view of this, Freud's (1940a) ideas are still pertinent: psychoanalytic hypotheses will be modified and justified after an experience has been shown to recur in the work of many analysts. After sufficient debate, validation will be achieved if there is a consensus or common sense within the analytic community (Botella & Botella, 2001)—or within a relevant part of that community.

On the other hand, the transformation of analysts' experience into texts and those texts' publication is the most important factor in fostering psychoanalytic debate. As we have seen, publication will be read, more or less depending on their accessibility. And their accessibility depends on the language in which they are published and their authors' scientific reputation. Of course, the more prolific and respected authors will have a better opportunity to have their observations and theories validated because they have more readers.

The clinical facts that I intend to validate in this article have been put to the test in scientific work that has been presented in publications and at scientific meetings and conventions. Their publication and translation into widely understood languages and their use by other researchers[2] in the psychoanalytic community suggests that they have been accepted in that community—or at least that they have not been refuted.

Here, I propose another type of validation. I shall see whether, in other psychoanalytic texts in which colleagues are testing out their own observations, they describe clinical facts similar to the ones I have observed. These researchers either were not familiar with my work or they did not take my work into account when they published their observations. In addition, I shall attempt to see to what extent my theoretical hypotheses might be useful to help to understand what these colleagues have set out. In this way, I shall also try to assess the power these hypotheses have achieved.

Criteria for selecting the material

From many different and interesting articles, I have chosen four by using the following criteria:

1. *Articles that a reader can easily find.* Since I am testing my attempt at validation, I hope that any of my readers who want to can evaluate my ideas by consulting the articles I use. Three of these texts (Bateman, 1998; Ivey, 2008; Yardino, 2008) have been published in the *International Journal of Psychoanalysis*. The other article (Sapisochin, 2007) is in Spanish and appears in the *Revista de Psicoanálisis de Madrid*. It has also been presented at international psychoanalytic meetings.
2. *Researchers from different psychoanalytic cultures.* I have chosen one Latin American (Yardino), one European-Spain (Sapisochin), one South African (Ivey), and one of the United Kingdom (Bateman). This variability in theoretical and cultural orientation is based on the principle that "facts are facts" and free from cultural biases.
3. *Detailed clinical reports.* Even though their degree of detail might be different, I have chosen reports that have sufficient data so that I can compare them with my own observations.

My approach is hampered because I do not have deeper access to what went on during my colleagues' sessions—either because there are no words to describe those goings-on, or because these authors did not feel it was important to include those details. This inadequacy could be remedied somewhat if I had contacted them. I decided not to do it for two reasons: a) because what I am working on is their reports, as they wrote them, and their form also expresses emotional experiences. I have, thus, put myself in the same position as any other reader; b) so as to avoid my being influenced by what these colleagues might tell me beyond what they have written down. It is, of course, the case that I have not taken advantage of the possibility that more information might enrich the validation process.

I should also point out that the clinical material I have chosen addresses factors of a nature other than mine, and they had no direct relationship with the facts I shall attempt to validate. Yardino's objective in presenting his patient was to stimulate the readers and commentators (Apfelbaum, 2008; Fogel, 2008) in the "Analyst at Work" section of the *International Journal of Psychoanalysis*. Yardino does not advance any specific psychoanalytic theory, ratherd she calls attention to what she believes is a significant moment in the transference. Using material from one of his patients, Sapisochin's objective was to discuss, in a post-Freudian frame of reference and at a deep level, metapsychological and technical aspects related to *Agieren*. Ivey, based on his work with a particular patient, produced a concentrated critical piece dealing with contemporary debates related to the function of enactment. Bateman sought to study thin- and thick-skinned defensive organisations in borderline patients and their relation to one of his patients' enactments.

The material is presented here in résumé so as to focus mainly on the features that are important for my validation.

Presentation and discussion of the clinical material

The first case: Ignacio (Yardino, 2008)

Ignacio got into analysis under pressure from his wife, who could no longer put up with him and demanded that he change his ways or leave. Ignacio was a self-described perfectionist—controlling and hard to deal with. He told his analyst that in his first analysis he would spar with the analyst and that the analyst may have grown weary. Ignacio reported that he told that analyst that the treatment was not going anywhere and dropped him.

In their first encounter, Ignacio came across as hostile, and he degraded women in various ways. Yardino, as a woman herself, was discouraged and thought that Ignacio would not come back—especially because Ignacio was seeing another analyst at the same time he was interviewing Yardino.

However, Ignacio chose Yardino, but he did not get into treatment until the two of them could agree on the terms of his analysis, which was difficult. Ignacio gave no evidence of anguish or affect—other than an intense rage. The boxing ring was set up and for three years Ignacio sparred with Yardino. He would come late to his sessions, miss them without telling her beforehand, and he often failed to pay her on time. He would either have aggressive reactions to her interpretations, or they made no sense to him. Still, once in a while his defensive carapace would waver, and he appeared to have some contact with his emotions.

Even after Ignacio would miss several sessions in a row, Yardino has no recollection of wanting him to stop. She thought her surviving his attacks and not fighting back was helping him.

One day, after two consecutive absences, Yardino waited for Ignacio for thirty-five minutes. His hour was the last one in an especially trying day, and she decided to leave. Once she had left the building, she felt uneasy. She knew that he still might come, but she did not go back.

That night, Yardino woke up in a fright. She had dreamed that her young son had broken loose from her hand at the supermarket and she lost sight of him. At that moment, she realised she had been mistaken. She had left at the beginning of Ignacio's session rather than at its end, as she had thought. That day Ignacio's hour began at 8:30 p.m. rather than at 8 p.m. as on other days.

Yardino blamed herself for leaving. She could not be happy with any of the explanations she thought of to account for her mistake. What she realised was that her dream revealed her acted countertransference, her desire to break loose from Ignacio, lose him, and never see him again.

At the next session, Ignacio arrived five minutes early—a first. Yardino saw him on schedule and she could not avoid giving him an apology. Ignacio answered that there was no problem, he had come early even though he had gone to bed late the night before. He had been at his children's school, at a party in the teachers' honour. He pealed back his prickly hide that Yardino had described in earlier sessions and told her how moved he had been with the "acts of love" he had witnessed at the school.

Yardino had expected a furious attack or a dead silence, but she was surprised—even more so by the words "acts of love" that she had said to Ignacio in other sessions. She believed that he had not taken them in.

Ignacio's silence about the missed session made Yardino ask: "What has happened to us?"

Ignacio answered that he too was surprised. He was often confused by this time for his hour and, for that reason, he had come without bathing or having breakfast so as to get there on time. He said "I broke loose", referring to his letting go of his rituals so as to have his whole analytic hour. Yardino was impressed by Ignacio's breaking loose and by his failure to mention the missed session.

Later in the session, Ignacio said that what he had experienced the day before "was important". He had felt affection and generosity and celebrated it all by coming early that day. But he also recognised that he could easily backslide.

When Yardino reminded him that the day before they had had no session, Ignacio laughed and said that she had left him standing on the pavement. This had to happen, he said, because he had often left her waiting in her office. He had gotten there late because he had mixed up the time. He saw Yardino off in the distance leaving. That time *he* had been stood up.

When Yardino told him that it had been her fault, Ignacio got upset and insisted that it was his fault, because he is sure his analyst would never abandon him. Yardino interpreted his difficulty in accepting that she could leave him by suggesting that that was how his mother had been when Ignacio was a child.

Then, extremely upset, Ignacio remembered an incident that had happened when he was three or four years old. He had been taken shopping with his mother, and she had become so absorbed in looking at display windows that he had gotten lost. Another lady took him to the police station. His mother showed up hours later. She had forgotten that she had taken Ignacio with her. "She clean forgot about me and I was a small child, being alone among so many people scared me." He started crying. After that, Ignacio remembered the film *Break Point* where surfers rob banks, and do daring, almost suicidal deeds. He brought up what he called his "crazy side": he takes risks both in sports and in life. During his adolescence, he took all kinds of risks hoping someone would stop him: "But no, I could break everything and no one would know or care."

Discussion

In the model I am proposing the acute enactment is when Yardino, induced by Ignacio's tardiness and his absences, left before the session was over.

On her way home, Yardino felt uncomfortable, but she was not clear about her feelings. Of course, in her mind, by trying to dream, she sought to find some meaning in her affect.

My position is that acute enactment does not only entail discharge, but also a movement in search of meaning. Yardino experienced that search as indecision and as a hint of guilt. Her work in dreaming non-dreams continued unconsciously, and it came to the fore when she went to sleep and had a night dream. In that dream, where she loses her son, traumatic affect (hate, vengeance, fear, guilt, a desire to break loose), which before could not be dreamed, turned into imagetic symbols with a specific meaning. That meaning also shows how difficult the contact with the triangular situation is. Yardino has a life of her own beyond Ignacio. Yardino was actually dreaming her own non-dream as well as Ignacio's. She transformed both of them into dreams-for-two. However, her dream was interrupted (Ogden, 2005), and she woke up in a fright because she could not go on with this traumatic perception of her hatred and with the separation in the triangular situation.

Even so, when she woke up, the possible dream had connected to the network of symbolic thought, and she was able to access her own repressed memory and realise she had made a mistake concerning when the session ended. And here we see "in living colour" the transformation of acute enactment's elements into more complex symbolic forms (Langer, 1942). These images called out for verbal symbols that Yardino could use to communicate with herself.

At their next session, Yardino was surprised that Ignacio was unaware of her abandoning him. He insisted on absolving Yardino and on blaming himself. It seems that Ignacio desperately tried to recapture the dyadic relationship by denying his contact with reality, that is, his contact with the separation of self and object. The dyadic relationship was a chronic enactment, as we shall see.

Yardino had avoided the seductive collusion, and when she blamed herself, she went on dreaming the traumatic situation's reality. Yardino's interventions connected to Ignacio's obstructed symbolic network and stimulated his daydream. And in this daydream, Ignacio remembered the time his mother had lost him. But, contrary to Ignacio's mother, Yardino was right there. The following scene brought on by *Break Point* revealed Ignacio's perception of breaking loose as self-destructive activity. This compulsive repetition of the traumatic situation had found someone to dream it.

My proposal is that an acute enactment can undo an established chronic enactment co-occurring along with an analytic dyad's successful endeavour. Thus, on the one hand, Yardino was aware of Ignacio's protective shell and tried to dream Ignacio's traumas. On the other hand, the dyad had manufactured of a sadomasochistic plot that in part was unperceived. Yardino tells us that she felt like she was in the ring with Ignacio, she was unhappy, in despair, worn-out, and could not find a way to get out of this predicament.

It may be that analysts do not become sufficiently aware of their involvement in chronic enactments or do not confront them so as to avoid contact with their own hatred, as Calich (2009) has also pointed out. Yardino maintains that she had never wanted Ignacio to disappear—she only became aware of this hidden desire after the acute enactment.

I think that in situations such as this, even though they are not totally clear about what is going on, analysts may intuit that their interpretations could be of a retaliatory nature and might re-traumatise their patients. The fact that these analysts are being constantly provoked is, in these cases, minimised. The greater or lesser denial of their hatred is also linked to the love all analysts feel for their work. This connection appears as an analyst's "necessary" masochism and is similar to what a mother feels when she puts up with her baby's abuse of her as she is trying to dream it. Analysts run the risk, however, of tolerating more masochism than they should.

I have proposed that during chronic enactment analysts both explicitly and implicitly use their alpha-function in parallel areas so as to weave meaning into traumatised regions. When patients cannot endure a meaningful dream, they revert back to non-dreams. When this happens, analysts intuit that the established tessitura was insufficient because these patients still experience reality as traumatic. Analysts go on working, dreaming, and weaving at the edges of the traumatic holes, and this process takes time and patience. At some point in the process, when the dyad intuits that both parties can come in contact with reality, even though it is somewhat traumatic, they try "to break loose". They test out whether they can live in triangular reality, and that requires them to intensify their dreaming the trauma in the here and now. This is when an acute enactment comes about, as an attenuated re-experiencing of the trauma being dreamed.

Thus I propose that, notwithstanding Yardino's hatred, she only let herself leave before the hour's end because she intuited that it was worthwhile running the risk of being a non-self. She may have felt like doing that earlier on, but she did not do it so as to avoid the risk of causing an unbearable re-traumatisation.

A large part of what I have described is the fruit of deep contact between the dyad's two unconscious minds. During chronic enactment, it seems that analysts unconsciously sound out their patients' symbolic resources and that patients do the same thing concerning their analysts' protective shields. They too intuit the extent to which their analysts can contain the potential trauma. An acute enactment occurs at a certain point, but neither before nor after the point that both unconscious minds perceive that it is worthwhile to relive the trauma. Fogel (2008) also identifies this when he comments on Yardino's material.

The above hypotheses help us to understand better the queasiness and guilt analysts feel even before an acute enactment is understood to have occurred. This queasiness and guilt will go on afterwards. Queasiness and guilt basically derive from an analyst's persecutory guilt owing to vengeful hatred and the patient's consequent re-traumatisation. But these factors also entail depressive guilt owing to patients' suffering from their exposure to reality. This guilt's origin is first attributed to the failure of the analytic function. But afterwards, analysts can access their deeper motives. In other words, analysts only have access to traumatic situations *après-coup*, that is, after they happen. I have now broadened the hypotheses I intend to validate.

The second case: Álvaro (Sapisochin, 2007)

This patient, age forty, has a chronic history of psychic and physical abuse as well as serious self-destructive conduct. During his analysis, Álvaro's internal sadistic saboteur object known as "Destroyer" (in Spanish, *tio cañero*) came to the fore. Destroyer was his own, as well as other people's, executioner. This object would show up during the analysis just before a vacation. It would attack whatever the dyad had accomplished up to that point.

During one session, a very depressed Álvaro told Sapisochin about some extremely serious acting he had done that endangered both his physical and financial health. Consequently, he had no money to go on vacation and once more had to assume his chronically weakened and helpless way of life. Sapisochin took what he said to mean: "Everybody else is going on vacation, and I'm stuck here in Madrid all alone."

Álvaro's analyst reminded him that the day before Álvaro had said that he could go to such and such a place and stay with what's-his-name, and so on. But this intervention sounded strange to Sapisochin. Álvaro scorned this intervention, and Sapisochin points out that his patient's response reminded him of a child's rapidly rejecting any of the available activities. After this, Álvaro produced an obsessive diatribe, and Sapisochin could not get back to what they had been talking about.

Uncomfortable with what had happened, Sapisochin re-examined his intervention. Even though its content and timing were appropriate, it seemed strange and out of character as far as his usual technique was concerned. While Álvaro was off in the world of his associations, what had first come to the analyst's mind was a scene in which a cranky child refused to play, but when he took his second look, he saw a busy adult who did not want to be bothered by the child, and, consequently, the child got even more cranky.

Sapisochin, in a sort of *déjà vu*, remembered that six months earlier, during the Christmas vacation, he had also surprised himself acting in a "manic" fashion and minimising Álvaro's helplessness as he faced an interruption in his treatment. As he tried to find his way, Sapisochin remembered one of his analyst's interpretations years ago concerning a part of his life Sapisochin would prefer not to remember. He realised that he had become identified with an object incapable of empathy with a child's feelings of helplessness.

Then Sapisochin remembered that during his childhood vacations, Álvaro would stay with his father who beat him while his mother went off with her own family. The analyst thought of his patient's mother as symbiotically united with her own mother. It occurred to him that Ignacio's father had been taking his frustrations out on his son.

The analyst concluded that he had acted his complementary identification with a manic object that could not invest in and empathise with a child's helplessness and lack of organisation. He had done this to protect himself from a guilty feeling for abandoning Álvaro's infantile side and for leaving him with someone who abuses him during vacations. He only became aware of his unconscious countertransference after this acting.

Then Sapisochin explained to Álvaro that a deriding malicious object had come between them, and this object was constantly at work. Sapisochin used one of the patient's own expressions (that means "someone in constant mockery") to describe that maternal object's manic and superficial state that was being recreated in the analytic space. This object was the opposite of Álvaro's "official" idea of his mother as an "affectionate and understanding mother".

Álvaro answered in an ironic tone and said "that may be", because when he came into the consulting room he saw a guidebook of Brazil on the table and thought: "this asshole (in Spanish, *tío pijo*) is already on vacation".

Discussion

It appears that for some time Sapisochin had been trying to dream Álvaro's dreams and non-dreams involving situations of helplessness or impotence struggling against destruction and sabotage. Sapisochin describes his listening in this area as empathic-intuitive. This is the same as my notion of dreams-for-two.

At the same time, Sapisochin refers to Álvaro's tedious repetitions as a "broken record". Thus, in areas parallel to his empathic-intuitive listening, a chronic enactment arose in which a cranky patient subjugates a cranky analyst and, perhaps, vice versa.

As we have seen, in situations such as this one, analysts have a hard time undoing a dyadic collusion because they intuit that they will make their patients relive traumatic situations of helplessness if they come in contact with reality—the self's separation from its object. Sapisochin's later perception, that he could "screw" Álvaro and abandon him so as to take care of himself, became congealed in their chronic enactment. At the same time, while he was binding Álvaro's traumatic wounds using his implicit and explicit alpha-function, the analyst was experiencing a necessary masochism and could not take care of his own needs.

An acute enactment occurred when Sapisochin discharged and became "manic". When he criticised Álvaro by saying that he had some options (i.e., "other friends and other toys"), Sapisochin denied his patient's disorganisation and helplessness as he faced the coming vacation and the interruption of his treatment. I think Sapisochin's uneasiness at having lost his analytic capabilities had combined with his intuition that he had traumatised his patient.

Then, based on his uneasiness, Sapisochin regained his ability to dream. And this ability enabled him to remember the Christmas vacation when something similar had happened, and when Sapisochin made little of his patient's suffering. This shows us that acute enactments occur more or less clearly intermingled with chronic enactments, but they may not always be useful, and the dyad's collusion goes on.

Sapisochin theorises that traumatic re-living is a case of *Agieren* and shows how it can only be understood *a posteriori*, in what he calls a transferential–countertransferential roundabout concomitant with empathic-intuitive listening. Sapisochin's theoretical position coincides with my own—there is a spectrum of elements between dream <–> non-dream, and in the analytic field these elements try to come out at the same time.

Then Sapisochin expanded his dream and with Álvaro he shared his perception of the constantly mocking object that had been congealed in their chronic enactment. The analyst's dream had connected to Álvaro's symbolic network, and Álvaro could access his having seen the guide book and his fantasy that his analyst was already on vacation. The dream-for-two went on, and Sapisochin realised that having the guide book out was the work of the manic and deriding object.

Sapisochin went on to understand more thoroughly Álvaro's destructive acts. They were seen as identifying stigmata with archaic objects including the continuously mocking object that Álvaro could not let go of and that made him a plot he compulsively repeated. Álvaro's fantasy that patient and analyst would be together "until death do them part" also became clearer. That fantasy was maintained in their chronic enactment.

In this material, Sapisochin reveals personal facts. The analyst's real person, with its intuitive capacity and its blind spots, contributes to the analytic process. Ideal analysts do not exist and any analyst's mental processes may mesh with their patients' processes—so much so that that analysts may experience them, but they run the risk of having their own acuity compromised. Sapisochin remembered his own analyst's interpretation concerning a period in his life he would prefer not to remember, which made him connect with his own difficulty in empathising with a helpless child. Sapisochin discretely spares us greater detail. I imagine he does the same in the analytic situation. Analysts should only play their cards face up (Renik, 1999) in very special circumstances and never more than is necessary so as to avoid overloading their patients with their personal conflicts.

Third case: P (Ivey, 2008)

P is a doctor who is constantly involved with women who use drugs, and who neglect him emotionally. These relationships repeat similar situations P experienced with his mother, who did not nurse him and who, at night, would shut him in his room with a baby bottle containing sugar water. Ivey reports that he had done considerable interpretive work with P concerning those relationships in which P would accept sugar water from girlfriends who could not nurture him emotionally. Understanding these facts, P felt he should end his relationship with his current girlfriend, R, but he did not feel strong enough to do it.

In one session, P once more told of how R neglected him, but he discounted his complaints in a typical fashion, saying that there were times in which she was considerate and that gave him hope. Ivey felt frustrated with P's habitual cycle, which had been interpreted over and over. He pointed out to P that R really showed scant evidence of an ability to change her ways, and he reminded P of R's shortcomings that P himself had identified. He added that P seemed to want to avoid the painful reality that R could not satisfy his adult needs in a relationship, just as his mother could not attend to his needs as an infant.

As he was saying this, Ivey felt that his interpretation sounded gruff, critical, and inept. But P sighed and said Ivey was right. He seemed defeated and sunk deep into the chair saying that he felt weak and pathetic. Ivey got even more uncomfortable, and that was how the session ended.

Some hours before P's next session, the patient called Ivey and said he was not sure if he should come because he remembered that Ivey had said that he would have to miss a session, maybe it was this one. Ivey could not remember having said any such thing. P came to his hour and said that in spite of R's ambivalence, their relationship was improving and he had decided to go on with the relationship, even though days before he had felt he should end it.

Ivey remarked that P had said nothing about the phone call earlier and suggested that because he had felt pathetic at the end of the last session, P may not have wanted to see him. And that was why P had convinced himself that Ivey would not be there. P admitted that Ivey was right. He added that his phone call would give the analyst a "way out", an opportunity to have a day off from him. P was convinced that Ivey was disappointed with him because he could not break up with R.

Ivey then asked P whether he had said something during the previous session that would make him feel that his analyst had become critical and disappointed. P said "no" and added that that was how he felt about himself. In truth, he had felt for some time that Ivey was disappointed in him because of P's "block" and that he had thought of ending his treatment. He felt this way even though Ivey had seemed understanding and accepting in the past. After a reflexive pause, P remembered that his father had been constantly critical of him and how he felt he had disappointed his father.

Discussion

In his article, Ivey refers to his gruff intervention as an interpretive enactment (Steiner, 2006). It was the fruit of the irritation Ivey felt owing to P's attachment to his girlfriend R. In the model I use, the collection of facts and the patient's reactions constitute an acute enactment.

With this material, Ivey shows that for some time he had been upset with P's relationships since he threatened to jeopardise their work in the analytic field by overvaluing P's external reality. It seems to me that this analytic dyad had established a chronic enactment containing sadomasochistic components, that is, his patient's complaining about his girlfriend made the analyst oppose R. P saw Ivey's point, but continued to frustrate him by his failure to end the relationship. The frustrated analyst persisted with his interpretive model, and time and again P agreed, but nothing happened. Without sufficiently recognising what was going on in the analytic field, both the analyst and the patient were frustrated and critical of one another, and critical of themselves.

The acute enactment, Ivey's gruff talk, and P's pathetic response and its sequelae could reveal and undo their underlying chronic enactment. That happened when Ivey got upset and realised how inadequate his critical intervention had been. Right after that, he was able to dream it and to connect it to the network of symbolic thought. Certainly, similar situations had been happening beforehand, but they did not go beyond stagnated non-dreams.

Remember that an acute enactment indicates, in an attenuated form, a traumatic recognition of the triangular situation. However, whenever that situation threatens them, the analytic dyad can try to reassume their chronic enactment relationship. We can see this in Ivey's clinical material.

Thus, after Ivey's gruff intervention, P felt defeated and agreed with Ivey and blamed himself. The analyst also blamed himself. At this point, they could once more reassume their chronic enactment, with a whining, victimised, and incompetent patient complementing a frustrated analyst.

However, Ivey was now both ill at ease and curious. He wanted to see how this situation would work out. At P's next session, after the confusing phone call, he once more complained about R, and Ivey could start his critical interventions again. But, thanks to his recognising the acute enactment, Ivey was alert and did not fall into that trap. Beginning to dream, he tried to find the meaning of that phone call. P confessed that he had sadistically invited the disappointed analyst to take "a day off". Of course, if that had happened, P would feel victimised and would later accuse Ivey of not caring.

The compulsive collusion entailing non-dreams-for-two simulates a traumatic non-dream where one relives a similar stagnated situation: P's attracting supposedly negligent women and then retreating, but also disappointing these women if they tried to get close to him. This plot is superimposed on top of other, more archaic situations, some of which cannot even be remembered. P's addiction to this object constellation that is repeated and congealed in the dyad's chronic enactment indicates that it was better for them to have a dyadic relationship in which the trauma was controlled than it would be to get out of that relationship and acknowledge the triangular relationship.

After the acute enactment, the dyad came in contact with memories and new facts, both of which broadened the network of symbolic thought.

However, once more they would try to revert the work dream. In his next session, P declared that he had broken up with R. Ivey carefully listened to P's complex associations. After an intense dialogue, Ivey showed P that he had had a hard time admitting that his analyst had criticised him. P agreed, but he also thanked Ivey for having alerted him concerning the self-destructive behaviour he was engaging in with R. Thus, even when Ivey was responsible for ending that relationship, the sadomasochistic situation turned into one of mutual seduction.

In his discussion of the clinical material, Ivey shows how P had submitted to his analyst's countertransferential desire and, in a very sensitive manner, he demonstrates how the dyad was hard-put to tell self from object.

As we have seen, attempts to revert back to chronic collusions indicate that the traumata experienced in the analytic field, the traumata being implicitly dreamed, had not been sufficiently dreamed. Since the triangular situation's framework was still intolerable, the would-be dreams turned back into non-dreams. However, little by little the symbolised areas get larger and larger, and the attenuated trauma comes out in an acute enactment that makes it possible to dream.

Ivey mentions nothing more about P's treatment, but he shows how the analyst himself was able to use this work to get in touch with his own issues. Reflecting on the personal factors that might have brought on the acute enactment, Ivey tells his readers that they became much clearer later on, when he talked to other colleagues about his work with P. And this confirms the notion that unconscious countertransference only comes into the light through the participation of another person. Ivey recollected a brief but intense relationship he had had with a heavy smoker. And in this recollection, he identified his unconscious connection to drug addiction. Ivey's relationship failed owing to this woman's ambivalence, which made him feel rejected and critical of himself and of how he had handled the affair—all of this was similar to what P was struggling with. Ivey reminds us how patients can project on some aspects of their analysts' specific unconscious (cf. Pick, 1985).

It appears that the analyst's personal history, which we learn about after an acute enactment, represents the last, but suddenly conscious, link in a mass of traumata, one on top of the other, forming a traumatic web. It is this web that makes us into specific individuals and that makes us repeat these traumata to a greater or lesser extent. Characterologic traumata are part of an analyst's real person. Because they are in tune with our ego, they can both help us in our analytic function, and, as blind spots, they can hinder us. The remaining traumata should have been identified and worked through in our personal analyses. But there are always some elements that hang on and try to take over when, as enactments, they get caught up in in a patient's conflicts. Once they are understood, they increase both the patient's and the analyst's symbolic capacities. It is far from rare that analysts sometimes gain more from a patient's analysis than the patient does. All analysts have come through sessions with our patients where we would like to pay them for their help rather than charge them our fees …

I think that no analyst can claim that a particular treatment was successful if that same analyst did not also gain something in the treatment. And that is why I wager that P went on being helped by his analytic work even though he often had to flee from any contact with reality.

Fourth case: Jane (Bateman, 1998)

I shall discuss both this material and Bateman's theoretical hypotheses. He describes three levels of enactment in his material. The so-called "first level of enactment—countertransferential collusion" reveals an analyst who was trying to reassure, relieve, and counsel Jane in her sadness, despair, and helplessness. Bateman would later realise that that he had not been able to recognise all of what was going on. He had become party to a "pathological object relationship". Simultaneously, he recognised in part what was going on and that his work had been satisfactory.

Using my model for his situation, the "first level of enactment" corresponds to what I call chronic enactment. Patient and analyst are caught up in non-dreams-for-two, even though, at the same time and in parallel channels, they experience oneiric transformations.

After two years of analysis, before a particular vacation time, Bateman shows that Jane felt abandoned and considered her analyst selfish since he would not put off his vacation until hers began. When Bateman came back to work, Jane appeared aggressive, arrogant, tense, and scornful. She degraded her analyst and maintained she had not missed him at all. Bateman writes that Jane's thin-skinned defence (Rosenfeld, 1987) had become thick-skinned. Shortly thereafter, however, Jane once more assumed her self-pitying position.

As the treatment went on, Bateman realised that he continued to feel sorry for Jane. He worried about a possible suicide, but his interpretations in that area were never accepted. Jane got more and more desperate, frightening, and threatening. Her wavering between thin- and thick-skinned organisations grew more intense and frequent. Little by little, Bateman realised how impotent he was feeling. He could not do his work, and he thought it might be better if Jane stopped her analysis and never came back.

At a certain point, an exasperated Bateman told Jane that she felt she had defeated the analysis, she had triumphed over his ability to help her, and that now she wanted her analyst to watch while she slowly committed suicide. He told her that she did not know whether she wanted to erase him from her mind and never come back, or if she wanted to push him into dropping her so she could go on feeling sorry for herself.

After Jane's arrogant response and a similar one by Bateman, Jane left the consulting room without saying a word. A few minutes later, Bateman went out, but Jane's car was no longer there.

This is an acute enactment. The analyst shows that he was exasperated, and Jane, feeling accused and perhaps misunderstood, left Bateman's consulting room. And this is when the chronic enactment we have been examining became undone. That is, the self-pitying, reassuring, defensive collusion exploded in a traumatic fashion and became its opposite. When Bateman went to see if Jane's car was still there, he revealed his worry and his guilty feelings. It seems to me that Jane's departure would gratify Bateman's wish to be rid of her, but at the same time the analyst's love would motivate his trying to dream the event.

This acute enactment indicates that both patient and analyst are both experiencing the trauma that had been congealed in their chronic enactment. That trauma revealed a fall into a "black hole", as Bateman points out, using Jane's phraseology. They had already tried in vain to dream that dream when Bateman vigorously insisted to Jane that he was a person separate from her. He pointed this out once again, but this time Bateman realised how exasperated he was. During their acute enactment, they created a mix of discharges and traumatic contact with the triangular situation's reality.

This is when Bateman introduces his "second level of enactment—defensive countertransference". He realised that their self-pitying and reassuring collusion was covering up his fear that Jane might kill herself. He then realised that his desire that Jane quit her analysis revealed that her fantasy had been projected onto him. He points out that only after that eruption was he able to understand that during Jane's entire analysis he had been afraid of her self-destructive behaviour. This was one of his "blind spots". However, after this acute enactment, Bateman broadened his ability to dream.

Bateman would later realise that Jane's mother's chronic threat of suicide controlled the entire family. Jane was sacrificing herself because she continuously worried that her mother might kill herself. The analyst had been recruited for a similar task—to stop Jane from hurting herself, but through a chronic enactment.

Bateman's second level of enactment seems to be another way of seeing the very same self-pitying and reassuring chronic enactment—both are defences against a threatened suicide. Such a suicide would be a flight from the "black hole". This suicide would be taken for traumatic contact with triangular reality. The suicide flees from the terrifying void searching for an idealised totality, a symbiotic life inside a uterine paradise where there are neither needs nor frustrations (Cassorla, 2010a).

And this is similar to a fantasised fusion with the analyst during the chronic enactment.

In a session after their acute enactment, Jane related a nighttime dream containing a mix of traumatic discharges and symbolic components. Her suicidal fantasies become evident, and Bateman suggested ways of understanding them. That is, after an acute enactment, as I propose, the dyad's dreaming gets stronger. Bateman understood his own fear that Jane might actually take her life and suggested that she be hospitalised. She refused and tried to reassume their old collusion. It was now she who tried to reassure Bateman that she was all right. Her analyst stuck to his guns.

Then, suddenly, Jane pulled a knife out of her purse and slit her wrists and her palms, drawing blood. Bateman made a clumsy attempt at interpreting this act, and Jane told him to "drop dead". Desperate, Bateman said that if she did not drop the knife, he would feel even worse, and would not be able to think of any way he could help her. Jane sprang off the couch like a mountain lion and said she would do whatever she felt like doing. She stalked around the room and rebuffed Bateman's suggestion that they both sit down and think this through. Jane pointed her knife at him, and Bateman said he was afraid she would kill herself or she would attack him. Surprisingly, Jane handed over her knife and ended up accepting her hospitalisation.

The analysis continued with Jane in the hospital. After getting out of the hospital, Jane revealed an embryonic capacity to keep in mind what had happened, and she began to recognise how important her analysis was.

Jane's further acts and more acute enactments produced a mix of discharges and symbolic elements placed within the analytic field. And Bateman shows that these enactments were the living consequence of the suicidal non-dream's being acted and dreamed at the same time. Jane had frightened her analyst and at the same time had validated her insight that she needed outside help.

Bateman's theoretical considerations are very similar to my own, and I am sorry not to have included them in my earlier writing. Bateman says that Jane had not developed the ability to leave her mother and re-evaluate their relationship from a different point of view. He points out that Jane was caught in a dyadic relationship and could not make it triangular. She was living this dyadic relationship with her analyst during their chronic enactment. After the acute enactment and what followed,

Bateman managed to think clearly and became a third person, separate from Jane.

Bateman describes a "third level of enactment", identifying the act in which he took the knife from Jane, asked her to sit down, and told her if she did not sit down, he could not manage to think. After that, he spent a good part of the session persuading Jane to commit herself, but Jane tried to reassure her analyst and reassume heir dyadic relationship. Bateman points out that as he got more and more terrified, Jane tried harder and harder to reassure him. And when he calmed down, Jane would get terrified once more. Only when he insisted on her hospitalisation could Bateman think clearly and reassume his analytic role without being "at the mercy of a projective pressure enactment".

It appears that the "third level of enactment" corresponds to the dreaming being done after the chronic collusion's dissolution, which began with the acute enactment. Dreaming like this comes and goes and includes attempts to revert to non-dreams, as well as threats of reliving the trauma. But in the end, this is the necessary road for working through the mourning for the dyadic relationship's loss and the assumption of oedipal triangularity.

Final considerations

Validation of clinical facts

This validation has been beneficial. In these four case reports have identified situations that can be described as chronic and acute enactments whose features are similar to what I described earlier.

As such, we have seen that chronic enactments *precede* acute enactments. The latter emerge in a greater or lesser intensity and threaten to destroy the analytic field. Analysts become aware of their failure and feel guilty. Then they try to understand what happened.

After the enactment is understood, the analytic dyad becomes sturdy and their dreams-for-two show them to be working in traumatic terrain where they broaden the network of symbolic thought. All of follows an acute enactment, which is a mix of discharged elements on their way to being transformed into dreams. At the same time, or shortly thereafter, analysts become aware of the situation's antecedent—a paralysing collusion, that is, a chronic enactment.

During chronic enactments, analysts are, to one extent or another, aware of the specific traumatic situations and try to dream them. But the stagnant areas, the non-dreams-for-two, are not sufficiently recognised.

Often, once an acute enactment has begun, the analytic pair tends to go back to their former chronic *modus operandi*. For example, Yardino reports Ignacio's desperate attempt not to acknowledge that his analyst had made a mistake—that is, that she is a separate person. But Ignacio went on trying to preserve their dyadic relationship. Sapisochin shows us an acute enactment that he had failed to see during the Christmas break, which resulted in the pair's taking up their chronic collusion once more. Ivey demonstrates how he and his patient tried to reassume their sadomasochistic collusion that from time to time would revert to a seductive collusion. And Bateman gives us several situations in which that pair, mainly Jane, behaved in such a way so as to reclaim their reassuring collusion whenever Jane realised that the analyst was an "other".

In every case these analysts describe their queasiness and guilty feelings when they intuited that there had been an acute enactment. They all became aware of their own specific issues that made them susceptible to the different collusions, and some of these analysts reveal intimate details to their readers. This reflects contemporary psychoanalysis' movement towards evaluating the analyst's real person as a facilitator or obstructer of the movements taking place in their analytic fields (Bonaminio, 2008; Levine & Friedman, 2000; Maruco, 2007).[3]

Validation of the theoretical hypotheses

If the clinical facts in case reports from several different analysts have jibed with my own clinical experience, their validation becomes more complicated as far as my theoretical hypotheses are concerned. As I have said, this complication is also related to the fact that the four works I have examined do not necessarily share similar objectives or theoretical outlooks—either to each other or to mine.

My theoretical hypotheses suggest that configurations identified through the clinical facts I have described come from these patients' difficulty in tolerating reality. They experience reality as traumatic because they are unable to dream it or think it, and this inability is what has been described as typical of borderline configurations. And that inability within the theory I am using comes from an inadequate introjection of alpha-function.

In the areas under investigation, the patients were not able to elaborate the oedipal situation, they were stuck in a dyadic one. The very failure to elaborate the triangular situation hinders symbol formation, that is, the ability to dream and think. A vicious cycle is formed in which reality is felt to be traumatic because these patients have no mind capable of dreaming it. Dreaming, then, is out of the question because the triangular situation has not been elaborated, and there is no space for dreaming. These patients live in an empty world without a cohesive self. Their self is split and projected onto objects they desperately depend on, but at the same time they feel that these objects are intrusive and threatening. Their identities' coherence depends on how they experience the external objects within whom they live in a projective fashion. Their lives take place in a sort of shell, within an external carapace. These patients have no "spinal column" (Rey, 1944). Living like parasites within their shells, they are constantly insecure.

In the analytic process, these patients fantasise that they go into their analysts and turn them into their protective shell in search of some would-be security. They immobilise their analysts, experiencing them as a part of themselves. Attaching themselves to their analysts, they avoid traumatic contact with the reality that their analyst is a separate person. These patients confuse the loss of the dyadic relationship, where they feel protected, with reliving traumata that earlier they could not dream because their minds were incapable of dreaming. That is why reality testing that occurs during their analytic process tends to be aborted and the dyadic situation prevails once more.

However, chronic enactments demonstrate defensive organisations that occur in the analytic field. There are three concomitant reasons why analysts fail to recognise them:

1. The overwhelming nature of patients' projective identifications attacks their ability to think.
2. These projective identifications "mesh" with analysts' own traumatic areas.
3. When analysts identify with their patients, they find it hard to bring reality into the picture because they intuit that reality could bring on unbearable trauma and, conceivably, madness, suicide, or the destruction of the analytic process.

Still, just like their patients, analysts can section off areas where there is reasonable contact with reality. In these areas, analysts try to re-dream their patients' dreams. They also have access to their non-dreams, which they try to dream. The hypothesis I have proposed is that during a chronic enactment, analysts implicitly use their alpha-function with their patients, who, also implicitly, introject it. Alpha-function can, little by little, rework the traumatic areas. When there is a hint of symbolic capacity, the dyad appears to risk a separation, and they relive the trauma in an attenuated form by creating an acute enactment.

Thus, I believe that acute enactments entail a starting to dream mixed with raw material that requires this sort of work, and this reflects the impact that the implicit alpha-function is making on the traumatised areas that are being reworked and fixed. The clinical data examined here support this hypothesis: in the four case studies we have identified a symbolic spectrum, that is, symbols (dreams) <–> non-symbols (non-dreams) that are being dreamed in real time within the analytic field.

The four analysts' theoretical hypotheses are consistent with their own objectives. Even though they cannot be compared to my hypotheses, they do not refute them. Quite to the contrary, they often strengthen and advance them. Sapisochin's interesting contributions broaden my ideas concerning symbol formation and technique. Within a contemporary Freudian frame of reference, he directs our attention to phylogenetic and archaic traumata as well as towards listening through a countertransferential detour as a means of accessing these areas.

On the other hand, following Rosenfeld (1987), Bateman has us focus on the vacillation between these patients' thick- and thin-skinned organisations. He shows us that the dyad becomes more susceptible to enactments when there is a change in their defences. In my work, I have seen that chronic enactments come with two main types of stagnation—a wavering between mutual idealisation and mutual sadomasochism. To a certain extent they correspond to Bateman's thin- and thick-skinned configurations. It may be that acute enactments occur during this fluctuation as the fruit coming from a hint of contact with reality. When reality cannot be sufficiently tolerated, the organisation re-establishes itself, sometimes in the opposite mode. There is also a similarity between my hypotheses and Bateman's position as far as the function of chronic enactments (Bateman's first- and second-level enactments) is concerned. First- and second-level enactments preserve the dyadic relationship by avoiding contact with a third person. And when analysts get incorporated into the paternal function (Bateman's third level), acute enactments come about.

Finally, Ivey's detailed observations concerning these controversies complement my hypotheses—especially when Ivey shows how important an analyst's subjectivity can be in the production of enactments.

Among the different researchers who have been studying enactments, Schrek's (2010) work is especially striking. She provides a finetuned description of how a dyad, almost unawares, got caught up in a chronic sadomasochistic enactment. The chronic enactment became undone and was understood after an acute enactment in which the analyst could not tolerate her patient's attacks and sent her away. When patient and analyst met once more, their work was strengthened, even though attempts at reassuming their chronic enactment were always present. Schreck's description and her use of my hypotheses support the theories' validation.

On the other hand, in my supervision of and discussions with colleagues, especially when the latter are beginners, one can identify enactments brought on mainly by the analyst. These enactments can be situated at the beginning of the spectrum containing "(the analyst's) acting out <–> (the dyad's) enactment". Situations such as these do not find their way into scientific papers. The same thing happens with extremely subtle interpretive enactments (Steiner, 2006, 2009). These enactments are almost undetected, but are part of an analytic dyad's daily fare. But even in these enactments, there seems to be an antecedent dyadic identification. Caper's (1995) ideas concerning the difficulty in making a mutative interpretation coincide with my hypotheses—a transferential interpretation confronts a patient with the triangular situation's reality.

In earlier work (Cassorla, 2001, 2005a), I proposed that enactments can be considered both normal and pathological. I considered normal enactments to be those facts that constantly occur in the analytic field, where patient and analyst experience or re-experience micro-traumas deriving from their being different people trying to identify themselves, to communicate, and to dream-for-two. Evidently, during this process, the extant triangular space obliges them to face reality. Normal enactments can be understood and undone almost instantaneously, and for that reason they do not stand out. They are the fruit of normal projective identifications or of massive projective identifications with which analysts can, on purpose, get themselves involved and become one with their patients. But these analysts realise what is going on and can undo these enactments when it seems appropriate to do so.

Acknowledging the triangular situation as greater or lesser trauma is an idea that implies that the analytic process is constituted by a continuous series of enactments and traumatic experiences. In this context, Hartke's (2005) ideas make a lot of sense. Hartke maintains that the basic traumatic situation's presence in the analytic relationship, with the dream of micro-traumata involving the failure to connect (my normal enactments), is part of the elaborative process. The trauma's violence is revealed by the enactment's intensity and its elaboration makes them normal or minimises them.[4]

The above observations lead me to propose that there is a continuous spectrum of enactments that emerge in the analytic field. At this spectrum's extremities, we have, on the one hand, subtle or minimal enactments and, on the other, we have intense acute enactments, with all sorts of enactments lying between these two extremes.

Of course, in my desire to validate my observations I may have committed some evaluation errors. For instance, I may have chosen material best suited for supporting my ideas, and I may have ignored material that could refute them. Or it may be that the case histories reported sought to illustrate clinical phenomena I was interested in and did not report any material that might refute them. In other words, the researcher's subjectivity, his investigative instrument, can also betray him and occasion something similar to observational and theoretical enactments. I hope that my being aware of this possibility has protected me from errors such as these, but I cannot be totally sure.

In this spirit, then, I put this paper to the test. I rely on my readers to take part in the validation process by using their subjective and objective observation instruments to criticise, refute, complement, or broaden my observations and hypotheses.

We search for the truth, but we know that as we seek it, it will always elude us. In our process of trial and error, we must remember, along with Freud, that "what is praised today as the highest wisdom will be rejected tomorrow and replaced by something else, though once more tentatively. The latest error is then described as the truth. And for this truth we are to sacrifice our highest good" (1933a, p. 172).

Notes

1. Tuckett (1994), Michels (1994), Azevedo (1994), Kernberg (1994), and Cassorla (1998a, 2004), among others, have studied the validation process in clinical psychoanalysis.
2. For example, Verissimo (2000), Sanchez Grillo (2004), Barros, Gabbard, and Williams (2005), Abreu (2006), Devereux (2006), Rocha (2009), Marchon (2006, 2009), Ribeiro (2007), Gus (2007), Paz (2007a, 2007b, 2009), Deserno (2007), Churcher (2008), Ivey (2008), Wieland (2009), Borensztejn (2009), Lothane (2009), Luz (2009), Galipeau (2009), Mann (2009), Schreck (2010), Gheller (2010), Brown (2010, 2011, 2013), Sapisochin (2011, 2013), Bernardi and de Bernardi (2012), Chaves (2012), Ponsi (2012), Strauss (2012), Bohleber et al. (2013), De Leon and de Bearnardi (2013), Greenberg (2013), Schwartz (2013), Steyn (2013), Yerushalmi (2013), Gastaud, Padovan, and Eizirik (2014), Marks-Tarlow (2014), Nos (2014), Ruvinsky (2014), and Katz (2014).
3. Analysts' self-revelations to their readers can be found in Levine and Friedman (2000), Jacobs (2001, 2006), Cassorla (2001, 2004, 2005b, 2008c), Sánchez Grillo (2004), Hartke (2005), Orbach (2009), Calich (2009), and Schreck (2010).
4. Friedman (2008) considers situations in which the analyst is as professional as possible with a patient who is maximally and objectively motivated to create "minimal enactments".

CHAPTER TEN

When the analyst becomes stupid: between Narcissus and Oedipus

An attack against the analyst's capacity for perception occurs in chronic enactment, as he fails to realise that he is involved in collusions with his patient. This reduction of perception or, we might say, this stupidity is usually associated with arrogance and it blocks the perception of the same stupidity. A study of clinical facts shows that this stupidity protects the dyad from traumatic contact with triangular reality. Paradoxically, its apparent accentuation shows that such contact is possible, and constitutes acute enactment.

Sometimes an analyst realises that he needs help from colleagues in order to perceive what is going on in his work. In this chapter, we will show how stupidity can also contaminate colleagues, who end up experiencing the same facts that are going on in the analytic dyad.

I use two complementary definitions for stupidity.

1. In the myth of Narcissus, the eponymous character falls in love with his own image reflected in the waters of a lake. Narcissus' inability to discern self from object reveals his numbed perception. In one version of the myth, this stupidity results in Narcissus drowning in an attempt to reach the idealised object, which he does not realise to be his own reflection.

Transposing this situation into the analytic field, we find ourselves in an area in which analyst and patient establish a fusional relationship through cross-identifications. Each feels the other to be an extension of their respective self. They may both be unaware that this is happening. When this occurs, the analytic process remains frozen in the dual area of fusion-confusion, even while development may proceed in other areas. This is what we call chronic enactment.

2. Another sense of the term "stupidity" refers to the impossibility of Narcissus accepting the love of Echo the nymph. We can consider Narcissus' rejection to be a result of his terror of coming into contact with the self/object differentiation. Thus the function of stupidity is to avoid contact with the triangular reality in seeking to maintain the fantasy of narcissistic completion.

The transposition of this second sense into the analytic field reveals situations in which the perception of the triangular reality is attacked. The threat of self/object differentiation triggers catastrophic anxiety, which is discharged at the same time as the analytic dyad returns to the fusional situation. When the patient (rightly) attributes this perception to the analytic work, this work will be attacked. The analyst's thinking capacity is blocked by massive projective identifications. This attack can be carried out by attacking links that have come up (Bion, 1959) and trying to reduce or block the analyst's capacity to think. Therefore, both the re-establishment of the dual relationship and the stupidity are preceded by the unbearable glimmer of contact with reality. Such situations are very similar to acute enactments but they are unbearable and the dyad returns to chronic enactment.

The Oedipus myth reveals situations to complement that of Narcissus. If the latter's initial state is one of undifferentiated fusion, with the triangular reality as threat, in the oedipal myth the acquired triangularity is what becomes dangerous. For this reason, it is reversed. This occurs, for example, when Sophocles (in *Oedipus the King*) describes the beginning of Oedipus' investigation in the search for Laius' murderer. As he is consulting Tiresias, they have a tense and aggressive exchange in which Tiresias "opens Oedipus's eyes". Oedipus defends himself from the threatening perception, accusing Tiresias of colluding with Creon (Jocasta's brother) to steal the throne from him. The projection of voracious and envious aspects within the Tiresias–Creon dyad liberates the Oedipus–Jocasta dyad; the true usurpers of Laius' throne.[1]

The configurations implied in these two senses of the term "stupidity" oscillate in a double meaning: frozen dual relationship <-> threat of perception of the triangular reality. Stupidity therefore manifests itself in two ways:

1. the impossibility of the dual relationship to perceive itself;
2. the impossibility of experiencing the triangular reality.

The models described relate to working with patients who present difficulties with perceiving and living in the triangular reality where self and object are distinct from one another. Of these patients, there are some for whom borderline configurations predominate, that is, where parts which were split off live in a world of dual relationships while others maintain contact with the triangular reality. These patients have been unable to develop oedipal situations in certain areas of their minds, and thus either return to or remain in narcissistic situations. On the other hand, attraction to narcissistic situations can reveal traumas that make this development difficult.

The clinic

Anne, a young psychotherapist, is a member of a supervisory group that I coordinate. Two years ago, she brought to the group clinical material about a patient named Paula. This patient was a young lawyer who constantly felt she was the victim of conflictive situations with her family and co-workers. Anne's material indicated that Paula sabotaged her own emotional and intellectual resources by projecting her self-devaluation into the surrounding environment, which she saw as threatening and frustrating. Her misery was also expressed through very serious financial difficulties. It was clear that Paula almost compulsively got herself into situations that accentuated her suffering and her identity as a victim.[2]

Paula (the patient) complained that Anne (the therapist) ignored her suffering and failed to help her enough. Little by little, Anne began feeling incompetent and guilty, but she was clearly aware that her feelings were intensified by Paula's projective identification. Anne interpreted these facts to Paula, and Paula seemed to understand, but she also seemed to absorb interpretations only minimally, and soon she would begin complaining again. However, at several different moments, Paula seemed to assume some responsibility for her life. My impression as supervisor was that, even though the analytic process was difficult, it was moving ahead adequately, and I felt it would become more productive with time.

After a few weeks, Anne began bringing other cases to the group, and we heard no more about Paula for the next two years.

Then one day, Anne arrived late, out of breath, and announced that she had some very interesting material on a patient whom we had discussed some two years earlier. The treatment was going along very well but, even so, Anne decided to talk to the group about a particular session with this patient. She was sure that I, the coordinator, would find something new to consider (though I felt uncomfortable about this remark).

Anne reminded the group about Paula, the patient who was always "on the border". Anne noted that, in the past, we had been confused about this patient and never knew whether she lived in R or in S, whether she was married, whether she was actually working as a lawyer, or whether she helped support her parents financially. Paula had come from a very poor family, Anne reminded us, and was unable to make use of her emotional resources. She complained about her financial situation and was constantly threatening to leave therapy. Then Anne described to the group a recent session she had had with Paula, as follows:

> Paula came into the consulting room with a happy expression on her face and told me [Anne] that she [Paula] had gone with her whole family to an event at the company where her father worked. She was pleasantly surprised to discover that her father was greatly admired and respected by his superiors and co-workers.

At this point, a member of the group interrupted Anne to ask what profession Paula's father practised, and Anne answered that he held an important administrative position. I was surprised because I remembered him as having very limited schooling and being an alcoholic, but I kept this to myself.

The account of the session continued:

> At the company party, Paula's father had proudly introduced his lawyer daughter to his fellow workers, and she had felt warmly received. Even her mother, who was continually depressed, said how happy she was to have such a beautiful and intelligent daughter.

I continued to seriously wonder about what I was hearing. I remembered sessions of two or more years earlier when Paula had complained bitterly about her parents. I noted that other members of the group were also uncomfortable about something that was hard to define. Anne went on:

> Paula said that her sister was also at the event and that the sister was going to take a trip abroad. There were a number of children at the party and Paula had a good time playing with them.
> After the party, the family went back to their car and headed home. Paula's husband was at the wheel and her sister-in-law sat in the back seat. By coincidence, they passed an obstetrician friend of theirs in another car, and Paula told her husband that, when she got pregnant, she would like this doctor to deliver the baby.

At this moment, Anne interrupted her account and stated that, earlier, Paula had been terrified at the idea of getting pregnant and having children. Then Anne went back to her account:

> Paula complained that her husband made no comment about this remark. Then Paula asked her sister-in-law in the back seat what she thought about her getting pregnant. The sister-in-law simply said to Paula's husband, "It's getting hot in here. Could you turn down the air conditioner?"

Anne once again interrupted her account and, referring to Paula's desire to get pregnant, delightedly told the group that this meant Paula was progressing. I felt irritated at this superficial comment about Paula's "progress". At the same time, I noticed that Anne's joy contrasted with the apparent mood of the rest of the group. We were uninterested, tired, and restless, and I realised this was because Anne's account was boring and unappealing, and included too many details. It was clear that we were anxious for the supervisory session to be over.

But there came a point when my sleepy disinterest was replaced by a feeling of alertness. Anne was describing an intense discussion between Paula and herself: "Paula complained that her mother did not back up her desire to get pregnant", she said. Anne then told Paula that she (Paula) always wanted everyone to agree with her. Paula disagreed, but Anne insisted that she (Paula) always had to be right. The climate in the analytic session had become tense and aggressive. Paula angrily said that Anne did not understand her. Anne reminded Paula about situations in which she (Paula) always wanted to be right, both at work and with her husband. Then Paula said that she was afraid her husband would leave her because of their financial problems. Anne made no further comments, and the session ended.

As I (the supervisor) listened to Anne, I realised how disappointed I was with her work. She had not listened to Paula and had wanted Paula to agree with her (Anne) and her own (Anne's) theories. It was clear that Anne had stepped out of her analytic function. I imagined that Paula's last words, about being afraid her husband would leave her, reflected the situation of helplessness she was experiencing due to her therapist's lack of understanding.

Trying not to show my disappointment, I said that what had most strongly caught my attention was the climate at the end of the session.

Anne became quiet and serious and, after a time, she said she had just remembered how uncomfortable she had felt at that moment. She had noticed her attacks on Paula and felt embarrassed and guilty. And she felt it strange that she did not remember this fact when she decided to bring the session to the group, nor as she was recounting it.

Then Anne spontaneously told us more about this analysis. She remembered that some time earlier, Paula had missed three consecutive sessions without calling. Anne had become concerned but waited to hear from her. When Paula did come back, she said casually that she had missed her sessions because she was having an expensive aesthetic treatment. Then Anne told us that Paula had traded in her old car and was now driving a sophisticated and expensive new model. Anne said that only at that moment in supervision had she become aware that Paula had been taking advantage of her financially: she said, "I only realised it just this minute, as I told you about it".

As Anne gradually became aware of her feelings, the group and I sat in silence. Anne remembered that, at the end of the analytic session, Paula had paid for all her previous sessions. Anne then said that she had been surprised because Paula had not complained about the cost. Up until then, whenever Paula paid for her sessions, she insisted on reducing their number or threatened to halt the treatment. In the group, Anne then vacillated and became embarrassed as she told us that she had charged Paula a lower price—far below what she usually charged patients—since she had felt moved by Paula's financial problems.

Finally, Anne told us that as soon as Paula left, she, Anne, decided to raise the price starting with their next session.

Dreaming the clinical material

In a supervisory process, through realistic projective identification and verbal symbols, the analyst communicates to the supervisor how he is dreaming the patient's dreams and non-dreams. The analyst hopes that the supervisor will re-dream these dreams from other angles, thus expanding the analyst's capacity to think.

But the supervisor's capacity to think can also be attacked through non-dreams discharged by the analyst. The supervisor does not always realise what is happening and, if this is the case, he, too, runs the risk of getting involved in non-dreams-for-two with the analyst being supervised. This situation constitutes *non-dreams-for-three*. When there are several different persons in the clinical discussion, as in the situation described here, this risk is lower but not eliminated.

The session and acute enactment

As mentioned, there was a two-year period in which Anne did not bring any clinical material about Paula to the supervisory sessions. When she finally did come rushing into the meeting that day, out of breath, she may have been discharging her non-dreams. But she may also have been trying, through actions, to represent her uneasiness related to the fact that she was "late" or "behind" in her analytic capacity. As long as these actions had no meaning, they consisted of non-dreams in search of dreamers.

Anne came in with the expectation that I, her supervisor, would find new elements in the material. Something was making me uncomfortable, and it continued to bother me all through her account. I felt an emotional experience whose meaning was escaping me. Only an outline of meaning came to me: I felt threatened by Anne's expectations of me. My dream could not seem to get beyond this point.

As Anne went on talking, I continued to visualise Paula at the party, enjoying her emotional resources. My visualisation, consisting of my experience with dreams-for-two that occur in the analytic field, was a mixture of facts as they had been told by Anne and other facts from my own personal history. But images and ideas related to poverty and scarcity also came to mind, related to earlier sessions and to personal experiences of mine. The contrast surprised me.

When Anne expressed her satisfaction at Paula's wanting to have a baby, I could not agree that this in itself should be considered a sign of "improvement". I felt that Anne's analytic function was out of kilter. In fact, I was disappointed with her. When it became clear to me that Anne's and Paula's desires were coinciding, I hypothesised that they might be operating in an idealised relationship. In what follows, we will be able to confirm that non-dreams-for-two were giving rise to chronic enactment of mutual idealisation. Anne's participation was obvious in her belief that the analytic work was "coming along very well".

My dream, which gave some meaning to the hypothesis of mutual idealisation, was pressuring my mind to broaden this meaning, like a conception in search of realisation (Bion, 1962a). A step further may have helped me realise that the collusion of idealisation between Anne and Paula was being repeated in the supervisory field, but I noted this only later.

Other, more basic affects were also demanding dream work at the same time. The climate in the supervisory group was one of restlessness and disinterest, and the participants were hoping that Anne's account would soon be over. In other words, there was something uncomfortable (beta-elements) going on, something that sought to be eliminated through the bodies of the participants of the group (indicated by the unrest and boredom) and through projection into the outside world (a hope that the meeting would soon be over).

My sleepiness had the same function of getting me away from this frustrating reality, but it also revealed my reverie. Suddenly I was warned by the absurd discussion I was hearing about between Anne and Paula.

Anne was being stupid and arrogant, and my disappointment with her was growing. I had two alternatives: I could either get away from the frustration or put up with it until it took on some meaning (Bion, 1962a, b). At this crucial moment, I became aware that my disappointment with Anne was related to the idealisation I had set up about her in the past and that was being abruptly and traumatically de-idealised. Again, I had two alternatives: to run away from this traumatic realisation or include it in my symbolic network of thinking.

One possible defence against frustrating reality is omniscience. It is accompanied by the splitting and projection of the perception of traumatic reality into the object. Since this perception threatens omniscience, it is moralistically censured. Discrimination between true and false, true reality and omniscient invention, is replaced by the dictatorial assertion that something is either right or wrong.

In the situation described above, it seems that I was moralistically reproaching Anne for my own disappointment (a moralistic position of the superego), but this constituted an inversion of truth and falsehood. In fact, both the idealisation and the disappointment were products of my own mind, and I was fully responsible for them. This moralistic reproach could have made me stupid and arrogant.

Freed from the moralistic moment, I returned to my function as supervisor and accepted getting closer to reality, that is, to Anne's shortcomings (and my own as well). I was led to wonder how her analytic capacity had been attacked.

Let us go back to the discussion between Anne and Paula. They had had conflicting ideas and were rejecting each other's positions. It was clear that, in this moralistic dispute, they both wanted to be right. We cannot rule out the possibility that each one wanted to think with her own mind, but the mutual criticism (especially Anne's of Paula) indicated resentment over their being in opposite camps, and this resentment reflected their disappointment with the destruction of the idealised dyadic relationship.

At this point, my perception of reality was broadened. If Anne had indeed lost her analytic function, this was the result of the power of this same function. This apparent paradox could be seen in the following way. At the start, Anne and Paula were in chronic enactment, that is, an idealised dual relationship (a *non-dream-for-two*). But since there was no dream, Anne was not aware of this. The discussion indicated that the idealised relationship had been undone. Once they began to disagree, Anne and Paula became aware of the triangular reality, that is, that they were separate human beings. I assumed that this perception of the triangular reality had resulted from the analytic work, but this hypothesis awaited confirmation. And, since their perception was traumatic, Anne and Paula tried to return to their idealised dual relationship.

In my view, the configuration expressed in the discussion between the two women should be classified as acute enactment. This means that the chronic enactment has been dissolved, and contact with triangular reality has begun. The trauma that accompanies this contact is highlighted, as well as the attempt to return to the dual relationship.

Acute enactment involves a mixture of facts all taking place at the same time:

1. beta-elements, non-dreams, are being discharged (through emotions, acts, and speech);
2. non-dreams are looking for dreamers;
3. non-dreams are being dreamed;
4. recently dreamed dreams are converting back into non-dreams;
5. dreams are seeking to be included in the symbolic network.

These new facts show that a double *reversion of perspective* had occurred (Bion, 1963). The apparent failure in Anne's analytic function during the acute enactment was in fact a return of this function. And the analytic process that had taken place before—a process that was apparently productive—had in fact been dominated by obstructive dual relationships that had gone unnoticed.

The consequences of acute enactment depend on which of two forces is predominant. The first includes trauma, psychological catastrophe, and the threat of destruction of the analytic field, while the second incorporates dream work and contact with reality. Since this contact is traumatic, it stimulates destructive forces. The second force, dream work, has the purpose of neutralising the destruction by trying to give meaning to the trauma. From this perspective, three possibilities arise:

1. the traumatic situation gets out of hand and the analytic process is destroyed;
2. the dual relationship is returned to, thus re-establishing the chronic enactment; or
3. the dream work of the analyst and the analytic dyad generates meaning, and thus brings the trauma into the symbolic network of thinking.

As we saw, the analytic session ended with Paula feeling depressed and worried about the possibility that her husband (who in the session represented Anne) might leave her because of their financial problems. Paula's sensitivity will become evident in what follows.

After the session with acute enactment

At the end of the analytic session, Anne was feeling guilty about the discussion they had had, but she soon attacked her own perception of this guilt. The feeling was unconscious, but it continued to pressure her mind to search for broader meaning. This compelled her to seek other dreamers in the supervisory group.

After describing the session, and encouraged by the group's containing attitude, Anne was able to link her experiences with elements in her symbolic network of thinking. She remembered the strangeness and guilt she felt over the discussion with Paula and realised that she had tried to forget this fact by escaping from reality.

As Anne shared her feelings in the group, she also expanded her overall ability to dream. She remembered situations in which she had felt disrespected, and she gradually realised that she had attacked her own perception of the fact that Paula had caused her to feel uncomfortable. As soon as she became aware of her feeling that Paula had taken advantage of her financially, she moved into a moment of depression, forced to admit that she had charged Paula much less than her other patients.

Now Anne realised that she had set up a sadomasochistic collusion. Paula had attacked her and had even cheated her financially and made her envious. In return, Anne attacked Paula for having blocked her from using her analytic capacity. Anne's stupidity had transformed violence into submissive idealisation, but the submission had gone unnoticed. That is, the analytic dyad defended itself from the persecutory collusion through manic defences.

When Paula paid Anne what she owed without complaining and without threatening to leave analysis, Anne then thought about upping Paula's fees. What might have precipitated this action and reaction? Either:

1. Paula was frightened by the fact that her therapist lost her temper and tried to calm her down in order to maintain the dual idealised relationship; or
2. The acute enactment was the first result of the dreamwork-alpha, that is, of a trial contact with reality. The continuation of this dream work could expand the capacity to think.

The sequence of events indicates that the second hypothesis is the correct one. In later sessions, when Paula showed that she was resentful, there could be a creative return to this discussion. Paula talked about her fantasies and recollections of early traumatic situations. Among them was a probably very intense depression suffered by her mother, and situations of helplessness that left her with a sense of abandonment—the perception of which she had denied. These situations may well have been reminiscences of other, even earlier scenes that would never be consciously remembered, but that had been relived in the analytic relationship. The traumas, which had been non-dreamed up to that point, took on figurability. At the same time, hypothetical constructions filled in lacunas in the symbolic network. For her part, Anne honed her listening to be able to hear possible early warning signs of a return to dual collusions. In short, the dyad's capacity to dream and to think had been strengthened.

Before the acute enactment

By the end of the supervisory session, we realised that Paula and Anne were living in an idealised collusion, alternating with or covering up a sadomasochistic collusion. We were led to suspect that this collusion might have been present before the analytic session but had gone unnoticed. Bion (1965) stirred up some curiosity when he stated that, once a psychological catastrophe is over, invariants that were already present in the pre-catastrophic phase can be identified.

When we reviewed the material brought to the group before the acute enactment had occurred, including facts that had come up as long as two years earlier, we noted that Anne and Paula had been working in both symbolic and non-symbolic areas. Paula brought in dreams that Anne re-dreamed and non-dreams that Anne tried to dream. Through them, Paula revealed her misery and attacked Anne by making her feel powerless, unhappy, and guilty. Anne realised what had taken place and continued to move on patiently.

At the same time, in a non-symbolic area, Anne had been pulled in to participate in a *sadomasochistic chronic enactment* that she was not aware of. Anne's analytic capacity had been neutralised by Paula's attacks and by the fear that Paula might abandon her. The fantasy of the dual relationship was reinforced by the constant reduction of fees. The patience that Anne needed had been transformed into masochistic patience. By idealising her patience and denying Paula's destructiveness, Anne had become involved in a collusion of idealisation that covered up and alternated with sadomasochistic collusion.

When Anne presented this material in supervision two years earlier, I was not able to realise what had happened. The fact that Anne had not told me about her fear of losing Paula, nor about her having lowered the price of the sessions, simply made things worse. I do not discard the possibility that my perception also failed due to my initial idealisation of Anne. In what follows, I will discuss the factors related to this idealisation in both areas, analysis and supervision.

What happens during the chronic enactment

As we saw in the session described earlier, clinical observation has shown that acute enactments indicate the beginning of contact with triangular reality. The fact that Anne and Paula had undone the idealised dual relationship led us to suppose that, during the obstructive collusion, an implicit development of the symbolic network in areas parallel to the obstruction occurred. The acute enactment followed due to this development.

My experience indicates that, during chronic enactment, an analyst can realise what is going on in areas parallel to the dual collusion and try to dream non-dreams. Many dreams are converted into non-dreams, and the analyst continues to try to dream them. The dream work may not be apparent because it is covered over by chronic enactment. The patient fantasises that he controls the analyst through the dual relationship, "but at the same time and on another level" (Grotstein, 2009) implicit alpha-function work is taking place, which covers over the traumatic holes in the symbolic network.

When triangular reality takes over, two possibilities come up. In one scenario, there is still not enough capacity to dream, and therefore the dual collusion is maintained or re-established. The other possibility is that, as of a certain moment, the patient can live in reality. In this case, the trauma is attenuated, but it continues to have traumatic effects. It emerges in the analytic field as acute enactment and may continue to be dreamed then and there by the analytic dyad.

As we saw, Anne and Paula had set up a persecutory/idealised chronic enactment, at the same time that the explicit and implicit alpha-function wove itself over traumatic areas. In the session described, Paula showed that she was then able to dream the triangular reality, making the best of her resources. This fact made clearer the collusion of victimisation and financial damaging that was being experienced at this moment, especially by Anne. The risk of discrimination and of contact with reality had become greater.

Anne recognised Paula's development but, in a parallel area, she was blind to her own feeling of having been taken advantage of financially. She also failed to perceive that envy had taken over the analytic field. The fact that Paula had clearly brought emotional and financial resources of her own to the session might have led us to think that she had induced Anne to become aware of the financial disadvantages involved. The discussion between them, which constituted the acute enactment, happened after they had realised that enough of a symbolic network had been constituted to run the risk of coming into contact with triangular reality. This contact was sustained and the dream work was broadened. If this had not been possible, the dyad would have returned to a dual relationship.

Anne later confessed to me that her happiness with Paula's possible pregnancy had covered up her own sadness. Anne had postponed her own wedding because of financial problems. Paula's complaint that others had not supported her in becoming pregnant called to mind Anne's own conflicts, since she herself had had to sacrifice her wishes without complaining. At another level, Anne complained about the fact that she had submitted to Paula's dictates.

Clinical experience leads me to think that chronic and acute enactments are part of the work with some patients, such as borderline patients, who experience reality as traumatic. To escape from this reality, the patient enters the analyst and takes him as a protective shield. The dual relationship protects the patient from contact with triangular reality at the same time that it enables the action of implicit alpha-function. A study of borderline configurations can be found in Chapter Seven.

Acute enactments become evident in a vaguer form when traumatic areas are less intense and there is more capacity for working through, such as when these enactments appear as micro-enactments. This is the case with certain interpretive enactments (Steiner, 2006) in which the analyst is surprised by his own tone of voice or by certain terms he would not normally use. These micro-enactments are easily identified and, in general, have no serious consequences, but they run the risk of being repeated, of becoming chronic.

The model proposed can help us understand events that take place in areas that are predominantly non-psychotic. Transference relationships with neurotic patients involve a certain degree of undifferentiation between patient and analyst, but a dual relationship can quickly be undone through an interpretation that reintroduces the patient into a triangular relationship. This contact with reality is traumatic, even if only slightly so. Therefore, there would seem to exist a basic traumatic situation in any analytic relationship (Hartke, 2005). The analyst's difficulty in making a mutative interpretation (Caper, 1995; Strachey, 1934) is related to this risk. In the model proposed, these situations involve normal (Cassorla, 2001, 2005a, 2012a), or minimal, enactments (Friedman, 2008).

Neurotic areas can sufficiently bear and dream reality, thus making mutative interpretations possible. But this is contraindicated in psychotic and traumatic areas, as long as a symbolic network has not yet been created that can bear the trauma of the contact with triangular reality.

How might an analyst fail to realise that he is involved in chronic enactment? As mentioned above, I suggest that there are three factors involved here:

1. the massive character of the patient's projective identification attacks the analyst's capacity to think;
2. such projective identifications are connected to traumatic situations of the analyst himself; and
3. the analyst is afraid to undo the dual relationship because he realises that this step would be highly traumatic for the patient (or for both of them).

Fortunately, analysts are now able to talk or write about their own involvement in analytic impasses, freed as they are from moralistic self-recrimination, and this allows psychoanalytic knowledge to advance. Anne, for example, noted the similarities between certain aspects of her life and Paula's, since they had both come from poor families and had struggled hard to move beyond these circumstances. Anne knew what it meant to have financial problems, so her identification with Paula made her feel happy with "[her] patient's progress". But the idealised relationship kept Anne from seeing that she was not taking care of herself, in that envious attacks by Paula and the action of internal objects of her own were ignored. Positively, Anne's personal analysis was certainly deepened.

The supervisor, in turn, knew that he was identifying with both Anne and Paula because he, too, came from a family that had had many financial difficulties during his childhood and youth. In fact, he was able to become an analyst only because, at a certain stage in his life, he found an analyst who charged him what he was able to pay.

Stupidity, arrogance, and curiosity

In his article "Hate in the countertransference", Winnicott (1949) states that, if the analyst does not show in some way the hate that the patient stirs up in him, the patient will also not believe that he can stir up love. That same article brought up the matter of the intersubjective point of view in contemporary psychoanalysis. In this text, I have shown this kind of emotion can undo collusions of the dyad even if the analyst appears to be stupid.

Bion (1958) wrote that allusions to stupidity, arrogance, and curiosity are indications of psychological catastrophe. In this article, I am dealing with less disturbed patients in whom borderline configurations are covered over. The triad appears when we come close to the psychotic (non-symbolic) area, and it becomes evident through enactments.

Patients express *curiosity* through a wish to continue their analyses, but the wish may mean running a serious risk of being unable to constantly maintain a fantasised fusion with the analyst. The risk of re-traumatisation, or of destruction of the dual relationship, is similar to the risk run by Adam and Eve when they listened to the serpent, that of Oedipus when he consulted the oracle and Tiresias, and that of Narcissus when stalked by Echo.[3]

The necessary fusion is accompanied by *curiosity* about the analyst, who is known through his reaction to the projective identifications that the patient throws into him. This knowledge has the purpose of paralysing the analyst, but the patient will be frustrated if the analyst holds his ground too insistently. The patient then runs the risk of being "expelled from the dual paradise" and having to face traumatic reality.[4]

Arrogance joins the omniscience and moralistic evaluation that replace the perception of reality with condemnatory judgement. Undifferentiated from the object, the patient dictatorially condemns everything that threatens the dual relationship. Any fact that might indicate the existence of the other, of triangular reality, is omnisciently considered bad and wrong, and what an observer might call arrogance is seen by the patient as the legitimate use of his rights.[5]

Stupidity has to do with the patient's difficulty in keeping contact with reality, and also involves failures in the capacity to symbolise, dream, and think. The patient therefore replaces these operations with discharge. The indiscrimination and deformation of reality, and a position of condemning anything that is frustrating, indicates that stupidity is close to arrogance.[6]

As we have seen, the analyst runs the risk of being recruited by the patient's non-dream and of *becoming* an aspect of the patient's psychotic part. In this case, prevented from dreaming, the analyst cannot be aware of what is going on. He thus becomes stupid, arrogant, and morbidly curious, like the patient. He becomes curious by the simple fact of being an analyst. He may also become the depositary of persecutory or depressive guilt, when he imagines that he is traumatising the patient by showing him the triangular reality.

In *Experiences in Groups*, Bion (1961) describes situations of this type. He says that the analyst fails to notice that his mind is becoming numb and takes as reality what is really the result of massive identifications. The analyst imagines that the strong feelings he is experiencing are quite adequately justified by the objective situation. Later, Bion attributed this numbing to the action of the beta-screen that stirs up in the analyst what the patient wants.

Joseph (1989) clearly shows us how an analyst is recruited to represent aspects of the patient in order to maintain the *status quo*. Besides Bion and Joseph, pioneer authors in studies on massive projective identification include Grinberg, Rosenfeld, Sandler, Grotstein, and Ogden. All of them show how the analyst is induced and recruited to become an aspect of the patient, a topic that Ferenczi suggested even earlier.[7]

If chronic enactment is inevitable, it can be diagnosed early on if the analyst keeps an eye on himself. The realisation that his mind is operating predominantly on the basis of memories, theories, and desires indicates that his analytic capacity is being obstructed. The analyst might question his impression that the analytic process is going well. He might also wonder whether he is fatigued. He may be proud about the vivacity of his own analytic capacity (in the first case), or his patience and capacity to contain (in the second case), with the result that he tends to be unaware of his arrogance and stupidity. Irritation with patients or constant self-admiration are other indications. The analyst should overcome any laziness related to resistance when he feels compelled to write down the clinical material, even though he might not know exactly why. This fact indicates the need for a "second look" (Baranger, Baranger, & Mom, 1983), for "listening to listening" (Faimberg, 1996). Countertransferential nighttime dreams and intuitions of daytime dreams can give us other clues.

Analytic work, especially with patients who have serious disorders, stimulates the analyst's self-knowledge. He comes into contact with some of his own traumatised areas. An analytical process fosters development in both members of the dyad. It is hoped that the patient can profit more than the analyst, but a lack of development in the analyst forces him to suppose that there is also something wrong going on in his own processes.

Notes

1. Tiresias latches onto Oedipus' dilemmas, which mobilises his own "oedipal" conflicts. These are mythically exposed in his interference with the Zeus–Hera couple and in his killing of snakes engaged in the sexual act (Cassorla, 2008b, 2010b).
2. The reader may not differentiate who is the analyst and who is the patient. Factors of this confusion will be indicated below. To facilitate understanding, the name Anne begins with the letter A, from analyst, and Paula, with the letter P, from patient.
3. The serpent, the oracle, and Tiresias can be understood as equivalent to the realisation of the oedipal preconception (Bion. 1962a). The traumatic becoming aware of triangular reality, including an awareness of death (Link K), is the result of disobedient curiosity (Cassorla, 2010a).
4. If this hell can be dreamed, it becomes the earth—reality, but infernal devils and idealised gods continue to haunt the patient (Cassorla, 2010b).
5. Bion shows us that when intolerance to frustration is not excessive, the personality develops omnipotence to replace the realisation of the preconception or conception with negative realisation. Omniscience replaces learning from experience. At the same time, a moralistic superego often evaluates reality as right or wrong, thus replacing the idea of true or false (Bion, 1962b).
6. In a previous article (Cassorla, 1993), I associated stupidity with *turning a blind eye*.
7. A review of the ideas of these authors can be found in Cassorla (1995, 1997, 2008c) and in Brown (2011). This latter author went deeply into the question of intersubjectivity. The evolution of the concept of projective identification can be seen in Spillius and O'Shaughnessy (2011).

CHAPTER ELEVEN

Oedipus, Tiresias, and the Sphinx: from non-dream to transformations into dreams

Mythical narratives condense humanity's ancestral aspects and fantasies and reflect complex emotional configurations. The practising psychoanalyst, who is able to access them, feels impelled to use these narratives and turn them into models that might allow for the transmission of the ineffable facets of emotional experience. The competence of the analyst should eliminate the risks of reductionism and concreteness inherent to any model, but these features must remain under constant consideration.

The aim of this chapter is to put forward models related to nameable configurations (and names reflect psychoanalytic cultures) such as *non-dreams-for-two, enactments*, countertransferential recruitments, and obstructions to thinking capacity. We will also engage with themes of death, suicide, victim-precipitated homicide, pathological mourning, and anniversary reactions (Cassorla, 1985, 1986, 1998b, 1998c, 1998d, 1998e, 2000, 2008b, 2008d). The models will have their origins in the oedipal myth (Brandão, 1986) and its theatrical transformation as proposed by Sophocles in *Oedipus the King*. The stories will be accompanied by conjectures and imaginative speculations from the author, stimulated by clinical events and by his experiences as an analyst, supervisor, and teacher. These speculations will adopt the characteristics of dreams seeking the development (in the photographic sense) of aspects that are obscured.

Let us cast our minds to Laius, king of Thebes, who was infertile and went in search of the oracle of Delphi, to be told that if he had a son he would die at his hands. His wife Jocasta gives birth to a baby, who is given to a servant to be killed, abandoned on Mount Cithaeron. But the servant takes pity on the baby, whose name is Oedipus ("swollen feet"), and places him in the care of a Corinthian shepherd. The rulers of Corinth, Polybus and Merope, adopt Oedipus, but they conceal from him the fact that he is adopted. As an adolescent, Oedipus is suspicious of his origins. When he meets the oracle, he discovers it has been predicted that he will kill his father and marry his mother. This is why he runs away from Corinth and travels apparently aimlessly in the direction of Thebes, at whose gates the Sphinx sets the young Thebans riddles, and kills those unable to decipher them. On his journey, Oedipus arrives at a crossroads where he meets an imperious man flanked by his personal guard. Neither wishes to allow the other to pass, so they fight. Oedipus kills the man and all of his guards (save one). The man killed by Oedipus was Laius, on his way to consult the oracle about the Sphinx terrorising his kingdom. Back in Thebes, the sole survivor of the attack tells everyone that Laius had fallen victim to bandits. Then Oedipus arrives at the gates of Thebes, solves the riddle of the Sphinx, and, as a reward, is made king and marries Jocasta.

The city is content and Oedipus is revered. Years later, a plague is ravaging Thebes, and the people demand that Oedipus make provisions (this is the moment at which the play *Oedipus the King* begins). Oedipus asks his brother-in-law Creon to go and consult the oracle. The oracle links the plague with Laius' murder and predicts that it will only cease once the murderer is discovered and brought to justice. Oedipus takes the task upon himself. He begins his investigation by consulting Tiresias, the blind prophet. Tiresias is noncommittal, vague, and unclear, and ends up accusing the king of the crime. Oedipus imagines himself to be a victim of a plot, with Creon seeking the throne for himself and Tiresias in his command. Jocasta tries to dissuade Oedipus from believing in oracles by telling him about her baby and the oracle's apparent error, since Laius had been killed by bandits. Oedipus links the death of Laius with the scene at the crossroads, and starts to suspect himself. The rest of the story portrays the fight between the truth as it tries to make itself known, and the various ways in which it is evaded. In the end, Oedipus realises that he is the murderer. After the revelation, Jocasta committed suicide and Oedipus blinds himself. Exiled, Oedipus is cared for by his daughter Antigone, who accompanies him until his death.

Non-dream-for-two 1: Oedipus and Tiresias

Location: Thebes. Laius' murderer must be discovered, for this is the first condition that must be met to put an end to the plague ravaging the city. Oedipus calls upon the blind prophet Tiresias, in the hope that he can identify the criminal.

Tiresias is annoyed upon arrival, and does not hide his irritation. He mutters something about wretched people who do not want to think, but no one understands what he is saying. He grudgingly refuses to respond to Oedipus' questions and makes only vague comments. He proclaims bad things for everyone, for Oedipus and for himself, showing that he is also frightened. He seeks to protect himself by avoiding going into detail about his visions. Oedipus is irritated, yet at the same time (I imagine), stares at him as though hypnotised. I think that he will later discover that he saw himself in Tiresias; he saw his own terror, his excessive pride, and his tendency to evade responsibility.

Tiresias continues to refuse to respond. Oedipus is enraged and suspects that Tiresias is in this state because the blind prophet is implicated in some way in Laius' death, and starts to think he may be guilty. At this point, the accused Tiresias loses control and hurls the same accusation back at Oedipus.

Tiresias' accusatory interpretation may have been correct but it came charged with hate, and so it transformed the truth into cruelty. For this reason, the truth will be of scarcely any use to Oedipus. The truth charged with hate only supports Oedipus' hatred of the truth, which will then make him discharge the guilt onto the Creon–Tiresias dyad, believing the accusations of murder to be designed to take the throne from him, which would then go to Creon.

Speculating, I propose that when Tiresias confronted Oedipus he felt irritated, because by seeing the king he is obliged to *re-see* himself. When Tiresias was young, he had the experience of being curious, arrogant, and imprudent (Bion, 1957) and was duly punished. The story goes that when he saw the sexual coupling of two snakes (we do not know if this was in his mind or outside of it …), he killed the female.

He carried her like a shadow within himself (Freud, 1917e) and turned into a woman. Seven years later, he had a relapse, and this time killed the male, thus returning to a man. There were ideograms that Tiresias' mind was unable to apprehend sufficiently to draw them into the symbolic thinking network. This prevented him from learning from the experience. This non-learning led him, years later, to become involved in a conflict, taking sides between the members of a divine couple, Zeus and Hera, and displaying arrogance once again. There is no doubt that Tiresias struggled with couples … (Tiresias participates, like Oedipus, in what psychoanalysis would centuries later refer to as *oedipal conflicts*.) Punished with blindness, his intuition sharpened as a result, he came to be known as a sage. Even now—confronting Oedipus—Tiresias, in all his wisdom, does not understand how the human being compulsively repeats his arrogant curiosity, as though attracted to death and destruction. In this way, Tiresias sees himself in Oedipus. And Oedipus sees himself in Tiresias.

Compelled by Oedipus' accusatory projection, Tiresias violently extricates himself from his reflected image by making Oedipus responsible for the crime, and paradoxically reveals a truth. Tiresias, in confusing himself with Oedipus, did not know how to be a good *therapist* and thus made him suffer unnecessarily. The identity confusion meant that the truth, contaminated by hate, became useless for stimulating thinking.

I imagine Tiresias to have been incapable of tolerating access to *his own* suffering and guilt, as elicited by aspects projected by Oedipus. If, in the intersection of their two minds, it had been possible to *re-see* repressed memories relating to sexual curiosity and homicidal impulses, the massive mutual identification prevented this from occurring. That is, each confused himself with the other: both are murderers and both are cursed but, by mutually projecting, confusing themselves with one another, they are unable to access themselves.

Centuries later, if Tiresias was a psychoanalyst he would theorise the incident (between himself and Oedipus and also between Oedipus and Creon) as non-dreams-for-two or enactments, complexes of crossed massive projective identifications resulting in attacks on thinking. The analytic field will reveal stagnant dramas, products of the externalisation of the patient's internal aspects interacting with those of the analyst, which establish identification complexities. During the enactment, a product of non-dreams, the analytic process is paralysed (within a parasitic container–contained relationship), and like a traumatic re-experiencing the non-dreams repeat themselves over and over, obstructing access to the symbolic network. When the analyst is able to maintain sufficient reverie and alpha-function capacity, the non-dreams can be dreamed, opening up the symbolic network and allowing meanings to glide in, newly acquired. Tiresias almost achieved this, but Oedipus was unable to dream his true dream because it was communicated to him contaminated with hate, thus reversing the alpha-function (Bion, 1963).

Non-dream-for-two 2: Oedipus and the oracle

Oedipus runs away from the oracle of Delphi after receiving the noxious news: he was fated to kill his father and marry his mother. He was even able to question it—let us imagine that guards ("security") forcibly escort him from the temple, while he can hear the crowd shouting that he is cursed. He is tired, miserable, frightened, and feels as though he is on the brink of madness. He wonders whether it would not be better to die.

Let us hypothesise: Oedipus walks, limping, to the road. He remembers his parents, Polybus and Merope, and their surprise at being questioned on his legitimacy. He sensed a lie in their response: he did not feel loved, like the future king of Corinth, as they assured him. That night (let's imagine), he has a terrible dream (his legs were cut off and he could only move by leaning on two people, who were negligent and let him fall ...), which makes him abandon Corinth in search of some legs of his own, in the direction of the oracle.

The journey to Delphi is hard, his feet and body are hurting and his soul seems to shrivel. He staggers into the temple and there, with a place to sleep and dream the dreams that he is obliged to tell the priests, he feels grateful to have found somewhere to rest.

The next day Oedipus wakes, terrified by his nightmares: dark images, clouds, thunder, violence, nothing was clear. He knows there was a battle, a castle, a tower that collapsed on him ... He was running in the darkness, fleeing the threat of death, strangely without limping—suddenly, he saw himself on a mountain (Cithaeron?) where he was faced with a woman's corpse, a ghost that raised itself up and offered him her frozen breast ...[1]

Oedipus enters the room where the priests are expecting him, terrified by the images still lingering in his mind, and feels like he is going mad. He no longer knows if it was a dream, memory, or madness.

Facing the priests, Oedipus realises that he cannot display fragility. Trained to be a valiant prince, and a vain one at that, he cannot humiliate himself by asking for help. For this reason, his request comes across as arrogant, masking his terror and suffering.

The priests are unimpressed with the way in which Oedipus presents himself and fail to perceive his terror and helplessness. They converse with him for some time (fifty minutes …), about his dreams and who knows what else, and suddenly the high priest advances towards Oedipus shouting "Cursed, cursed, be gone, you cannot stay here. This is a sacred temple; it is no place for people like you." As the guards take him outside, Oedipus is astonished to hear the priests shouting: "take this patricide away from here, take him away this cursed man who will marry his mother after murdering the man who made him". The voices get louder, they become a chorus (the crowd, internal "voices" …), and Oedipus can only despair, as the guards carry him out of the temple.

These conjectures describe emotional configurations present in the myth. I think that the expulsion from the temple, a failure of the alpha-function, would stem from the priests' recruitment by Oedipus' arrogant aspects, constituting an enactment in which mutual identification transitions into attacks on thinking, excessive pride, arrogant curiosity, super-superego. We know little about the priests' own aspects, but the final outcome will be a *hostile reverie*, to quote Ribeiro (1999), also intuited in models such as atomic bombs, dinosaur attacks, internal stonings (Bion, 1975; Sapienza, 2009), taking place *for-two*.

Victim-precipitated homicide: Oedipus and Laius

Let's imagine: Oedipus is crying. His soul is unbearably painful. His incomprehension and his expulsion from the temple are not sufficient to justify his pain. It goes much deeper. He no longer knows what he feels and thinks (if he is able to do so); he does not even know who he is. He has the impression that he is merely a shadow, soon to be effaced. Why did the priest not listen to him? He wanted to have had the opportunity to talk about his pain, about his suffering, so many questions … that he barely knew how to phrase. In a glimmer of sanity, he perceives that they were questions that he had always been trying to formulate, but found himself unable to …

Oedipus walks along the road, weeping, travelling as far away from Delphi as possible. He keeps his distance from other travellers, some of whom sympathetically try to approach him. He feels like a leper. He wants to be alone, and does not believe anybody would be willing to listen to him or to tolerate his curse.

He thinks about his parents, Polybus and Merope. He would like to return to them, to be looked after. But Oedipus knows that if he were to return, *he* would be the one to have to look after his sad parents. He fears killing them with misery if they were to learn of his suffering.

At this moment, Oedipus remembers the oracle and feels even more frightened—perhaps the priest was right. Yes, he could kill his father, Polybus, and marry Merope, his mother! These thoughts make him stop short. He decides not to return to Corinth, and takes the other direction instead. Oedipus continues along the road, limping, suffering, and crying. He wants death; it would be better than the madness threatening to consume him completely.

Oedipus tries to sleep, hidden alone in the corner of a roadside inn. The other travellers around him irritate him with their animated conversations. Oedipus cannot help overhearing about a monster, half woman half animal, who waits at the entrance to the city of Thebes. She strangles all the young people who pass by. Soon Thebes will be populated exclusively by the elderly, and the city will disappear.

Oedipus' interest in the story gradually grows. The monster, the Sphinx, sets people riddles that nobody can solve. Oedipus smiles for the first time in weeks. It is a sad smile, the smile of someone who has discovered a way to die. His death will be heroic, not an assassination or a suicide, but what in future will be known as victim-precipitated homicide (Cassorla, 1998e). Oedipus, as a future victim of the Sphinx, finally feels like somebody. Somebody destined for death. Had this not always been the destiny from which he fled?

Oedipus follows the road towards Thebes, and towards his destiny. Along the way, he meets terrified people who inform him of more deaths caused by the Sphinx. This spurs him on all the more. He feels curious: what will the monster be like? Why is it doing this? He even wonders whether the Sphinx might be suffering, like him. Was there a form of suffering that made her homicidal? Suddenly, Oedipus sees how killing someone could be a relief, a substitute for the desire to die.

At this point in his journey, Oedipus finds himself at a crossroads. An imperious, arrogant man, accompanied by an entourage, denies him passage. The man draws his sword. And Oedipus, instead of fleeing or allowing himself to be killed, without knowing how, becomes strong, stronger than he had ever imagined. He kills his adversaries, including the imperious man. And thus Oedipus, without knowing it, kills his true father, Laius, king of Thebes, who was on his way to see the same oracle of Delphi, to consult the oracle about the Sphinx.

Oedipus feels relieved and proud. He continues walking. Despite some injuries, he walks better, his steps are firm and his posture is straight. He no longer feels despair. It must be a miracle. When night comes, Oedipus dreams that he is mad. The terrifying nightmare is transformed when, in the dream, he finds someone who is unafraid of his madness and welcomes him, listening attentively and saying words that indicate understanding. Now, the dream is a relief.

Yet on resuming his journey, melancholy takes hold of him once more. More intensely than before, Oedipus wishes to die. He wants to meet the Sphinx so that he will meet his death. But it is no longer a death whose sole purpose is to escape from madness—now Oedipus has the impression, almost the certainty, that there is justice in this act of dying, despite the reason for it being unclear. So despite his feelings of melancholy, he feels a strange urge to travel to the gates of Thebes, towards an encounter with the Sphinx.

Reverie, alpha-function, transformations into dream, and symbolic suicide: Oedipus and the Sphinx

Oedipus finally finds himself before the Sphinx. A small crowd has gathered around the two of them. He is told that if he can solve the riddle, then he will inherit the throne of Thebes and marry the queen Jocasta. Now Oedipus feels something confusing: although he desires to die, it seems as though some doubts are emerging. The idea of a new home almost attracts him, but he soon extinguishes this desire in his mind.

He stares at the terrifying Sphinx and is surprised by the gentleness of the monster's gaze. At the same time, he perceives a shadow in this gaze that frightens him. But the sensation of relief is greater. The Sphinx's face seems familiar, he is no longer terrified. Observing her, he feels that her monstrosity makes her suffer. Could she have been made a monster as a result of other suffering? Oedipus is now certain that the Sphinx's arrogance, positing herself as the owner of truth, of life and death, reveals nothing more than a flight from monstrous pain. Oedipus feels the same as her—he may look like a prince, but he is a monster just the same as the Sphinx. The more he looks at the Sphinx, the more he sees himself, pieces of animal and of human being, strange and agglomerated, confused and bizarre. And like someone seeing themselves in a mirror that reflects the unknown, Oedipus *re-sees* himself. But strangely with less fear, perhaps even with hope …

While the Sphinx and Oedipus converse, she sings softly, and he looks upon his whole life as though in a mirror. An asphyxiated baby, disintegrating into pieces, abandoned and despairing, animals devouring him in the real world and in his mind. He is dying, terrified, and suddenly there is a miracle, someone is holding the parts of him that were almost shattered, containing them and giving them a form. Someone is saving him from death. An immense gratitude spreads through the world, even though sometimes the memory of the terror tries to reappear. The gratitude revolves around the Sphinx, who continues with her gentle eyes, listening attentively. With each one of her whispers, Oedipus' mind is illuminated. He is overcome with emotion, and cries, but this time crying is comforting. The Sphinx observes him with a caring expression, and encourages him to look at himself more and more. And Oedipus sees suffering in the eyes of the Sphinx, the suffering of a monster desperately in need of someone to make it feel like it exists. He realises that, like her, he began his journey through life crawling on a painful ground, then he learned to limp, with the cane as his companion, walking through life as a baby-adult-old-man, lame and confused, searching for himself.

At this moment, Oedipus realises that he has solved the riddle. What animal goes on four feet in the morning, two feet at noon, and three feet in the evening? He no longer knows whether it was the Sphinx who proposed it or whether he himself did. It doesn't matter. Oedipus is an expert in feet, in foundations, since he has suffered so much from their flaws. Oedipus knows that man, at the dawn of life, supports himself crawling on all fours, and uses the support of his parents' minds. Later, he can break free of them and walk on two feet. And at the dusk of life, he needs a stick, three feet, in the form of a daughter-mind on whom he can rely. At this moment, Oedipus becomes aware of the vicissitudes of the journey through life, from birth and the need for support, to adequate and limping development, the expulsion with his despair, envy, and jealousy, the sexuality that fertilises and can kill, to the passage of time, the destruction that comes from without and mainly from within, to death.

The Sphinx feels content, seeking to transform herself and to transform minds. She will not need to devour yet another failed part of becoming human, which would attack her from within, battling other parts and reinforcing her monstrosity. She will no longer need to drown herself, asphyxiating so as to not disintegrate. Now she can live like Oedipus, as one being, as a human being, enriching herself and enabling the other's life, as something separate. Now the Sphinx finally feels like a *therapist*, knowing this is only because she could feel what Oedipus was feeling. And this feeling occurred because it resonated with the vicissitudes of her own life.

Now the Sphinx is no longer necessary. The monstrous part of her has died and her love has become part of Oedipus. The Sphinx kills herself. Like a mother, like parents, the couple who must also symbolically kill themselves when their baby-child detaches and walks on its own two legs towards adulthood.

Returning to our times, I propose that we consider the Sphinx's generous suicide, which some would consider *rational* (Cassorla, 1998c), as equivalent to the analyst's capacity to enable the patient's development and detachment, jettisoning components of envy that could attack the analysis, resulting in something akin to a filicide. The analyst withdraws, "killing" parts of himself and fostering the development of the other, his patient. At the same time, he is containing his own fears and making use of his capacity for reverie and his alpha-function.

Aniversary reaction: the plague

But what Oedipus does not know is that, in the depths of his mind, there remains an area that is destroyed and destructive, as though sealed off. In this area, there are still traces of murderous aspects. When some of these aspects threaten to surface, they are repressed or deflected. And this is not difficult for Oedipus to do, since in a kingdom there are so many enemies …, upon whom it is possible to project … and transform hate into hallucinosis. Yes, sometimes Oedipus believes he is threatened by them, by the external enemies as well as the internal ones, and this gives him nightmares. He used to dream that he had died and his sons Polynices and Eteocles were killing each other over his inheritance. He would awake in despair, imagining it to be a warning, but his wife Jocasta would convince him not to pay his dreams any heed.

Let's speculate: Oedipus will now be forty-two years old, with twenty-one years of reign (Brandão, 1986, p. 241), during which time Thebes had been a happy city. Curiously (let's imagine) close to his birthday, he notices that his nightmares are becoming more frequent. An old dream resurfaces, in which his daughter Antigone is a dying prisoner, and merges with a new one, in which he, Oedipus, blind and helpless, desperately needs his daughter to guide him. But he does not know whether he will be able to rely on her.

Gradually, however, the dreams no longer have a narrative: all he feels is terror, the feeling of catastrophe, of death. He realises the risk of going mad—he imagines Thebes being destroyed, people, animals, and plants dying, and no way to stop it. The sensation is as though his mind, his kingdom, is disintegrating and going to pieces. He cannot bear it.[2]

When Oedipus realises that his dream-nightmare has become a reality and the plague is sweeping the city, he no longer knows what is dream and what is real. He only knows that he needs help, because death and madness are consuming everything. This is why he orders the counsel of the oracle of Delphi. While all this is happening, as king he seeks to remain strong and composed, intimately concealing his madness.

The plague only comes to an end when Oedipus discovers that it was he who had killed his father. But he never discovered why the plague broke out at that particular time, and not at some other point over the course of his twenty-one-year reign.

Years later (we imagine), Antigone is guiding her blind old father, listening once again to his story of the vicissitudes of why it happened. Oedipus liked to tell and re-tell his story, because every time he told it, he saw fascinating new dimensions to it. This time, talking about the plague, Oedipus remembers that his children were young at the time, and greatly resembled him. He says they reminded him greatly of the time when he had left Corinth in search of himself. But now he sees that the madness, the plague, had been gradually triggered in his mind by the terrifying sight of himself in the mirror. Oedipus saw a man, he saw himself, with the same features and the same build as the victim at the crossroads (cf. Sophocles, p. 57). More than once he had considered breaking the mirror. He began to avoid looking at himself, because he had so often felt terrified to "see" the shattered mirror beside his own reflection.

This image of someone who resembles him in age and in build, reflecting his accusatory gaze, has pursued him inside, although he had not clearly perceived it. Now he is certain that this was what had triggered the plague, the madness. It is only now that Oedipus realises that he had reached the same age, he had the same kind of build as his father Laius, whom he had killed. And coincidentally his oldest son was about to be twenty years old, almost the same age as he, Oedipus, had been at the time of the murder.

Oedipus is convinced (although he does not know why) that these coincidences had mobilised the sealed-off areas, where the traces of feelings relating to the murder had been deposited. The time and the ages had been the triggers that had caused these dormant areas to stir. Now that Oedipus has deciphered this new riddle, he can die in peace.

Let's return to our time. The features described here are known, today, as "anniversary reactions", which are the re-experiences of encysted pathological mourning, triggered by external situations relating to dates, anniversaries, similar ages, and other temporal factors (Cassorla, 1986, 1998b). The psychoanalyst who is familiar with this phenomenon will have a greater chance of dreaming it during the dream-for-two that occurs during the analytic process.

Hope: Antigone

When Antigone awakes (let's imagine), she sees her elderly father, close to death, looking at her. And in his eyes, she sees peace. But suddenly a question surfaces in her mind. She wants Oedipus to tell her how he viewed, such a long time afterwards, the episode with the oracle, when he was expelled from the temple. Surely Oedipus continues to resent the priest-therapist who failed to tolerate his terror and suffering and thus expelled him. Oedipus smiles, thinks, and remains silent. Antigone insists. Oedipus tells her, with amusement, that he is increasingly convinced that there never was an oracle. That he, Oedipus, had had a nightmare, and the priest who had failed to tolerate his curse was, in fact, himself. He could no longer be his own therapist, just like his father, Laius, had been unable to deal with his own maledictions. Antigone is disappointed. Oedipus embraces her and tells her that a nightmare is very important ..., so as to find the other who will help us to dream it ... And, with affectionate sadness, he announces to Antigone that now that he is about to die, she must prepare herself to confront the nightmares she will encounter on her own journey to find herself. As a father, he hopes to have planted the seeds to allow her to dream her own nightmares and to re-encounter herself. And he hopes she will seek help, find a good *therapist*, not like the priest and better than Tiresias—someone like the Sphinx. Antigone wants to know why the Sphinx did not warn Oedipus about his future, but knows that her father will say that life can sometimes be beyond even the greatest of therapists.

Oedipus blesses Antigone and tells her that she, like every human being, deserves to live her life, this suffered, fascinating life, whose purpose is … to make it one's own … so that we shall serve as an example to our children … so that they can make their lives their own … and so on, down the generations …

Notes

1. We are speculating about "non-dreams" as fruit of initial traumas, looking for dreamers to dream them.
2. We are speculating in the area of non-dreams with the threat of psychotic disintegration, the internal plague.

REFERENCES

Abreu, A. A. (2006). The act of interpretation. *International Journal of Psychoanalysis, 87*: 953–964.

Apfelbaum, L. (2008). Some comments on *Break Point* by Stella M. Yardino. *International Journal of Psychoanalysis, 89*: 249–252.

Austin, J. L. (1962). *How To Do Things with Words*. New York and London: Oxford University Press.

Azevedo, A. M. A. (1994). Validation of the psychoanalytical clinical process: the role of dreams. *International Journal of Psychoanalysis, 75*: 1181–1192.

Azvaradel, J. R. (Ed.) (2005). *Linguagem e construção do pensamento*. São Paulo: Casa do Psicólogo.

Baranger, M., & Baranger, W. (1961–1962). The analytic situation as a dynamic field. *International Journal of Psychoanalysis, 89*: 795–826. [Reprinted, 1968, 2008.]

Baranger, M., Baranger, W., & Mom, J. (1983). Process and non-process in analytic work. *International Journal of Psychoanalysis, 64*: 1–15.

Barros, E. M. R. (2000). Affect and pictographic image: the constitution of meaning in mental life. *International Journal of Psychoanalysis, 81*: 1087–1099.

Barros, E. M. R. (2002). An essay on dreaming, psychical working out and working through. *International Journal of Psychoanalysis, 83*: 1083–1093.

REFERENCES

Barros, E. M. R. (2005). Trauma, símbolo e significado. In: M. O. A. França et al., *Trauma psíquico: uma leitura psicanalítica e filosófica da cultura moderna* (pp. 109–127). São Paulo: SBPSP (Acervo Psicanalítico).
Barros, E. M. R. (2011). Reflections on the clinical implication of symbolism. *International Journal of Psychoanalysis, 92*: 879–901.
Barros, E. M. R. (2013). Formlessness: deformation, transformations, dream, figurability and symbolic transformation. *Bulletin of the European Psychoanalytical Federation Association, 63*: 107–120.
Barros, E. M. R., & Barros, E. L. R. (2016). The function of evocation in the working-through of the countertransference: projective identification, reverie and the expressive function of the mind. Reflections inspired by Bion's work. In: H. B. Levine & G. Civitarese (Eds.), *The Bion Tradition: Lines of Development—Evolution of Theory and Practice over the Decades* (pp. 141–153). London: Karnac.
Barros, E. M. R., Gabbard, G. O., & Williams, P. (2005). IJP Rio Conference. *International Journal of Psychoanalysis, 86*: 609–613.
Bateman, A. W. (1998). Thick and thin-skinned organisations and enactment in borderline and narcissistic disorders. *International Journal of Psychoanalysis, 79*: 13–25.
Bernardi, R., & De León Des Bernardi, B. (2012). The concepts of vínculo and dialectical spiral: a bridge between intra- and intersubjectivity. *Psychoanalytic Quarterly, 81*: 531–564.
Bianco, S. M. (1996). Distúrbios do sono, um fértil campo para investigação psicossomática. *Boletim de Psiquiatria (São Paulo), 30*: 37–40.
Bion, W. R. (1957). Differentiation of the psychotic from the non-psychotic personalities. In: *Second Thoughts: Selected Papers on Psycho-Analysis* (pp. 43–64). London: Heinemann, 1967.
Bion, W. R. (1958). On arrogance: In: *Second Thoughts: Selected Papers on Psycho-Analysis* (pp. 86–92). London: Heinemann, 1967.
Bion, W. R. (1959). Attacks on linking. In: *Second Thoughts: Selected Papers on Psycho- Analysis* (pp. 93–109). London: Heinemann, 1967.
Bion, W. R. (1961). *Experiences in Groups*. London: Tavistock.
Bion, W. R. (1962a). A theory of thinking. In: *Second Thoughts: Selected Papers on Psycho-Analysis* (pp. 102–119). London: Heinemann, 1967.
Bion, W. R. (1962b). *Learning from Experience*. London: Heinemann.
Bion, W. R. (1963). *Elements of Psychoanalysis*. London: Heinemann.
Bion, W. R. (1965). *Transformations*. London: Heinemann.
Bion, W. R. (1967). Notes on memory and desire. In: E. B. Spillius (Ed.), *Melanie Klein Today, Volume 2: Mainly Practice* (pp. 17–21). London: Routledge, 1988.
Bion, W. R. (1970). *Attention and Interpretation*. London: Tavistock.
Bion, W. R. (1975). *A Memoir of the Future—The Dream*. Rio: Imago.

Bion, W. R. (1977). *Two Papers: The Grid and Caesura*. Rio: Imago.
Bion, W. R. (1980). *Bion in New York and São Paulo*. Pertshire: Clunie Press.
Bion, W. R. (1992). *Cogitations*. London: Karnac.
Bohleber, W., Fonagy, P., Jiménez, J. P., Scarfone, D., Varvin, S., & Zysman, S. (2013). Towards a better use of psychoanalytic concepts: a model illustrated using the concept of enactment. *International Journal of Psychoanalysis, 94*: 501–530.
Bokanowski, T. (2005). Variations on the concept of traumatism: traumatism, traumatic, trauma. *International Journal of Psychoanalysis, 86*: 251–265.
Bollas, C. (1989). *The Shadow of the Object*. New York: Columbia University Press.
Bollas, C. (2007). *The Freudian Moment*. London: Karnac.
Bonaminio, V. (2008). The person of the analyst: interpretation, not interpretating and countertransference. *Psychoanalytic Quarterly, 77*: 1105–1146.
Borensztejn, C. L. (2009). El enactment como concepto clínico convergente de teorías divergentes. *Revista de Psicoanálisis (Buenos Aires), 46*: 177–192.
Botella, C., & Botella, S. (2001). De la recherche en psychoanalyse. *Revue Française de Psychanalyse* (hors de serie): 355–372.
Botella, C., & Botella, S. (2005). *The Work of Psychic Figurability*. New York: Routledge.
Botella, C., & Botella, S. (2013). Psychic figurability and unrepresented states. In: H. B. Levine, G. S. Reed, & D. Scarfone (Eds.), *Unrepresented States and the Construction of Meaning* (pp. 95–120). London: Karnac.
Brandão, J. S. (1986). *Mitologia Grega, Volume 1*. São Paulo: Vozes.
Britton, R. (1998). *Belief and Imagination: Explorations in Psychoanalysis*. London: Routledge.
Britton, R. (1999). Getting on the act: the hysterical solution. *International Journal of Psychoanalysis, 80*: 1–14.
Brown, L. J. (2005). The cognitive effects of trauma: reversal of alpha function and the formation of a beta screen. *Psychoanalytic Quarterly, 74*: 397–420.
Brown, L. J. (2010). Klein, Bion, and intersubjectivity: becoming, transforming, and dreaming. *Psychoanalytical Dialogues, 20*: 669–682.
Brown, L. J. (2011). *Intersubjective Processes and the Unconscious: An Integration of Freudian, Kleinian and Bionian Perspectives*. New York: Routledge.
Brown, L. J. (2013). Bion at a threshold: discussion of papers by Britton, Cassorla, Ferro and Foresti. *Psychoanalytic Quarterly, 82*: 413–433.
Calich, J. C. (2009). What do our patients think when we do not think? Panel, IPA Congress, Chicago.
Canelas Neto, J. M. (2003). Comentário sobre o caso Bernardo supervisionado por André Green. *Revista Brasileira de Psicanálise, 37*: 53–67.

Caper, R. (1995). On the difficulty to make a mutative interpretation. *International Journal of Psychoanalysis, 76*: 91–101. [Reprinted in *A Mind of One's Own: A Kleinian View of Self and Object* (pp. 31–39). New York: Routledge, 1999.]

Caper, R. (1996). On alpha function. In: *A Mind of One's Own: A Kleinian View of Self and Object* (pp. 121–129). New York: Routledge, 1999.

Caper, R. (1999). *A Mind of One's Own: A Kleinian View of Self and Object*. New York: Routledge.

Cassorla, R. M. S. (1985). Depression and suicide in adolescence. In: Pan American Health Association (Ed.), *The Health of Adolescents and Youths in the Americas* (pp. 156–169). Washington: PAHO.

Cassorla, R. M. S. (1986). Reações de aniversário: aspectos clínicos e teóricos. *Jornal de Psicanálise (São Paulo), 19(38)*: 25–39.

Cassorla, R. M. S. (1993). Complexo de Édipo, vista grossa, curiosidade e catástrofe psicológica. *Revista Brasileira de Psicanálise, 27*: 607–626.

Cassorla, R. M. S. (1995). Comunicação primitiva e contra-reações na situação analítica. *Arquivos de Psiquiatria, Psicoterapia e Psicanálise (Porto Alegre), 2*: 11–33.

Cassorla, R. M. S. (1997). No emaranhado de identificações projetivas cruzadas com adolescentes e seus pais. *Revista Brasileira de Psicanálise, 31*: 639–676. [Reprinted as: Der Verwicklung von projectiven Kreuzidentifizierungen mit Adoleszenten und ihren Eltern. *Kinderanalyse* (Stuttgart, 2004), *12*: 183–230.]

Cassorla, R. M. S. (1998a). Objetividade, confidencialidade e validação: três problemas e uma surpresa na apresentação de material clínico. *Jornal de Psicanálise (São Paulo), 31(57)*: 93–112.

Cassorla, R. M. S. (1998b). O tempo, a morte e as reações de aniversário. In: *Do suicídio: estudos brasileiros* (2nd edn., pp. 107–116). Campinas: Papirus.

Cassorla, R. M. S. (1998c). *Do suicídio: estudos brasileiros* (2nd edn.). Campinas: Papirus.

Cassorla, R.M.S. (1998d). Suicídio, homicídio precipitado pela vítima e totalitarismo. In: Associação Brasileira de Psiquiatria (Ed.), *Cidadania e direito à saúde mental* (pp. 1–14). São Paulo: Próxis.

Cassorla, R. M. S. (1998e). Psicanálise e surto psicótico: considerações sobre aspectos técnicos. *Revista Brasileira de Psicanálise, 32*: 721–746.

Cassorla, R. M. S. (2000). Reflexões sobre teoria e técnica psicanalítica com pacientes potencialmente suicidas. *Alter: Revista de Estudos Psicodinâmicos (Brasilia), 19(1)*: 169–186 (part 1); *19(2)*: 367–386 (part 2).

Cassorla, R. M. S. (2001). Acute enactment as resource in disclosing a collusion between the analytical dyad. *International Journal of Psychoanalysis, 82*: 1155–1170.

Cassorla, R. M. S. (2003). Estudo sobre a cena analítica e o conceito de "colocação em cena da dupla" (enactment). *Revista Brasileira de Psicanálise, 37*: 365–392.

Cassorla, R. M. S. (2004). Procedimentos, colocação em cena da dupla (enactment) e validação clínica em psicoterapia psicanalítica e psicanálise. *Revista de Psiquiatria do Rio Grande do Sul (Porto Alegre), 25*: 426–435.

Cassorla, R. M. S. (2005a). From bastion to enactment: the "non-dream" in the theatre of analysis. *International Journal of Psychoanalysis, 86*: 699–719. [Reprinted: *L'Année Psychanalytique Internationale, 4*: 67–86, 2006; *Revista Brasileira de Psicanálise, 41*: 51–68, 2007; *L'Annata Psicoanalitica Internazionale, 3*: 75–94, 2008; *Revista de Psicoanálisis (Buenos Aires), 62*: 137–161, 2010.]

Cassorla, R. M. S. (2005b). Considerações sobre o sonho-a-dois e o não-sonho a dois no teatro da análise. *Revista de Psicanálise da Sociedade Psicanalítica de Porto Alegre, 12*: 527–552.

Cassorla, R. M. S. (2007). The analyst, his "Mourning and Melancholia", analytical technique and enactment. In: L. G. Fiorini, T. Bokanowsky, & S. Lewkowicz (Eds.), *On Freud's "Mourning and Melancholia"* (pp. 71–89). London: IPA Publications.

Cassorla, R. M. S. (2008a). The analyst's implicit alpha-function, trauma and enactment in the analysis of borderline patients. *International Journal of Psychoanalysis, 89*: 161–180. [Reprinted: *Internationale Psychoanalyse, 4*: 83–112, 2009; *Livro Anual de Psicanálise, 24*: 61–78, 2009; *Libro Anual de Psicoanálisis, 24*: 55–70, 2009.]

Cassorla, R. M. S. (2008b). Desvelando configurações emocionais da dupla analítica através de modelos inspirados no mito edípico. *Revista Brasileira de Psicoterapia (Porto Alegre), 10*: 37–48.

Cassorla, R. M. S. (2008c). O analista, seu paciente e a psicanálise contemporânea: considerações sobre indução mútua, enactment e não-sonho-a-dois. *Revista Latinoamericana de Psicoanálisis, 8*: 189–208. [Reprinted: *Alter: Revista de Estudos Psicanalíticos-Brasília, 27*: 19–40, 2009.]

Cassorla, R. M. S. (2008d). Depressão e suicídio no estudante de medicina e no médico. In: K. B. S. Guimarães (Ed.), *Saúde mental do médico e do estudante de medicina* (pp. 171–188). São Paulo: Casa do Psicólogo.

Cassorla, R. M. S. (2009a). Reflections on non-dream-for-two, enactment and the analyst's implicit alpha-function. In: H. B. Levine & L. J. Brown (Eds.), *Growth and Turbulence in the Container–Contained: Bion's Continuing Legacy* (pp. 151–176). London and New York: Routledge, 2013.

Cassorla, R. M. S. (2009b). O analista, seu paciente adolescente e a psicanálise atual: sete reflexões. *Revista de Psicanálise da Sociedade Psicanalítica de Porto Alegre, 16*: 261–278.

References

Cassorla, R. M. S. (2009c). Transtorno de pânico e estados primitivos da mente. In: M. T. B. França & T. R. L. Haundenschild (Eds.), *Constituição da vida psíquica* (pp. 169–202). São Paulo: Hirondel.

Cassorla R. M. S. (2010a). A leste do Éden: loucura, feitiço e suicídio. *Revista Brasileira de Psicanálise, 44*: 147–157.

Cassorla, R. M. S. (2010b). Édipo, Tirésias, o oráculo e a esfinge: do nãosonho às transformações em sonho. In: C. J. Rezze, E. S. Marra, & M. Petricciani (Eds.), *Psicanálise: Bion. Teoria e Clínica* (pp. 110–131). São Paulo: Vetor.

Cassorla, R. M. S. (2012a). What happens before and after acute enactment? An exercise in clinical validation and broadening of hypothesis. *International Journal of Psychoanalysis, 93*: 53–89. [Reprinted: *Libro Anual de Psicoanálisis, 28*: 57–78; *Livro Anual de Psicanálise, 28(1)*: 77–101.]

Cassorla, R. M. S. (2012b). Transferindo aspectos inomináveis no campo analítico: uma aproximação didática. *Revista de Psicanálise da Sociedade Psicanalítica de Porto Alegre, 19*: 61–98.

Cassorla, R. M. S. (2013a). In search of symbolization: the analyst's task of dreaming. In: H. B. Levine, G. Reed, & D. Scarfone (Eds.), *Unrepresented States and the Construction of Meaning: Clinical and Theoretical Contributions* (pp. 202–219). London: Karnac.

Cassorla, R. M. S. (2013b). When the analyst becomes stupid: an attempt to understand enactment using Bion's theory of thinking. *Psychoanalytic Quarterly, 82*: 323–360.

Cassorla, R. M. S. (2013c). Afinal, o que é esse tal enactment? *Jornal de Psicanálise (São Paulo), 46(85)*: 183–198.

Cassorla, R. M. S. (2013d). O analista, seu paciente adolescente e a estupidez no campo analítico. *Calibán-Revista Latinoamericana de Psicanálise, 11*: 43–65.

Cassorla, R. M. S. (2013e). El trabajo de sueño del analista: en busca de la simbolización. *Revista de la Asociación Psicoanalítica de Madrid, 69*: 75–109.

Cassorla, R. M. S. (2014a). Em busca da simbolização: sonhando objetos bizarros e traumas iniciais. *Revista Brasileira de Psicanálise, 48*: 141–153.

Cassorla, R. M. S. (2014b). Commentary to case Ellen: the silent movies. *International Journal of Psychoanalysis, 95*: 93–102.

Cassorla, R. M. S. (2014c). Cuando el analista se torna estúpido: enactment como manifestación de dificultades en el proceso de simbolización. In: A. Vertzner Marucco (Ed.), *Metapsicología: Una clínica con fundamentos* (pp. 95–114). Buenos Aires: Lugar Editorial y APA.

Cassorla, R. M. S. (2015). Commentary on Supervision A34. In: H. B. Levine & G. Civitarese (Eds.), *The W. R. Bion Tradition* (pp. 73–77). London: Karnac.

Cassorla, R. M. S. (2016a). The dreaming field. In: S. M. Katz, R. M. S. Cassorla, & G. Civitarese (Eds.), *Advances in Contemporary Psychoanalytic Field Theory* (pp. 91–112). New York: Routledge.

Cassorla, R. M. S. (2016b). Dreaming the analytical session: between pleasure principle and reality principle. In: G. Legorreta & L. J. Brown (Eds.), *On Freud's "Formulation on the Two Principles of Mental Functioning"* (pp. 85–104). London: Karnac.

Cassorla, R. M. S., & Smeke, E. L. M. (1995). Autodestruição humana. *Cadernos de Saúde Pública, 10(1)*: 61–73.

Cavell, M. (1998). Triangulation, one's own mind and objectivity. *International Journal of Psychoanalysis, 79*: 449–467.

Chaves, L. P. (2012). Recent contributions from clinical research: on mental processing, on dreams and dreaming, and on the role of phantasies about parental couple relationships. *International Journal of Psychoanalysis, 93*: 750–775.

Churcher, J. (2008). Some notes on the English translation of "The analytic situation as a dynamic field" by W. and M. Baranger. *International Journal of Psychoanalysis, 89*: 785–793.

Chused, J. F. (1991). The evocative power of enactments. *Journal of the American Psychoanalytical Association, 39*: 615–639.

Chuster, A. (2003). *A psicanálise: dos princípios etico-estéticos à clínica*. Rio: Cia de Freud.

Civitarese, G. (2013a). The inaccessible unconscious and reverie as path of figurability. In: H. B. Levine, G. S. Reed, & D. Scarfone (Eds.), *Unrepresented States and the Construction of Meaning* (pp. 220–239). London: Karnac.

Civitarese, G. (2013b). *The Violence of Emotions: Bion and Post-Bionian Psychoanalysis*. New York: Routledge.

De León de Bernardi, B. (2013). Field theory as a metaphor and metaphors in the analytic field and process. *Psychoanalytic Inquiry, 33*: 247–266.

Deserno, H. (2007). Traumdeutung in der gegenwärtigen psychoanalytischen Therapie. *Psyche—Z Psychoanalyse, 61*: 913–942.

Devereux, D. (2006). Enactment: some thoughts about the therapist's contribution. *British. Journal of Psychotherapy, 22*: 497–508.

Ellman, S. J., & Moskovitz, M. (Eds.) (1998). *Enactment: Toward a New Approach to the Therapeutic Relationship*. Northvale: Jason Aronson.

Faimberg, H. (1996). Listening to listening. *International Journal of Psychoanalysis, 77*: 667–677.

Feldman, M. (1997). Projective identification: the analyst's involvement. *International Journal of Psychoanalysis, 78*: 227–241.

Ferro, A. (1992). *The Bipersonal Field: Experiences in Child Analysis*. London: Routledge, 1999.

Ferro, A. (1996). *In the Analyst's Consulting Room*. Hove: Brunner-Routledge, 2002.
Ferro, A. (1999). *Psychoanalysis as Therapy and Storytelling*. Hove: Brunner-Routledge, 2006.
Ferro, A. (2002a). Some implications of Bion's thought: The waking dream and narrative derivatives. *International Journal of Psychoanalysis*, 83:597–607.
Ferro, A. (2002b). *Seeds of Illness, Seeds of Recovery: The Genesis of Suffering and the Role of Psychoanalysis*. Hove: Brunner-Routledge, 2005.
Ferro, A. (2006). Clinical implications of Bion's thought. *International Journal of Psychoanalysis*, 87: 989–1003.
Ferro, A. (2009). Transformations in dreaming and characters in the psychoanalytical field. *International Journal of Psychoanalysis*, 90: 209–230.
Figueiredo, L. C. (2003). *Elementos para a clínica contemporânea*. São Paulo: Escuta.
Figueiredo, L. C. (2006). Sense of reality, reality testing and reality processing in borderline patients. *International Journal of Psychoanalysis*, 87: 769–787.
Fogel, G. T. (2008). The origins of acts of love: a discussion of *Break Point* by Stella M. Yardino. *International Journal of Psychoanalysis*, 89: 253–258.
Fonagy, P. (1991). Thinking about thinking: some clinical and theoretical considerations in the treatment of a borderline patient. *International Journal of Psychoanalysis*, 72: 639–656.
Franco Filho, O. M. (2000). Quando o analista é alvo da magia de seu paciente: considerações sobre a comunicação inconsciente de estado mental do paciente ao analista. *Revista Brasileira de Psicanálise*, 34: 687–709.
Freud, S. (1900a). The Interpretation of Dreams. *SE 4, 5*. London: Hogarth.
Freud, S. (1905a). On psychotherapy. *SE 7*. London: Hogarth.
Freud, S. (1905e). Fragment of an analysis of a case of hysteria. *SE 7*. London: Hogarth.
Freud, S. (1911b). Formulations on the two principles of mental functioning. *SE 12*. London: Hogarth.
Freud, S. (1912b). The dynamics of transference. *SE 12*. London: Hogarth.
Freud, S. (1912e). Recommendations to physicians practising psychoanalysis. *SE 12*. London: Hogarth.
Freud, S. (1913c). On beginning the treatment. *SE 12*. London: Hogarth.
Freud, S. (1914g). Remembering, repeating and working-through. *SE 12*. London: Hogarth.
Freud, S. (1915e). The unconscious. *SE 14*. London: Hogarth.
Freud, S. (1917e). Mourning and melancholia. *SE 14*. London: Hogarth.

Freud, S. (1918b). From the history of an infantile neurosis. *SE 17*. London: Hogarth.
Freud, S. (1920g). *Beyond the Pleasure Principle*. *SE 18*. London: Hogarth.
Freud, S. (1923b). *The Ego and the Id*. *SE 19*. London: Hogarth.
Freud, S. (1926d). *Inhibitions, Symptoms and Anxiety*. *SE 20*. London: Hogarth.
Freud, S. (1930a). *Civilization and its Discontents*. *SE 21*. London: Hogarth.
Freud, S. (1933a). *New Introductory Lectures on Psycho-Analysis*. *SE 22*. London: Hogarth.
Freud, S. (1937d). Constructions in analysis. *SE 23*. London: Hogarth.
Freud, S. (1940a). *An Outline of Psycho-Analysis*. *SE 23*. London: Hogarth.
Friedman, L. (2008). Is there life after enactment? The idea of a patient's proper work. *Journal of the American Psychoanalytical Association, 56*: 431–453.
Gabbard, G. O. (1995). Countertransference: the emerging common ground. *International Journal of Psychoanalysis, 76*: 475–485.
Gabbard, G. O. (2000). Disguise or consent: problems and recommendations concerning the publication and presentation of clinical material. *International Journal of Psychoanalysis, 81*: 1071–1086.
Gabbard, G. O. (2006). Enactment contratransferencial e violação de fronteiras. In: J. Zaslavsky & M. J. P. Santos (Eds.), *Contratransfêrencia: teoria e prática clínicas* (pp. 236–243). P. Alegre: Artmed.
Galipeau, S. (2009). Journal review papers on enactment: Cassorla, Ivey, Morgan. *Journal of Analytical Psychology, 54*: 561–564.
Galvez, M. J. (2004). A paciência na elaboração psicanalítica. *Revista Brasileira Psicanálise, 38*: 895–914.
Gastaud, M. B., Padoan, C. S., & Eizirik, C. L. (2014). Initial improvement in adult psychodynamic psychotherapy. *British Journal of Psychotherapy, 30*: 243–262.
Gheller, J. H. (2010). Um après-coup do analista. *Revista Brasileira de Psicanálise, 44*: 61–72.
Guignard, F. (1997). Universalidade e especificidade das contribuições de W. R. Bion a uma teoria psicanalitica do pensamento. In: M. O. A. França (Ed.), *Bion in São Paulo: Ressonâncias* (pp. 253–262). São Paulo: SBPSP.
Green, A. (1973). *The Fabric of Affect in the Psychoanalytic Discourse*. London: Routledge, 1999.
Green, A. (1983). *Narcissisme de vie, narcissisme de mort*. Paris: Minuit.
Green, A. (1986). *On Private Madness*. London: Karnac, 1996.
Green, A. (1993). *The Work of the Negative*. London and New York: Free Association, 1999.
Green, A. (1998). The primordial mind and the work of the negative. *International Journal of Psychoanalysis, 79*: 649–656.
Green, A. (2002a). *La Pensée Clinique*. Paris: Odile Jacob.

Green, A. (2002b). *Key Ideas for a Contemporary Psychoanalysis*. Hove: Routledge, 2005.

Greenacre, P. (1950). General problems of acting-out. *Psychoanalytical Quarterly, 19*: 455–467.

Greenberg, J. (2013). Editor's introduction: Bion across cultures. *Psychoanalytical Quarterly, 82*: 271–276.

Grinberg, L. (1957). Perturbaciones en la interpretación por la contraidentificación proyectiva. *Revista de Psicoanálisis, 14*: 23–30.

Grinberg, L. (1967). Función del soñar y clasificación clínica de los sueños en el proceso analítico. In: *Psicoanalisis-Aspectos teóricos y clinicos* (pp. 187–208). Buenos Aires: Alex Editor, 1976.

Grinberg, L. (1982). Más allá de contraidentificación proyectiva. *Actas XIV Congreso Latinoamericano de Psicoanálisis*.

Grinberg, L. (1996). *El Psicoanalisis es cosa de dos*. Valencia: Promolibro.

Grotstein, J. S. (1984). A proposed revision of the psychoanalytic concept of primitive mental states, Part II: the borderline syndrome, Section 2: the phenomenology of the borderline syndrome. *Contemporary Psychoanalysis, 20*: 77–119.

Grotstein, J. S. (1990). Nothingness, meaningless, chaos and "the black hole", Part I: The importance of nothingness, meaningless and chaos in psychoanalysis; Part II: The black hole. *Contemporary Psychoanalysis, 26*: 257–290 (Part I); *26*: 337–407 (Part II).

Grotstein, J. S. (2000). *Who Is the Dreamer Who Dreams the Dream? A Study of Psychic Presences*. Hillsdale: Analytic Press.

Grotstein, J. S. (2007). *A Beam of Intense Darkness*. London: Karnac.

Grotstein, J. S. (2009). *"But at the same time and on another level…", Volume 1: Psychoanalytic Theory and Technique in the Kleinian/Bionian Mode*. London: Karnac.

Gus, M. (2007). Acting, enactment e a realidade psíquica em cena no tratamento analítico de estruturas borderlines. *Revista Brasileira de Psicanálise, 41*: 45–53.

Hartke, R. (2005). The basic traumatic situation in the analytical relationship. *International Journal of Psychoanalysis, 86*: 267–290.

Heimann, P. (1950). On countertransference. *International Journal of Psychoanalysis, 31*: 81–84.

Hinshelwood, R. D. (1999). Countertransference. *International Journal of Psychoanalysis, 80*: 797–818.

Imbasciati, A. (2006). Uma explicação da gênese do trauma no quadro da Teoria do Protomental. *Revista de Psicanálise da Sociedade Psicanalítica de Porto Alegre, 13*: 75–102.

Isaacs, S. (1948). The nature and function of phantasy. In: J. Riviere (Ed.), *Developments in Psycho-Analysis* (pp. 67–201). London: Hogarth, 1952.

Ivey, G. (2008). Enactment controversies: a critical review of current debates. *International Journal of Psychoanalysis, 89:* 19–38.

Jacobs, T. (1986). On countertransference enactments. *Journal of the American Psychoanalytical Association, 34*: 289–307.

Jacobs, T. (2001). On misreading and misleading patients: some reflections on communication, miscommunication and countertransference enactments. *International Journal of Psychoanalysis, 82*: 653–669.

Jacobs, T. (2006). Reflexões sobre o papel da comunicação inconsciente e do enactment contratransferencial na situação analitica. In: J. Zaslavsky & M. J. P. Santos (Eds.), *Contratransferência: teoria e prática clínica* (pp. 81–97). Porto Alegre: Artmed.

Joseph, B. (1982). Addiction to near-death. *International Journal of Psychoanalysis, 63*: 449–456.

Joseph, B. (1985). Transference: the total situation. *International Journal of Psychoanalysis, 66*: 447–459.

Joseph, B. (1989). *Psychic Equilibrium and Psychic Change: Selected Papers of Betty Joseph* (Edited by M. Feldman & E. B. Spillius). London: Routledge.

Junqueira Filho, L. C. U. (2003). *Sismos e acomodações: a clinica psicanalitica como usina de ideias.* São Paulo: Rosari.

Kafka, F. (1961). *Parables and Paradoxes in German and English.* New York: Schocken.

Katz, G. (2014). *The Play within the Play: The Enacted Dimension of Psychoanalytic Process.* London and New York: Routledge.

Keller, H. (1908). *The World I Live In.* In: www.gutenberg.org/files/27683

Kernberg, O. (1980). *Internal World and External Reality.* New York: Jason Aronson.

Kernberg, O. (1994). Validation in the clinical process. *International Journal of Psychoanalysis, 75*: 1193–1200.

Khan, M. R. (1963). The concept of cumulative trauma. *Psychoanalytical Study of the Child, 18*: 286–306.

Klein, M. (1932). *Psychoanalysis of Children.* London: Hogarth.

Klein, M. (1940). Mourning and its relation to manic-depressive states. In: *Love, Guilt and Reparation, and Other Works, 1921–1945* (pp. 344–378). New York: Free Press, 1975.

Klein, M. (1952). The origins of transference. In: *Envy and Gratitude, and Others Works 1946–1963* (pp. 48–53). London: Hogarth and Institute of Psychoanalysis.

Klein, M. (1957). Envy and gratitude. In: *Envy and Gratitude, and Others Works, 1946–1963* (pp. 176–234). London: Hogarth and Institute of Psychoanalysis.

Korbivcher, C. F. (2013). *Autistic Transformations: Bion's Theory and Autistic Phenomena.* London: Karnac.

Langer, S. K. (1942). *Philosophy in a New Key: A Study in the Symbolism of Reason, Rite and Art* (3rd edn.). Cambridge, MA: Harvard University Press, 1975.

Levine, H. B. (2010). Partners in thought: working with unformulated experience, dissociation, and enactment, by Donnel B. Stern (Review). *Psychoanalytic Quarterly, 79*: 1166.

Levine, H. B. (2012). The colourless canvas: representation, therapeutic action and the creation of mind. *International Journal of Psychoanalysis, 93*: 607–629.

Levine, H. B., & Brown, L. J. (2013). *Growth and Turbulence in the Container/Contained: Bion's Continuing Legacy*. New York: Routledge.

Levine H. B., & Friedman, R. J. (2000). Intersubjectivity and interaction in the analytic relationship: a mainstream view. *Psychoanalytic Quarterly, 69*: 63–92.

Levine, H. B., Reed, G., & Scarfone, D. (2013). *Unrepresented States and the Construction of Meaning: Clinical and Theoretical Contributions*. London: Karnac.

Levy, R. (2012). From symbolizing to non-symbolizing within the scope of a link from dreams to shouts of terror caused by an absent presence. *International Journal of Psychoanalysis, 93*: 837–862.

Loewald, H. W. (1975). Psychoanalysis as an art and the fantasy character of the psychoanalytic situation. *Journal of the American Psychoanalytical Association, 23*: 277–299.

López-Corvo, R. (2006). *Wild Thoughts Searching for a Thinker: A Clinical Application of W. R. Bion's Theories*. London: Karnac.

Lothane, Z. (2009). Dramaturgy in life, disorder and psychoanalytic therapy: a further contribution to interpersonal psychoanalysis. *International Forum of Psychoanalysis, 8*: 135–148.

Lutenberg, J. (2007). *El vacío mental*. Lima: Siklos.

Luz, A. B. (2009). Truth as a way of developing and preserving the space for thinking in the minds of the patient and the analyst. *International Journal of Psychoanalysis, 90*: 291–310.

Mann, D. (2009). Enactment and trauma: the therapist's vulnerability as the theatre for the patient's trauma. In: D. Mann & V. Cunningham (Eds.), *The Past in the Present: Therapy Enactments and the Return of Trauma* (pp. 9–30). New York: Routledge.

Mann, D., & Cunningham, V. (2009). *The Past in the Present: Therapy Enactments and the Return of Trauma*. New York: Routledge.

Marchon, P. (2006). Beyond transference, countertransference, the silences and the opinion. *International Journal of Psychoanalysis, 87*: 63–81.

Marchon, P. (2009). Roosevelt Cassorla e os enactments mútuos. In: *Flutuando atentamente com Freud e Bion* (pp. 157–160). Rio: Imago.

REFERENCES

Marks-Tarlow, T. (2014). Brain science as the analytic fourth: commentary on paper by Michael J. Gerson. *Psychoanalytical Dialogues, 24*: 236–246.
Marucco, N. C. (1998). *Cura analítica y transferencia. De la represión a la desmentida*. Buenos Aires: Amorrortu.
Marucco, N. C. (2007). Between memory and destiny: repetition. *International Journal of Psychoanalysis, 88*: 309–328.
McDougall, J. (1982). *Théatres du je*. Paris: Gallimard.
McDougall, J. (1999). *Theaters of the Body: A Psychoanalytic Aproach to Psychosomatic Illness*. New York: Free Association.
McLaughlin, J. T. (1991). Clinical and theoretical aspects of enactment. *Journal of the American Psychoanalytic Association, 39*: 595–614.
McLaughlin, J. T., & Johan, M. (1992). Enactments in psychoanalysis. *Journal of the American Psychoanalytic Association, 40*: 827–841.
Melsohn, I. (2001). *Psicanálise em nova chave*. São Paulo: Perspectiva.
Meltzer, D. (1975). *Explorations in Autism*. Perthshire: Clunie Press.
Meltzer, D. (1978). *The Kleinian Development, Volume 3: The Clinical Significance of the Work of Bion*. Perthshire: Clunie Press.
Meltzer, D. (1983). *Dream-Life: Re-Examination of the Psycho-Analytical Theory and Techniques*. Strath Tay: Clunie Press.
Meltzer, D. (1986). *Studies in Extended Metapsychology: Clinical Applications of Bion's Ideas*. Reading: Clunie Press.
Meltzer, D. (2005). *The Vale of Soul-Making: The Post-Kleinein Model of the Mind*. London: Karnac.
Mendonça, B. H. C. (2000). A identidade de ficção. In: *Anais do II Encontro do Núcleo de Psicanálise de Campinas e Região* (pp. 22–32). Campinas: NPCR.
Michels, R. (1994). Validation in the clinical process. *International Journal of Psychoanalysis, 75*: 1133–1140.
Minerbo, M. (2009). *Neurose e não neurose*. São Paulo: Casa do Psicólogo.
Money-Kyrle, R. E. (1956). Normal counter-transference and some of its deviations. *International Journal of Psychoanalysis, 37*: 360–366.
Nos, J. P. (2014). Collusive induction in perverse relating: perverse enactments and bastions as a camouflage for death anxiety. *International Journal of Psychoanalysis, 95*: 291–311.
Ogden, T. (1989a). The concept of an autistic-contiguous position. *International Journal of Psychoanalysis, 70*: 127–140.
Ogden, T. (1989b). *The Primitive Edge of Experience*. Northvale: Jason Aronson.
Ogden, T. (1994a). The analytic third: working with intersubjective clinical facts. *International Journal of Psychoanalysis, 75*: 3–19.
Ogden, T. (1994b). The concept of interpretative action. *Psychoanalytic Quarterly, 63*: 219–245.
Ogden, T. (1994c). *Subjects of Analysis*. London: Karnac.

Ogden, T. (1999). *Reverie and Interpretation: Sensing Something Human*. London: Karnac.
Ogden, T. (2005). *This Art of Psychoanalysis: Dreaming Undreamt Dreams and Interrupted Cries*. Hove: Routledge.
Orbach, S. (2009). Enactment and informative experience in the light of the analyst as a new object. Paper presented at IPSO, Chicago.
Panel (1999). Enactment: an open panel discussion. *Journal of Clinical Psychoanalysis, 8*: 7–92.
Paz, C. A. (2007a). Desde el baluarte al enactment. El no sueño en el teatro del análisis, de Roosevelt M. Smeke Cassorla. *Revista de Psicoanálisis (Madrid), 50*: 218–225.
Paz, C. A. (2007b). Del Agieren al Enactment: un siglo de cambios y avances. *Revista de. Psicoanálisis (Madrid), 50*: 59–71.
Paz, C. A. (2009). Lugar e importancia de los sueños en los pacientes borderline: acerca de nuestras posibilidades interpretativas en estos análisis. *Revista de Psicoanálisis (Madrid), 57*: 109–125.
Person, E. S., & Klar, H. (1994). Establishing trauma: the difficulty distinguishing between memories and fantasies. *Journal of the American Psychoanalytic Association, 42*: 1055–1081.
Pichon-Rivière, E. (1980). *Teoría del Vínculo*. Buenos Aires: Nueva Visión.
Pick, I. B. (1985). Working through in the countertransference. *International Journal of Psychoanalysis, 66*: 157–166.
Pistiner de Cortiñas, L. (2011). *Sobre el crecimiento mental: ideas de Bion que transforman la clinica psicoanalitica*. Buenos Aires: Biebel.
Ponsi, M. (2012). Evoluzione del pensiero psicoanalítico: acting out, agire, enactment. *Rivista di Psicoanalisi, 58*: 653–670.
Racker, H. (1948). La neurosis de contratransferencia. In: *Estudios sobre Técnica Analítica* (pp. 182–221). Buenos Aires: Paidós, 1977.
Racker, H. (1953). Los significados y usos de la contratransferencia. In: *Estudios sobre Técnica Analítica* (pp. 225–295). Buenos Aires: Paidós, 1977.
Reed, G. S. (2013). An empty mirror: reflections on non-representation. In: H. B. Levine, G. S. Reed, & D. Scarfone (Eds.), *Unrepresented States and the Construction of Meaning: Clinical and Theoretical Contributions* (pp. 18–41). London: Karnac.
Renik, O. (1998). The analyst's subjectivity and the analyst's objectivity. *International Journal of Psychoanalysis, 79*: 487–497.
Renik, O. (1999). Playing one's cards face up in analysis: an approach to the problem of self-disclosure. *Psychoanalytic Quarterly, 68*: 521–539.
Rey, H. (1994). *Universals of Psychoanalysis in the Treatment of Psychotic and Borderline States*. London: Free Association.
Rezende, A. M. (1995). *Wilfred R. Bion: Uma psicanálise do pensamento*. Campinas: Papirus.

Rezze, C. J. (2001). O sonho, o quase sonho e o não sonho. In: M. O. A. França, M. C. I. Thomé, & M. Petricciani (Eds.), *Transformações e Invariâncias. Bion <-> SBPSP. Seminários Paulistas* (pp. 97–116). São Paulo: Casa do Psicólogo.
Ribeiro, M. M. M. (1999). Rêverie hostil e rêverie benigno. *Revista Brasileira de Psicanálise, 33*: 431–447.
Ribeiro, P. M. M. (2007). Sonhando sonhos com quem não aprendeu a sonhar. In: Associação Brasileira de Psicanálise, *Prática psicanalítica: especificidade, confrontações e desafios. Anais do Congresso Brasileiro de Psicanálise* (pp. 1–16). São Paulo: Casa do Psicólogo.
Rocha, N. J. N. (2009). Enactment como modelo para pensar o processo analítico. *Revista Brasileira de Psicanálise, 43*: 173–182.
Rosas de Salas, C. (2010). *Dolor psíquico en las fronteras de lo analizable*. Buenos Aires: Psicolibro.
Rose, J. (Ed.) (2007). *Symbolization: Representation and Communication*. London: Karnac.
Rosenfeld, H. (1987). *Impasse and Interpretation*. New York: Tavistock.
Roughton, R. E. (1993). Useful aspects of acting-out: repetition, enactment, and actualization. *Journal of the American. Psychoanalytic Association, 41*: 43–471.
Ruvinsky, D. (2012). "What happens before and after acute enactments?" An exercise in clinical validation and the broadening of hypotheses of Roosevelt M. S. Cassorla. *Revista de Psicoanálisis (Madrid), 66*: 228–229.
Sanchez Grillo, M. R. (2004). Juego y "enactment" en psicoanálisis de niños. *Psicoanálisis (Asoc Psicoanal Buenos Aires), 26*: 407–419.
Sandler, J. (1976). Countertransference and role-responsiveness. *International Review of Psychoanalysis, 3*: 43–47.
Sandler, J. (1993). On communication from patient to analyst: not everything is projective identification. *International Journal of Psychoanalysis, 74*: 1097–1107.
Sandler, P. C. (1997). The apprehension of psychic reality: extensions in Bion's theory of alpha-function. *International Journal of Psychoanalysis, 78*: 43–52.
Sandler, P. C. (2005). *The Language of Bion*. London: Karnac.
Sandler, P. C. (2009). *A Clinical Application of Bion's Concepts, Volume 1: Dreaming, Transformation, Containment and Change*. London: Karnac.
Sandler, P. C. (2011). *A Clinical Application of Bion's Concepts, Volume 2: Analytic Function and the Function of the Analyst*. London: Karnac.
Sandler, P. C. (2013). *A Clinical Application of Bion's Concepts, Volume 3: Verbal and Visual Approaches to Reality*. London: Karnac.
Sapienza, A. (2001). O trabalho de sonho-alfa do psicanalista na sessão: intuição-atenção-interpretação. In: M. O. A. F. França, M.C.I. Thomé & M. Petricciani (Eds.), *Transformações e invariâncias: Bion-SBPSP, seminários paulistas* (pp. 17–25). São Paulo: Casa do Psicólogo.

Sapienza, A. (2009). Função alfa: ansiedade catastrófica-pânico-continente com rêverie. In: C. Rezze, E. S. Marra, & M. Petricciani (Eds.), *Psicanálise: Bion-transformações e desdobramentos* (pp. 51–59). São Paulo: Casa do Psicólogo.

Sapisochin, G. (2007). Variaciones post-freudianas del Agieren: sobre la escucha del puesto en acto. *Revista de Psicoanálisis (Madrid), 50*: 73–102.

Sapisochin, G. (2012). A escuta da regressão no processo analítico. *Revista Brasileira de Psicanálise, 46*: 90–105.

Sapisochin, S. (2013). Second thoughts on *Agieren*: listening the enacted. *International Journal Psychoanalysis, 94*: 967–991.

Scarfone, D. (2013). From traces to signs; presenting and representing. H. B. Levine, G. S. Reed, & D. Scarfone (2013). *Unrepresented States and the Construction of Meaning: Clinical and Theoretical Contributions* (pp. 75–84). London: Karnac.

Schreck, A. (2010). Eugenia: la "puesta en acto" en el proceso analítico. *Publicación del Instituto de Psicoanálisis, Asoc Psicoanal Mexicana*, México.

Schwartz, H. P. (2013). Neutrality in the field: alpha-function and the dreaming dyad in psychoanalytic process. *Psychoanalytic Quarterly, 82*: 587–613.

Segal, H. (1957). Notes on symbol formation. *International Journal of Psychoanalysis, 38*: 391–397.

Segal, H. (1981). The function of dreams. In: *The Work of Hanna Segal: A Kleinian Approach to Clinical Practice* (pp. 89–100). New York: Jason Aronson.

Sophocles (c. 429 BC). *Edipo Rei* [Oedipus Rex]. Rio: Jorge Zahar, 1989.

Spillius, E. B., & O'Shaughnessy, E. (Eds.) (2012). *Projective Identification: The Fate of a Concept*. New York: Routledge.

Steiner, J. (1993). *Psychic Retreats: Pathological Organizations in Psychotic, Neurotic and Borderline Patients*. London: Routledge.

Steiner, J. (1996). The aim of psychoanalysis in theory and in practice. *International Journal of Psychoanalysis, 77*: 1073–1083.

Steiner, J. (2000). Containment, enactment and communication. *International Journal of Psychoanalysis, 81*: 245–255.

Steiner, J. (2006). Interpretative enactments and the analytic setting. *International Journal of Psychoanalysis, 87*: 315–320.

Steiner, J. (2009). Can the analyst think while enacting? Panel, IPA Congress, Chicago.

Stern, D. N., Sander, L. W., Nahum, J. P., Harrison, A. M., Lyons-Ruth, K., Morgan, A. C., Bruchsweilerstern & Tronick, E. Z. (1998). Non-interpretative mechanisms in psychoanalytic therapy: the "something more" than intepretation. *International Journal of Psychoanalysis, 79*: 903–921.

Steyn, L. (2013). Tactics and empathy: defences against projective identification. *International Journal of Psychoanalysis, 94*: 1093–1113.

Strachey, J. (1934). The nature of the therapeutic action of psycho-analysis. *International Journal of Psychoanalysis, 15*: 127–159. [Reprinted: *50*: 275–292, 1969.]

Strauss, L. (2012). Sexuality in analysis: analytic listening and enactment. *International Journal of Psychoanalysis, 93*: 753–754.

Symington, J., & Symington, N. (1996). *The Clinical Thinking of Wilfred Bion*. London: Routledge.

Symington, N. (1983). The analyst's act of freedom as agent of therapy change. *International Review of Psychoanalysis, 10*: 283–291.

Tabak de Bianchedi, E. (Ed.) (1999). *Bion Conocido, Desconocido*. Buenos Aires: Lugar.

Tuckett, D. (1994). Developing a grounded hypothesis to understand a clinical process: the role of conceptualisation in validation. *International Journal of Psychoanalysis, 75*: 1159–1180.

Verissimo, L. (2000). Comentarios del trabajo de R. Cassorla. *Revista Uruguaya de Psicoanálisis, 92*: 63–68.

Wieland, C. (2009). Chronic and acute enactment: the passive therapist and the perverse transference. In: D. Mann & V. Cunningham (Eds.), *Past in the Present: Therapy Enactments and the Return of Trauma* (pp. 182–196). New York: Routledge.

Winnicott, D. W. (1949). Hate in the countertransference. *International Journal of Psychoanalysis, 30*: 69–75.

Winnicott, D. W. (1974). Fear of breakdown. *International Review of Psychoanalysis, 1*: 103–107.

Yardino, S. (2008). Break point: a significant moment in the transference. *International Journal of Psychoanalysis, 9*: 241–247.

Yerushalmi, H. (2013). On the therapist's yearning for intimacy. *Psychoanalytic Quarterly, 82*: 671–687.

INDEX

Abreu, A. A., 146
acting out, 3, 14, 43–47, 50, 56, 112, 144
acute enactment (*see* enactment)
affect, 4, 8, 12, 35, 40–41, 47, 79, 88, 114–115, 118, 121–122, 125, 127, 154
affective, 5, 40, 66, 99
   holograms, 7
   pictograms, 5, 40
   states, 41, 108, 111
alpha-elements, 2–4, 11–12, 29, 65–67, 74, 99, 101–102, 114
alpha-function, xviii, 2–5, 8, 11, 15, 40, 49, 66–67, 73–74, 90, 92, 94–95, 104, 110, 115–116, 128, 141, 143, 169, 172, 174
   analytic, 5
   explicit, 96, 131
   implicit, 89–92, 94, 110, 116–117, 131, 143, 159–160

   reversal of, 4–5, 49, 73–74, 169
   synthetic, 5
analyst, 147
   best colleague, 9, 121
   critical capacity, 37, 41, 76
analyst as a real person, xxiv, 9, 28, 36–37, 141
analytic capacity, 19, 28, 109, 112, 120, 153, 155, 157–158, 163
analytic dyad, xxiii–xxiv, xxix, 2–3, 9–10, 15, 28, 44, 46–48, 50, 52, 55, 63, 67, 90, 110–111, 119, 122, 128, 134, 140, 144, 147–148, 156–157, 159
analytic field, xxiii–xxiv, xxix–xxx, 1–2, 4, 6, 13, 23, 27–28, 32, 34, 36–37, 39, 41, 43, 46–48, 54, 64, 79, 103–104, 114, 121, 132, 134–135, 139–145, 148, 153, 156, 159–160, 168

analytic process, xxiv, xxvi, 1, 7,
    9–10, 19, 36, 40, 46, 49,
    51–52, 63–64, 66, 73, 75,
    79, 116, 120–121, 132, 142,
    145, 148, 150, 156, 163, 168,
    176
analytic self-criticism, 113
annihilation anxiety, 88
anti-alpha function, 5
Antigone, 167, 175–177
Apfelbaum, L., 124
arrogance, 147, 162–163, 168, 172
attacks, 14, 16, 18, 52, 68, 71–72, 81,
    83, 113, 125, 142, 144, 152,
    158, 161
    on thinking, 48, 89, 168, 170
Austin, J. L., 47
autistic barriers, 103
autistic-contiguous, 31
awareness, 48, 72, 81–82, 104, 164
Azevedo, A. M. A., 146
Azvaradel, J. R., 118

Baranger, M., 2, 19, 65–66, 75–76, 97,
    120, 164
Baranger, W., 2, 19, 65–66, 75–76, 97,
    120, 164
Barros, E. L. R., 15
Barros, E. M. R., 5, 15, 25, 40,
    101–102, 118, 146
bastion, 64–67, 72, 75–76, 97
Bateman, A. W., 45–46, 58, 123–124,
    137–141, 143–144
    levels of enactment, 137–141,
    143–144
beliefs, 4–5, 18, 24, 31
Bernardi, R., 146
beta-elements, 2–4, 12, 14, 31,
    40, 66, 67, 72–74, 99,
    102–104, 110, 112–114,
    154, 156
Bianco, S. M., 118

Bion, W. R., xxiv, 2–4, 8–10, 12–21,
    27–29, 31, 38–39, 49, 64–67,
    72–73, 79, 85, 95, 97, 113, 118,
    120–121, 148, 154, 156, 158,
    162–164, 167, 169–170
    Bion's container-contained
    model, 3, 31, 41, 66–67, 73,
    76, 168
    grid, 3
    reversal of alpha-function, 4, 73
    theory of thinking, 4, 17
    transformation in hallucinosis, 4,
    13, 16, 31, 74, 86
bizarre objects, 5, 31, 106, 108
Bokanowsky, T., 103, 118
Bollas, C., 3, 24
Bonaminio, V., 141
borderline configuration, 46, 80, 141,
    148, 160, 162
borderline patient, 59, 80, 93, 124, 160
Borensztejn, C. L., 146
Botella, C., 25, 103, 118, 122
Botella, S., 25, 103, 118, 122
Brandão, J. S., 165, 174
Britton, R., 49, 94
Brown, L. J., 10, 15, 49, 99, 102, 146,
    164

Calich, J. C., 128, 146
Canelas Neto, J. M., 40
capacity, 4, 12, 15, 17, 38, 42, 45, 90,
    99, 101, 105, 109, 110, 112,
    115–116, 120, 139, 143, 147,
    153, 155, 157–158, 163, 169,
    174
    analyst's critical, 37, 41, 76
    connection, 4, 79, 99
    containing, 16, 19, 23, 91, 163
    discrimination, 90
    dreaming, xxviii, xxx, 9–10, 13–
    14, 19, 35, 79, 106, 110–111,
    116, 119, 158–159, 163

INDEX

intuitive, 132
linking, xxv, 4, 79, 99
negative, 18, 104
normal masochism, 92, 97
not-knowing, 17
observation, xxiv, 38
reverie, 15–18, 28, 31, 103, 174
symbolization, xxv, 8, 12–13, 19, 27, 31, 79, 88, 94, 99, 101, 117, 163
thinking, xxviii–xxx, 4, 9, 11, 17, 19, 28, 35, 48–49, 72, 85–86, 88–89, 113–114, 116, 148, 153, 157–158, 161, 163, 165
thought, 4, 17
tolerate fluctuations PS<->D, 17
working through, 160
Caper, R., 5, 36, 144, 161
Cassorla, R. M. S., xxix–xxx, 3, 5–6, 15, 19–20, 46–47, 59, 76, 99, 118–119, 138, 144, 146, 161, 164–165, 171, 174, 176
catastrophic anxiety, 148
catastrophic change, 64, 97
Cavell, M., 121
Chaves, L. P., 146
chronic enactment *see* enactment
Churcher, J., 146
Chused, J. F., 45
Civitarese, G., 10, 15, 36
clinical facts, xxv, xxviii, 111, 119, 122–123, 140–141, 147
collusion, 10, 14, 22, 24, 46, 48–49, 51, 58–59, 61, 69, 72, 74–75, 81, 85–90, 92, 96, 111, 127, 131–132, 135, 137–141, 147, 154, 157–159, 162
common sense, 8, 120, 122
communication, xxv–xxvi, 2, 9, 32, 57, 65, 84, 95, 104
artistic, xxiv, xxvi
symbolic, 57, 60, 75

unconscious, 90–91, 95, 104
verbal, 46, 75
conscious/unconscious, 31, 38, 74
contact barrier, 2, 29, 74
container, 3, 12, 31, 41, 66–67
container–contained model, 3, 31, 41, 66–67, 71, 73, 76, 168
pathologies, 76
relationship, 67, 73, 168
contemporary psychoanalysis, xxiii, xxv, 15, 141, 162, 168
continuum dream <-> non-dream, 14, 99
counteridentification, 65, 104
countertransference, xxiii, 12, 14–15, 42, 60, 64, 72, 75, 118, 125, 130, 136, 138, 162 *see also* transference
Creon, 148, 166–168
cumulative trauma, 102
curiosity, 106, 158, 162, 164, 168, 170

daydreaming, 8, 13, 15
daydreams, 3, 9, 15, 19, 23, 27, 35, 84, 101, 105, 110, 121, 127, 165
De León de Bernardi, B., 146
delirium, xxviii, 5
delusions, 13, 31
Deserno, H., 146
desire-dream, 9
desire suspension, 3, 8–9, 19, 21, 111
Devereux, D., 146
dream<->non-dream, 14, 99
dreaming, xxviii, xxx, 2–4, 8–11, 13, 17–19, 27, 32, 94, 100–101, 104, 108, 117, 119, 127–128, 139–140, 142
anti, 74
apparatus, 30, 101
dream-like memory, 9, 20

dreams, xi, 2, 9–10, 12–13, 24, 27–32, 36, 38, 41–42, 46, 49, 67, 79–80, 84–86, 91, 100, 102, 104, 112, 122, 131, 135, 140, 143, 153, 156, 159, 169–170, 172, 174–175
    evacuative dreams, 31
    false dreams, 99, 116
    mixed dreams, 31, 103
    night dreams, 3, 27, 164
    predictive dreams, 118
    psychotic dreams, 31, 103
    traumatic dreams, 6, 87
dreams-for-two, xxviii, 7, 10, 13, 28, 39, 108, 116, 121, 127, 131, 140, 153
dreamwork-alpha, 2, 157
dual, 47, 115, 148, 162
    collusions, 14, 24, 158–159
    identification, xxix
    relationship, xxviii, xxx, 119, 148–149, 155–157, 159–162

Echo, 148, 162
Ellman, S. J., 43
emotional experience, xiv, xxv–xxvi, xxx, 5, 11, 15, 20, 27–28, 40, 67, 106, 109–111, 114, 123, 153
emotions, xxiv–xxv, xxvii, 2, 8, 14, 34–36, 39–41, 64–65, 106, 125, 156
emphatic-intuitive listening, 131–132
enactment, xxix–xxx, 3, 10, 20, 22, 24, 43–49, 56–57, 59–60, 66, 72, 74–76, 80, 95–97, 124, 136–137, 144–146, 148, 158, 161–162, 165, 168, 170
    acute, xxx, 24, 46, 48–49, 51–52, 54–55, 58–60, 67, 73, 75, 81, 84–92, 96–97, 114–117, 120–121, 126–129, 132, 135–136, 138–141, 143–145, 147–148, 153, 155–160
    chronic, 22, 46–49, 51, 56, 58–60, 67, 74–75, 80–81, 86–96, 101, 111, 114, 117, 119–120, 127–129, 131–132, 134, 137–144, 147–148, 154–156, 158–159, 161, 163
    collusive, 59
    interpretative, 134
    mutual idealization, 56, 60, 81, 86, 154–155, 159
    normal, 46, 60, 75, 144–145
    obstructive, 73, 81, 86
    pathological, 60, 75
    sadomasochistic, 143–144, 158
    symbiotic, 49
envy, 39, 54, 87, 89, 105–107, 160, 173–174

Faimberg, H., 19, 120, 164
fanaticism, 13, 31, 48
fantasy, xxvii, 3, 14–15, 48, 56–57, 64–66, 114, 132, 138, 148, 158
feelings, xxiv, 2, 4, 12, 15, 19, 21, 32, 34–35, 41, 54, 64, 68, 70, 94, 106, 108–109, 113, 121, 127, 130, 138, 141, 149, 152, 157, 163, 172, 176
Feldman, M., 49
Ferro, A., 7–8, 10, 18, 25, 28, 31, 101–102, 118
Figueiredo, L. C., 93
figurability, 5, 11, 15, 73, 103–104, 158
Fogel, G. T., 124, 129
Fonagy, P., 93
Franco Filho, O. M., 47, 104
Freud, S., 3, 5, 9, 11, 14–17, 19, 25, 36, 44–45, 47–49, 63–64, 88, 90, 102, 121, 145, 168
Friedman, L., 28, 141, 146, 161
frustration, xxviii, 16, 19, 21, 52, 95, 97, 130, 138, 154, 164

Galipeau, S., 146
Gastaud, M. B., 146
Gheller, J. H., 146
Green, A., 17, 25, 35, 93, 102–103, 118
Greenacre, P., 44
Greenberg, J., 146
Grinberg, L., xxiii, 14, 31, 65, 103, 163
Grotstein, J. S., 8, 10, 12, 93, 102, 118, 159, 163
Guignard, F., 102
guilt, 39, 54, 57, 68, 71, 80, 82, 84, 86, 89, 97, 106, 112–113, 115, 127, 129–130, 138, 140–141, 149, 152, 156–158, 163, 167–168
Gus, M., 146

hallucinations, 5, 31, 41, 101
hallucinosis, 4, 13, 16, 31, 74, 86, 174
Hartke, R., 145–146, 161
hate, xxv, 5, 36, 40, 127, 162, 167–169, 174
 negative of, xxv
Heimann, P., 14, 64
Hinshelwood, R. D., 49

idealisation, xxv, 81, 143, 154–155, 157–159
images, 3, 5–6, 8–9, 14–15, 18, 22, 28–29, 31–32, 35–36, 40, 100–101, 103, 106, 11, 115, 127, 154, 169
imagetic, 5
 symbols, 4, 11, 18, 127
Imbasciati, A., 18, 102
implicit alpha-function, 89–92, 94, 110, 115–117, 131, 143, 159–160
insight, 38, 139
interpretation, 7, 19, 23, 28, 40–41, 46, 56, 68–69, 72, 84, 87, 89–90, 106, 117, 121, 125, 128, 130, 132–133, 137, 144, 149, 161

mutative, 161
intersubjective models, 63–66
intersubjectivity, xxvi, 65, 164
intuition, xxiv, 17, 19, 35, 90, 131, 164, 168
 psychoanalytically trained, xxiii, 10, 38
intuitive capacity, 132
Isaacs, S., 9
Ivey, G., 123–124, 132–136, 141, 144, 146

Jacobs, T., 43, 146
jealousy, 54–55, 173
Jocasta, 166–167, 172, 174
Johan, M., 43
Joseph, B., 2, 36, 67, 72, 77, 163
Junqueira Filho, L. C. U., 10

Kafka, F., 63
Katz, G., 146
Keller, H., 6–7, 100
Kernberg, O., 93, 146
Khan, M. R., 102
Klar, H., 97
Klein, M., 2, 12, 27, 36, 47
knowledge, xxiv–xxvi, 8, 16, 19–20, 37–38, 41, 76, 161–162, 164
Korbvicher, C. F., 103

Laius, 148, 166–167, 170, 172, 175–176
Langer, S. K., 127
learning from experience, 164
Levine, H. B., 10, 25, 28, 118, 141, 146
Levy, R., 25, 92, 102, 118
linking, xxv, 2, 4, 31, 35, 40, 49, 54–56, 74, 101, 106, 115, 117, 157, 166
 attacks on, 147
listening, 8, 76, 120, 143
listening to listening, xxix, 19, 164

Loewald, H. W., 36
López-Corvo, R., 10
Lothane, Z., 36, 146
love, xxv, 36, 107, 128, 138, 162, 174
    negative of, xxv
Lutenberg, J., 102
Luz, A. B., 146

M moment, 71–73, 80–81, 84–87, 90
macro-validation, 121
    peer, 122
Mann, D., 146
Marchon, P., 146
Marks-Tarlow, T., 146
Marucco, N. C., 25, 102, 118
McDougall, J., 36
McLaughlin, J. T., 43
meaning, 3–7, 9, 12, 16–18, 20, 22, 24, 28, 39–40, 43–46, 49–50, 52, 67, 71, 75, 79, 85, 99–100, 102–103, 108–111, 113–114, 117, 120, 127–128, 135, 149, 154, 156–157, 169
    no, 4, 14, 74, 87, 153
Melsohn, I., 118
Meltzer, D., 7, 10, 12, 17, 31, 103
memory, 2–3, 8–9, 16, 19–21, 44, 47, 54, 111, 127, 169, 173
memory in feelings, 47
memory suspension, 3, 9, 19, 21, 111
Mendonça, B. H. C., 34
mental, 2, 5, 8, 14, 17, 19, 24, 41, 52, 54, 63, 67, 71, 74, 83–84, 88–90, 93, 100–101, 108, 117, 121, 132
    apparatus, 16, 103
    functioning, 1, 43, 89, 91, 99, 102, 104
    gestures, 101
    health, xxx, xxxviii, 44
    representation, 5, 40, 67
    states, 5, 15, 36, 79

mentalization, 99, 118
metabolisation of emotional life, 5
Michels, R., 146
micro-validation, 121
Minerbo, M., 118
model of observation, 41, 76
Money-Kyrle, R. E., 14, 64
moralistic superego, 19, 113, 155, 161–162, 164

Narcissus, 147–148, 162
negative, 59, 106, 118
    capability, 17
    capacity, 18, 104
    experience, 59
    links of hate, xxv
    links of knowledge, xxv
    links of love, xxv
non-dream, 3–4, 127–128, 131–132, 134–136, 139–140, 143, 153, 156, 158, 163, 168, 177
non-dream-for-two, 10, 13, 18, 49, 86, 88, 107, 111, 135, 137, 141, 153–155, 165, 167–169
non-existence, 93, 103, 110, 114, 116
non-psychotic, 79, 100, 117
    part of personality, xxix, 6, 13, 19, 27–28, 117–118, 160
non-representation, 3, 103
non-symbolic areas, 104, 158, 162
non-symbolised, 4, 99, 109
Nos, J., 146
nothingness, 88, 110
not-knowing, 9, 16–18

observation, xxiii, 17, 35, 37–38, 48, 82, 85, 88, 91–92, 120–123, 144–145
    capacity, xxiv
    clinical, 119, 159
    model, 41, 76

theory, 119, 121
vertex, 41, 101, 102
obstructive collusion, 81, 86, 88–90, 92, 111, 156, 159
oedipal
   conflicts, 28, 168
   desires, 57
   preconception, 164
   situation, 59, 94–95, 142, 149
   triangulation, xxix, 12–13, 27, 140
Oedipus, 162, 164, 166–177
   investigation, 148
   myth, 148, 165
Oedipus the King, 148, 165–166
Ogden, T., 7, 10, 12, 15, 27–28, 31, 56, 79, 100, 118, 127, 163
omnipotence, 164
omniscience, 13, 19, 21, 154, 162, 164
oneiric, 35, 137
   flashes, 101
   holographic field, 18
   thinking, 5, 8, 11
Orbach, S., 146
O'Shaughnessy, E., 164

patient's mental functioning, 1, 41, 43, 90–91
Paz, C. A., 146
peer macro-validation, 122
perception, xxiv, 3, 5, 15, 40–41, 56, 59, 68, 85–86, 88, 94, 115, 117, 120, 131–132, 147–149, 155–159, 163
   numbed, 19, 147
   traumatic 127, 154
persecutory, 19, 30
   anxiety, 70
   atmosphere, 82
   collusion, 157
   dual relationship, xxiii
   enactment, 159
   guilt, 129, 163

   object, 18, 68, 93
Person, E. S., 97
Pichon-Rivière, E., 64
Pick, I. B., 136
pictographic images, 5–6
Pistiner de Cortiñas, L., 10
Ponsi, M., 146
preconception, xxviii, 21, 164
primordial mind, 14, 103, 118
projective identification, xxviii, xxxix, 3, 9, 14–15, 17, 19, 47, 64–65, 104, 110, 161, 164
   crossed 47, 49, 60
   massive, 3–4, 10, 45, 60, 66, 72–73, 75, 94, 107, 110, 119, 145, 148, 161
   normal, 28, 60, 65
   realistic, 46, 65, 75, 153
propaganda, 9
PS<=>D, 12, 17, 79, 99, 118
psychoanalysis, xxvi–xxvii, xxix, 1, 8, 14, 19, 49–50, 77, 113, 118, 120–122, 141, 146, 162, 168
   as a thing for two, xxiii–xxiv
   as science-art, xxiv
psychological catastrophe, xxix, 156, 158, 162
psychotic, xviii, 3, 6, 13, 18–19, 28, 31, 71–72, 100, 103–105, 117–118, 161–162
   break, 51
   configurations, 14, 46
   disintegration, 177
   dreams, 31, 103
   functioning, 21, 79
   part of mind, xviii, 3
   part of personality, 6, 13, 18, 27–28, 31, 102, 162–163

Racker, H., 14, 64
Reed, G. S., 25, 118
re-enactment, 43

Renik, O., 46, 121, 132
representation, 5, 13, 18, 32, 40,
    43–44, 67, 88, 100–101, 110,
    112, 118
representational deficit, 103
reverie, 8, 15–18, 21, 28, 31, 74, 103–
    104, 154, 169, 172, 174
  hostile, 170
reversal of alpha function, 4–5, 49,
    73–74
Rey, H., 93, 142
Rezende, A. M., 10
Rezze, C. J., 100
Ribeiro, M. M. M., 146, 170
Rocha, N. J. N., 146
Rosas de Salas, C., 118
Rose, J., 118
Roughton, R. E., 45
Ruvinsky, R. E., 146

sadomasochistic collusion, 69, 74,
    85–86, 141, 157–158
  components, 134
  conspiracy, 72, 81
  enactment, 143–144, 158
  plot, 128
  situation, 145
Sandler, P. C., 5, 8, 10, 45, 47, 99, 102,
    104, 120, 163
Sapienza, A., 10, 38, 170
Sapisochin, G., 3, 102, 123–124, 129–
    132, 141, 143, 146
Scarfone, D., 25, 49, 118, 146
Schreck, A., 144, 146
Schwartz, H. P., 146
second look, xxix, 19, 76, 120–121,
    130, 164
Segal, H., 31, 80, 99, 101, 118
self and object, xvii–xviii, xxix–xxx,
    12, 24, 27, 30, 48, 149
  differentiation, xxix–xxx, 48, 148
  indistinction, 30

separation, 94, 114–115, 127, 131,
    147
self-knowledge, xxiv, 8, 20, 164
sense or common sense, 8
shame, 21, 97
signal anxiety, 88
simbolopoese, 18
somatisation, 5, 16, 31
Sophocles, 148, 165, 175
Sphinx, 166, 171–174, 176
Spillius, E. B., 164
Steiner, J., 49, 94, 134, 144, 160
Stern, D. N., 91
Steyn, L., 146
Strachey, J., 36, 64, 161
Strauss, L., 146
stupidity, xxx, 19, 147–149, 157,
    162–164
symbiotic
  enactment, 49
  fantasy, 56
  interaction, 74
  life, 138
  phase, 59
  relationship, 56, 58–59
symbolic, 14, 84–85, 92, 101, 139
  area, 19, 28, 100, 117, 158
  capacity, 13, 136, 143
  communication, 57, 60, 75
  component, 110, 139
  connections, 5, 18
  dreams, 104, 194
  equations, 18, 79, 99, 101, 106
  form, xxix, 127
  formation, 4, 74
  framework, 102
  function, 89
  network, 4, 7, 12, 14, 19, 21–22,
      28, 41, 80, 87, 97, 100–101,
      108, 114, 117, 127, 132, 154,
      156–161, 168–169
  spectrum, 143

thinking, 100
thoughts, 121, 127, 134–135, 140
web, 4, 6, 85
symbolic forms, xxix
symbolisation, xxv, xxix, 4, 6, 8, 13, 15, 17, 22, 28, 35, 47, 49, 79, 88, 91, 94, 99, 102, 115, 117–118
   in action, 22
   mental gestures, 101
symbols, xxv, 4–5, 11, 18, 28, 31–32, 40–41, 49, 79, 105, 108, 127, 142–143, 153
   quasi-, 101
Symington, J., 10
Symington, N., 10, 86

Tabak de Bianchedi, E., 10
theatre, 5, 29, 31–36, 40, 43
   analysis, 5, 33, 73
   critic, 37, 41, 76
   dreaming, 27, 33
   generator of meaning, 12
   metaphor, 36
   miming, 22
   mind, 33
   model, 31, 35, 37, 40
   movie, 28–29
   script, 40
"thing for two", xxiii–xxiv
thinkability, 4, 40, 67
thinking, xxv–xxviii, xxx, 2–4, 6–8, 10–11, 14, 16–19, 22, 28, 48–49, 70–71, 94, 109, 111, 113, 116, 118
   apparatus, 79, 101
   capacity, xxvii, xxix–xxx, 4, 9, 11, 17, 19, 28, 35, 48–49, 72, 85–86, 88–89, 113–114, 116, 148, 153, 157–158, 161, 163, 165
   emotional process, xxiv
   network, 100, 154, 156–157, 168, 170
   theory of, 4, 17

Tiresias, 148, 162, 164, 166, 167–169, 176
transference, xxviii, 2, 36, 40, 44–46, 64, 118, 124, 160 *see also* countertransference
transference, total situation, 2
transference/countertransference phenomena, xxiii, 12, 15
transformations, xxv, xxvii, xxix, 2, 4, 6, 11, 40, 72, 102, 120, 122, 127, 137
   in hallucinosis, 4, 13, 16, 31, 74, 86
   into dreams, 165, 172
trauma, 6, 51, 84, 88–93, 95–96, 99, 104, 108, 110, 114–116, 118, 129, 135–136, 138, 140, 142–145, 149, 156, 158–159, 161, 177
   cumulative, 102
traumatic, 39, 51, 87–88, 91, 110, 115, 127, 132, 134, 138–140, 154–156, 162, 164, 168
   areas, 6, 14, 19, 89–90, 93, 102–103, 110, 117, 142–143, 159–161
   childhood, 51, 84
   contact, 48, 138, 142, 147
   dream, 6, 87–88
   fabric, 91–92
   holes, 128, 159
   injury, 90, 92
   non-dream, 12, 88, 103, 135
   situations, 46, 51, 88–91, 96–97, 107–108, 117, 119, 127, 129, 131, 141, 145, 156–157, 161
triangular, xxix, 139
   reality, xxviii, xxx, 24, 128, 138, 144, 147–149, 155, 159–164
   relation, xxix, 115, 119, 135, 138, 161
   situation, 94, 116, 127, 134–135, 138, 142, 144–145
   space, 94–95, 144

truth, 8, 12, 15, 36, 59, 120, 133, 145,
     166–168, 172
Tuckett, D., 146
turbulence, 1, 42, 52

unconscious *see* conscious/
     unconscious
unconscious waking thoughts, 3

validation, xxx, 19, 119–124, 140–141,
     144–146

Verissimo, L., 146
void, 4, 16, 88, 101–104, 108, 138

Wieland, C., 146
Winnicott, D. W., 102, 162
working through, 59, 64, 92–95, 108,
     140, 160

Yardino, S. M., 122–129, 141
Yerushalmi, H., 146